Post-modernism for Psychotherapists

Post-modernism crucially describes a changing cultural world. This book is the first to explore the implications of the post-modern for those professionals who may not be aware of how it can help inform their work in a time of radically altering conditions.

Post-modernism for Psychotherapists is a critical reader which:

- Presents and examines extracts from original texts by a range of influential Continental post-modern thinkers: Lyotard, Baudrillard, Lacan, Derrida, Foucault, Kristeva, Irigaray, Cixous, Deleuze and Guattari, Levinas, Žižek, Wittgenstein.
- Discusses the history of key ideas through the exploration of some of the roots of post-modernism: phenomenological and existential roots, with extracts from Kierkegaard, Husserl, Heidegger and Merleau-Ponty, and other roots: Hegel, Marx, Nietzsche, Freud and Saussure.
- Offers a critique of post-modernism, with extracts from Sokal and Bricmont, Habermas, Rorty and Eagleton.
- Provides extensive suggestions for further reading as a basis for following through these ideas.

Post-modernism for Psychotherapists is essential reading for psychotherapists and counsellors, as well as those in training, who need an accessible text covering post-modern ideas and how they can challenge and inform theory and practice.

Dr Del Loewenthal is Director of the Centre for Therapeutic Education at the University of Surrey, where he is a Reader. He originally trained as a psychotherapist with the Philadelphia Association, and he is the editor of the *European Journal of Psychotherapy, Counselling and Health* (Routledge). He is also a Chartered Psychologist.

Dr Robert Snell is a psychoanalytic psychotherapist (London Centre for Psychotherapy) in private practice. His first training was in the history of art. He teaches at the Centre for Therapeutic Education at the University of Surrey, and he also works as an individual and group therapist in the counselling service at the University of Sussex.

Post-modernism for Psychotherapists

A critical reader

Del Loewenthal and
Robert Snell

Routledge
Taylor & Francis Group

LONDON AND NEW YORK

First published 2003 by Routledge
27 Church Road, Hove, East Sussex BN3 2FA

Simultaneously published in the USA and Canada
by Routledge
270 Madison Ave, New York NY 10016

Routledge is an imprint of the Taylor & Francis Group

Transferred to Digital Printing 2008

Typeset in Times by Keystroke, Jacaranda Lodge, Wolverhampton
Paperback cover design by Lisa Dynan

British Library Cataloguing in Publication Data
A catalogue record for this book is available from the British Library

Library of Congress Cataloging in Publication Data
Loewenthal, Del, 1947–
   Post-modernism for psychotherapists : a critical reader / Del
Loewenthal and Robert Snell.
      p. cm.
Includes bibliographical references.
   ISBN 1-58391-100-6 – ISBN 1-58391-101-4 (pbk.)
   1. Psychology and philosophy. 2. Psychology–Philosophy.
3. Postmodernism. I. Snell, Robert, 1951– II. Title.

BF41.L64 2003
149′.97′02415–dc21

                                          2003000323

ISBN 978–1–58391–101–3 (pbk)

Contents

Preface

The post-modern challenges the modernist assumptions that prevail in so much of psychotherapy, counselling, psychology and psychoanalysis. We suggest that in some important senses the work of psychotherapists, counsellors, psychologists and psychoanalysts may be out of touch with current cultural practices, and thus the world from which our patients/clients come. The book is written by two psychotherapists for practitioners and trainees who wish to examine how post-modernism can help inform their work and how they think about it. What is proposed here is not that people necessarily change to a new 'post-modern school' of therapy, but that they examine the implications of post-modern Continental philosophy for current practice. These implications may, however, be profound.

Acknowledgements

We wish to thank Ilse Niemela, at the University of Surrey, for the work of getting the extracts into publishable order, and Eric Abrahams and Philip Channer for their careful readings of an earlier version of the text. It is hard to imagine how this book could have come into being at all without the good humoured secretarial and moral support of Helen McEwan, or the challenges and enthusiasm, over many years, of our students and staff at the Centre for Therapeutic Education at the University of Surrey. The teaching and thinking of Steve Gans, John Heaton, and Chris Oakley, of the Philadelphia Association, have been important background stimuli. Thanks, too, to Lola and Lucy Loewenthal for their help, and, finally and most warmly, to Jane Loewenthal and Kim Crewe, for all their encouragement and long forbearance.

Permissions

Psychological Works of Sigmund Freud translated and edited by James Strachey. Reprinted by permission of The Random House Group Limited.

From *Course in General Linguistics* by F. de Saussure (1916). Reprinted with permission by Philosophical Library, New York.

From J-F. Lyotard (1984) *The Post-Modern Condition: A Report on Knowledge.* Copyright © 1984. Reprinted with permission by Manchester University Press.

From J. Derrida (1987) 'Du tout', from *The Postcard. From Socrates to Freud and Beyond.* Copyright © 1987. Reprinted with permission by Chicago University Press.

From *Powers of Horror: An Essay on Abjection* by J. Kristeva © Copyright 1982 Columbia University Press. Reprinted with the permission of the publisher.

From *The Newly Born Woman* by H. Cixous and C. Clémente (1986). Reprinted with permission.

From *Anti-Oedipus* by Gilles Deleuze and Felix Guattari, translated by Helen Lane, Mark Seem, and Robert Hurley, copyright © 1977 by Viking Penguin Inc., English language translation. Used by permission of Viking Penguin, a division of Penguin Group (USA) Inc.

From *To The Other* © 1993, E. Levinas, Purdue University Press. Reprinted by permission.

From S. Žižek (1991) *Looking Awry: An Introduction to Jacques Lacan through Popular Culture.* Copyright © 1991. Reprinted with permission by MIT Press.

From *Philosophical Investigations* by Ludwig Wittgenstein (2001[1958]). Reprinted with permission by Blackwell Publishing.

From *Intellectual Impostures* by Alan Sokal and Jean Bricmont. Copyright © 1998. Reprinted with permission by Profile Books Ltd.

From J. Habermas (1987) *The Philosophical Discourse of Modernity.* Copyright © 1987. Reprinted with permission by MIT Press.

From *The Illusions of Postmodernism* by T. Eagleton (1996). Reprinted with permission by Blackwell Publishing.

We have also approached the relevant publishers for permission to use the following quotes:

From *Symbolic Exchange and Death* by J. Baudrillard (1993), pp. 8–10, 10–12, 50, 73–76. Copyright held by Sage Publications Ltd.

From *Objectivity, Relativism and Truth* by R. Rorty (1991), pp. 22–34. Copyright held by Columbia University Press.

From *The Seminar of Jacques Lacan, Book 1, Freud's papers on techniques* by J. Lacan (1988), pp. 1–3, 73–78. Copyright held by W.W. Norton & Co.

From 'This Sex Which Is Not One' by L. Irigaray, in *New French Feminisms: An Anthology* by E. Marks and I. De Courtivron (eds) (1981). Copyright held by Cornell University Press.

From *The Discourse on Language* by M. Foucault (1971). Copyright held by Pantheon Books, Random House Inc.

Chapter 1

Introduction

The post-modern challenges, and through this, potentially stimulates, in a variety of ways. Crucially, it attacks the 'modernist' ego-centric/person-centred approaches of much psychoanalysis, counselling, psychotherapy and psychology. Post-modern Continental philosophers suggest that we are 'subject to'. For example, for Lacan we are subject to language, for Levinas we are subject to the other and to difference, for Foucault we are subject to power/knowledge relationships, for Derrida we are subject to undecidability and the constant deferral of meaning, for Kristeva we are subject to strange, disruptive and potentially creative forces. In that he insisted that we are subject to the unconscious, Freud himself is a foundational post-modern thinker.

We are not trying to peddle something called 'post-modern therapy', as yet another 'school', theoretical breakthrough or new market brand. Rather we are looking at the implications of some Continental, post-modern thinking for practice – we are interested in implication rather than application, in thoughtfulness rather than technique. We feel, however, that the post-modern shift in European thinking reflects values and attitudes which are important for any therapeutic practice, of whatever theoretical bias. We believe post-modern thinking can provide useful pointers as to what may most help us within our current culture – for example, to respond more appropriately to the world from which patients/clients come. It helps raise important questions, especially in a climate of evidence-based practice, as to what the good life is. What is our attitude to this ancient question, as therapists? It can encourage scepticism and questioning, particularly towards the status and function of theory itself. It can help us be wary of closure, and invite openness – to hearing stories, to the unforeseeable. It underlines the importance of putting the other (the client/patient) first, and it emphasises the inter-subjective, what can emerge 'in the in-between'. By reminding us that we are 'subject-to(o)', it can be a challenge to omnipotence, both the patient's and the therapist's, and it can be a plea for humility. It can induce a sense of wonder. It questions whether language and speech are ever neutral or transparent, merely pointing to meanings outside themselves. It can alert us to the fact that language is never static, but always changing, within the culture which language also shapes. It can remind us that our words and gestures are cultural, personal and inter-subjective *acts*.

We are psychotherapists who became interested in philosophy; we are writing both as psychotherapists and as teachers. Between us we have experience of the main counselling and psychotherapy regulatory bodies in the UK, as members of them, or as tutors on courses accredited by them: the United Kingdom Council for Counselling and Psychotherapy (UKCP), the British Confederation of Psychotherapists (BCP), the British Association for Counselling and Psychotherapy (BAPC), and the British Psychological Society (BPS).

The book has been written and compiled collaboratively; it echoes conversations we have had, and it emerges from a particular context. On the four-year MSc in Counselling and Psychotherapy as a Means to Health and Learning at the University of Surrey, Centre for Therapeutic Education, where we both teach, we spend part of our time reading philosophical texts with a large group, struggling to find some shared/sharable meaning. This is with students who are typically from nursing or related, non-academic backgrounds. The nature of the reading we do with the group is reflected in the structure and contents of this book; it might thus constitute a kind of course in itself, providing the texts necessary for a long-term reading group. Our reading at Surrey takes place within a course structure which, in other ways too, emphasises the importance of the struggle to stay open (a typical day would consist of case presentations in a group, large group reading/seminar, large therapeutic/community group, group/individual tutorial, small therapeutic/peer group, business/housekeeping meeting).

The programme's historical roots lie in the therapeutic community movement of the 1960s, as exemplified particularly by the Philadelphia Association and the work of R. D. Laing, and in John Heron's humanistic psychology of the 1970s. Does this seem old-fashioned? We hope the ethos of this book, like that of the Surrey programme, may act as a necessary challenge to current scientism and the culture of privatisation. If we suggest that one way of using this book might be to read it in a group, this is because we support a practice of reading which can be both political and therapeutic, encouraging multiple critical perspectives, within a sense of the collective.

The book is thus an introduction to post-modern Continental philosophy, and its major roots, as understood by us in relation to our own practices and teaching. It is intended to assist students to carry out course work and research, and to be a source book for those who wish to follow these thinkers in more depth. It aims to meet the interest, curiosity and, perhaps, discomfort which many therapists may experience with regard to post-modernism. A common reproach levelled at post-modernism is that it is about style rather than substance, that it simply removes foundations, and disorients. We hope to help people to be able to speak and think more freely about these anxiety-provoking matters. This, we believe, requires some examination of the history of the European thought which has led to this particular phase of intellectual and cultural development. Uniquely and, we feel, crucially for any useful understanding, the book provides readings from some of the earlier literature out of which post-modern philosophy has emerged, from phenomenology, psychoanalysis, linguistics, and the writings of Hegel, Marx and

Nietzsche. Without some background to our thinking we are relatively disabled; what post-modernism can show up is how modernism, the dominant cultural movement of the twentieth century, with its emphasis on social and technological progress, can, in the name of abling, also disable thinking.

While this thinking from continental Europe has been widely discussed in architecture, art, English, modern language and cultural studies departments for at least a couple of decades, it has been largely avoided in therapeutic theorising and trainings. Indeed, the term 'post-modernism' probably arose in relation to literature and to architecture, in the 1960s and 1970s (Jameson, 1985: 111). It is a term with broad echoes. It can stand for extreme modernity, and the mind-set of a new kind of avant-garde; or it can suggest extreme relativism, and an abnegation of moral and political responsibility, within an anarchic or reactionary agenda (see Jencks, 1992). The word 'post-modern' has been used to designate a style (architecture), and/or a historical period, although there is variation of opinion as to where this would start or end. Some see Franz Kafka, who died in 1924, as post-modern (Lechte, 1994; and see Žižek, below). Other commentators regard post-modernism as a phenomenon of the 1980s and 1990s, which has subsequently been overtaken by a new category, 'post-post-modernism' (see, for example, Moss, 2000).

One important definition of the post-modern, as a radically sceptical and questioning attitude of mind, is that provided by the philosopher Jean-François Lyotard (1984), who wrote of it in terms of 'the death of grand narratives', with Marxism and Freudianism particularly in mind. Lyotard would see as futile attempts to consider the modern and post-modern in terms of historical periodisation. For him, the post-modern implies an intensely critical and reflective relationship with the modern, which we are far from having left behind (Elliott and Spezzano, 2000: 1–2). While agreeing with Lyotard, and without wishing to claim that one ism simply supersedes the other, we shall briefly attempt to think about post-modernism in terms of the modernist attitudes and world-views it critiques and with which it can sharply contrast.

Modernism has its historical roots in the philosophy of Descartes in seventeenth-century Europe. Descartes's famous 'I think, therefore I am' encapsulated a very particular view of what it is to be human. This view gave primacy to consciousness and reason. It postulated the human being as a mind free to ponder an 'outside' world, a mind housed in a machine-like body, able to contemplate its own being, and indeed defined *as* a being by its ability to contemplate itself. Descartes thus viewed the human being as a discrete and bounded entity (although his thinking also contains a fundamental split, mind–body, which subsequent thinkers within modernism have tried to heal by promoting an idea of human wholeness, 'holism').

This kind of thinking flowered, in eighteenth-century Europe and in the New World, as the intellectual and cultural movement known as the Enlightenment. Philosophers of the Enlightenment, from Locke, Voltaire and Rousseau, to Kant, shared a view that, through the application of Reason, man (Reason was generally a male attribute) would find himself in productive harmony with tamed Nature. The philosophy of the Enlightenment was generally, although not always, atheistic;

the project of driving out irrational beliefs and superstitions involved what the sociologist Max Weber called a process of 'disenchantment' (Weber, 1974: 155). Progress towards justice, liberty and happiness would follow. The American Declaration of Independence of 1776 is a classic statement of Enlightenment social and political ideals. These ideals, in spite of the bloody experiences of the French Revolution in the 1790s, and subsequently repeated social and political traumata, have vigorously subsisted into the twenty-first century.

Enlightenment faith in the progressive, explanatory, pattern-finding power of human consciousness has found clear expression in the social and political ideal of a coherent, even utopian social and political order – Fascism and Soviet Communism are two of the more extreme twentieth-century manifestations of this. Such faith can also be found in the field of artistic and cultural production – for example, in the modernist architectural idea of form following function, as in the work and theories of Le Corbusier, or of the Bauhaus, and the 'International Style'. It is echoed in the notion that there are 'core' or universal values and truths, transcending historical contingencies. It is present in the idea that as humans we are autonomous, and inherently health-seeking – in, for example, the humanist view that found its clearest expression, in the world of counselling and therapy, in the work of Carl Rogers (Rogers, 1961), with its implication that 'you can be who you want to be'. Implicitly or explicitly valued, in this post-Enlightenment, modernist vision, would be qualities such as lack of ambiguity, clearly articulated relations between elements, control, a sense of fitting in, of knowing the norms. Above all there would be a view of technology and its products, reason's most visible achievements, as 'progressive' and benign.

There is another kind of 'modernism', that of the radical avant-garde in late nineteenth- and early twentieth-century Europe and America, associated with such figures as Picasso, Duchamp, Stravinsky, Schoenberg, Joyce, Pound and Woolf, artists, composers and writers who questioned and subverted traditional forms of representation, notation and expression. Post-modernism would seem to draw from rather than stand in opposition to this tradition – Jacques Lacan, for example, was a friend of the Surrealist artists and poets in Paris in the 1930s – and to share many of the characteristics of a rebellious avant-garde: iconoclastic, deliberately provocative, critical of accepted values, courting new sensations and experiences. Perhaps what makes post-modernism more than just a new avant-garde, and distinguishes it from the old avant-garde, is its relation to tradition. Where Picasso or Joyce struggled with the pictorial and literary heritage, and paid passionate if sometimes ironic tribute to certain of their precursors, post-modernists do not tend to engage with the past in the same selective spirit. Rather the notion of tradition or heritage itself is made suspect.

The post-modern would certainly oppose the over-arching visions of 'rational' or late Enlightenment modernism. Post-modern thinking has coincided with the rise of local, interest-group politics since the 1960s: the green movement and feminism, in their various forms, and the confluence of ecological and liberation movements in the Third World (on the latter, see Esteva and Prakesh, 1998). It has accompanied the breakdown of the great political systems and ideologies of the earlier twentieth century, symbolised by the fall of the Berlin Wall in 1989. The events of 11 September 2001, were of course a further, massive blow to previously held certainties.

Post-modernism has developed alongside and through the new information technologies and the invention of cyberspace (triumphs of rationality, defenders of Enlightenment might argue). Post-modern thinking would tend to favour diversity, multiplicity and uncertainty, over system, ideology and generalisation; play, decoration and idiosyncrasy, over coherence and transparency; irony and questioning, over received wisdom or established authority. It would be circumspect about any notion of historical progress or patterning. It would question the supremacy of reason and consciousness, offering instead a 'decentred' vision of what it is to be human – even if it continued to believe such a vision was remotely possible or worth trying to grasp. Subject to contingency and, in the end, to our own deaths, that over which we have no control, it would see 'autonomy' and 'wholeness' as illusions; we are displaced, split, fractured and changeable, our messages to each other never leading to any finally consensual meaning, always open to slippage and variable readings.

Within the views outlined above, an existentialist philosopher like Jean-Paul Sartre, who saw the human being as struggling and failing to connect in an absurd world, would still be a modernist, in that he considered humans as discrete, bounded and autonomous islands of consciousness. His compatriot Lacan might superficially seem to have something in common with Sartre, in that he believed we are caught in a constant misrecognition; yet he would not be modernist. He would emphasise that we interpenetrate in complex ways, and have no inherent wholeness or 'centre' from which to speak, except as a wishful fantasy (although the current in Lacan's thinking that led him to try to construct a comprehensive, explanatory algebra and geometry for all this might be seen as more 'modern').

There are many useful post-modern readers and introductions to post-modern philosophy; a selection is listed at the end of the introduction to Chapter 4. We have found Sarup (1993) especially helpful, and we draw on him in our introductory comments on Kristeva, Baudrillard, Derrida and Foucault, for example, and elsewhere in the book. There is also, of course, no shortage of writers from within psychoanalysis, psychotherapy and counselling who think philosophically, and use philosophical texts to examine aspects of theory and practice. Two recent examples would be Symington (1999), in his study of psychoanalysis and religion, and Brooke (1999), in his edited book on the links between phenomenology and analytical psychology.

However, considering the vast quantity of books published annually in the field, only a relatively small number of writers from within, or non-practitioner commentators on, counselling, psychotherapy and psychoanalysis have specifically engaged with post-modern thinking – although the proportion is increasing.

Elliott and Spezzano's (2000) *Psychoanalysis at its Limits. Navigating the Post-modern Turn* is a useful and challenging collection of essays for those who wish to explore current debates on the relationship between psychoanalysis and post-modern philosophy in depth and detail. Members of the Philadelphia Association were among the first active practitioners to introduce thinkers such as Derrida, Levinas and Lyotard, as well as Lacan, into philosophical thinking about psychoanalysis and healing (Cooper *et al.* 1989). Forrester (1990) undertook a scholarly examination of the lineage from Freud to Lacan and Derrida, with an important concluding chapter on Foucault and the history of psychoanalysis. Kvale (1992) and Shamdasani and Munchow (1994) edited pioneering and cosmopolitan collections of essays, the latter including papers by Kristeva, Castoriadis, Spivak and Lingis, among others. O'Connor and Ryan (1993) considered the work of Kristeva and Irigaray, as well as of Lacan, in their study of psychoanalytic understandings of lesbianism; Frosh (1994) drew on Irigaray, Kristeva and Cixous in his critical exploration of psychoanalytic theories of sexual difference. Barratt (1993) argued that psychoanalysis should now redefine itself as a post-modern method, while Campbell (2000) linked psychoanalysis and post-structuralism in her re-thinking of the politics of gender and sexuality. DiCenso (1998) used Lacan and Kristeva to re-examine Freud's attitudes to religion, and Hauke (2000) aligned Jung's ideas to a post-modern critique of contemporary society. Parker (1999) made an important plea for a 'non-regulative' practice: he applied the post-modern turn in philosophy to psychotherapy, making particular use of Derrida and Foucault, to deconstruct power (including gender) relations within psychotherapy's institutions and discourses. Fiumara (2001) drew on a range of contemporary philosophy and feminist theory to explore the relationship between thinking and feeling.

Writing with a particular clinical focus, Malson (1997) brought post-structural and feminist ideas to bear in a discussion of anorexia, and, in the field of art therapy, Adams (1998) used Kristeva's thinking to inform her exploration of femininity and creativity. Layton (1999) sought to bring together clinical practice and post-modern gender theory. Timimi (2002) has made a passionate and reasoned appeal for a 'non-expert' post-modern stance, in relation to the practice of child and adolescent psychotherapy. Timimi's challenge to prevailing medical assumptions, in favour of greater attention to cultural and ethnic diversity and to the practitioner's as well as the client's values and beliefs, deserves the widest readership.

We have not included in this sampling, which is intended to be illustrative rather than exhaustive, writers who are also 'mainstream' Lacanian psychoanalysts (such as Darian Leader and Bice Benevenuto) – they are, by definition, exceptions within the relative scarcity, in so far as Lacan can be viewed, as the present writers view him, as predominantly post-modern.

What has not up to now existed is an introductory reader on post-modernism compiled specifically with psychoanalysts, psychotherapists, counsellors and psychologists in mind. Howard's (2000) *Philosophy for Counselling and Psychotherapy. Pythagoras to Postmodernism* sounds promising, but it starts out from a more modernist and cognitive place, and his book ends not with post-modernism at all, but with Sartre.

The present book also follows the launch in 1998 of the *European Journal of Psychotherapy, Counselling and Health* (Routledge), which has demonstrated the existence of widespread interest in this area. We hope it might become the first in a series of books examining the various implications of post-modern Continental philosophy for psychotherapeutic, counselling, psychological and psychoanalytic practice. As well as for practising counsellors, psychotherapists and psychoanalysts, whatever their orientation, the book is intended for students, trainers and lecturers, and those in related professions such as psychiatrists, nurses, health visitors, midwives and social workers, as well as for patients/clients. It is designed so that it can be used as a main text for counselling and psychotherapy, psychoanalytic and counselling psychology programmes.

The book is divided into five chapters: the introduction; the roots of post-modern thinking in phenomenology and existentialism; the roots of post-modern thinking in the works of Hegel, Marx, Nietzsche, Freud and Saussure; selected Continental post-modern philosophers, including, for good reasons, Wittgenstein; and a brief final survey of some critiques of post-modernism. Each chapter is divided into sections containing key extracts from the work of the philosophers in question. Each section has an introduction, which offers a brief account of the selected writer's key ideas and their implications for psychotherapeutic practice, and some thoughts on our reading of the text or texts that follow.

One of our most difficult tasks was the selection of extracts. Anthologists differ in their views of who is post-modern or not; our selection of writers is based on what has moved us, in our practice as therapists, and on what our psychotherapy and counselling students have found most useful. In choosing the extracts we had to decide whether we should dwell on that which is most central to the philosopher's thinking, or that which is most pertinent to therapists, or that which seems most readily understood. Inevitably in making such choices there will be omissions. We hope that what has been selected will provide readers with the inspiration to explore further. While we have acknowledged, above, some of the most useful commentaries on the post-modern turn in relation to psychotherapy, and while we make occasional references to these in our own notes, it has not been our intention to provide an overview or synthesis of such commentaries, but rather to encourage a return to the challenges of the original texts. We would welcome suggestions for alterations or improvements for future editions.

What follows is a book that aims to bring counselling, psychotherapy and psychoanalysis into lively contact with some current and recent thinking and cultural practice. It is hoped that engaging with it will help practitioners to be all the more alert to their own and their clients'/patients' worlds.

Some of the extracts are from works previously published using a philosophy convention in which the author has single quotes for the 'use' of a term and double quotes for the "mention" of the word or words. US-published work would have the reverse convention. In order to preserve the intended distinctions of the original authors, we maintain these conventions, but adhere to the UK version of the convention.

Chapter 2

Phenomenological and existential roots

Kierkegaard, Husserl, Heidegger, Merleau-Ponty

Introduction

The aspects of European thought which we consider to have been most important for the development of post-modernism fall under the headings phenomenology, psychoanalysis, and the legacies of Hegel, Marx, Nietzsche and Saussure. As teachers we feel that students need some notion of how post-modern ideas have evolved, in order to help them feel that they have somewhere to argue and speak from. Our purpose is to emphasise that post-modernism, far from being merely about veneer, is deeply rooted in European thinking. It has a rigour of its own, which is different from scientific rigour, but in no way inferior for that. In our view phenomenology, alongside psychoanalysis, is the crucial element underpinning post-modernism, and is of paramount importance to psychotherapy.

The question of where we are coming from is crucial – unless we accept an idea of ourselves as neutral observers. Our selection of texts inevitably involves our own value system, both with regard to our chapter headings, and what we select from within them. This chapter includes extracts from Kierkegaard, Husserl, Heidegger and Merleau-Ponty. Space has not permitted us to provide extracts from other important thinkers, such as Camus, Sartre, or de Beauvoir (although we briefly discuss the contributions of the last two below), nor from the writings of existential/phenomenological psychotherapists such as Binswanger, Boss, Buber, Frankl, Laing or May (we list key publications by these authors at the end of this introduction); we feel, however, that the four philosophers we have selected represent the key strands and debates within the existential/phenomenological tradition.

Phenomenology has directly influenced many schools of psychotherapy and in our view has (or should have) an important impact on other schools. It has led to a descriptive psychology (Giorgi, 1970); Koning and Jenner (1982) provides a good source of references on phenomenology and therapy. Phenomenology does not accept the way we perceive things as natural or neutral in any naïve sense; it pays special attention to the way in which we perceive; we are, furthermore, always implicated and, in a special sense, 'intentional' in what we perceive; the notion of 'objectivity' is therefore problematic. Once one has begun to think in this way it is much harder to embrace theory unquestioningly or uncritically, or to make a theory one's starting point. Thus such post-modern ideas as the death of grand narratives, and post-modern distrust of master theories (Lyotard, 1984), can be seen as deriving from phenomenology.

Why start with phenomenology? If we began anywhere else we would be starting from theory. Not that phenomenology is not theory, but it is arguing for something else. It is a theory that throws theorising into question. It attempts to start with phenomena, with a return, in Husserl's phrase, 'to the things themselves', in their unique particularity, in the present moment. There is a surprising lack of literature on the history of phenomenology, and little reference to such a history in the psychotherapeutic literature. It is easier to find reference to existentialism, and what reference there is to phenomenology tends to be humanistic and reductionist. Existentialism can provide a useful way in to an exploration of phenomenology. We would agree with Macquarrie (1972: 8): 'Most existentialists are phenomenologists, though there are many phenomenologists who are not existentialists'. Thus we are primarily interested here in phenomenology, and in existentialism only in so far as it sheds light on phenomenology. Yet an existentialist attitude would seem to be something likely to open up for the phenomenological enquirer. In asking the phenomenological question 'How is this table given to my experience?' (rather than the 'scientific' questions 'How much does it weigh? What are its dimensions?'), I find myself implicated in a relationship with the table – I do not objectify it – and this might lead me further to question, 'If the table is here and I am here, then what are we both doing here?'.

Heaton (1990) puts the case for existentialism being something that is forever changing and astonishing. He illustrates this by starting with Aristotle (384–322 BC). Aristotle argues that what is important is the thing *as* it is. Questions as to '*if* it is' (i.e. does it exist?) and '*what* it is' are secondary (Heaton, 1990: 2). There is, however, the further question of how we perceive the thing 'as it is'. Our perception of the same thing will change, for our culture changes how we describe what we perceive. This inevitably involves us in the question of where we are coming from.

Heaton continues his examination of different ways of contemplating being by turning to Thomas Aquinas's (1225–1274) notion of God being in all things, and therefore in us (which may also, arguably lead to modernist narcissism and egocentricity). Heaton next discusses the philosophy of René Descartes (1596–1650) and what could be seen as the Cartesian antithesis to phenomenology, in which the researcher/psychotherapist would be an objectifying person of science. 'I will now shut my eyes, stop my ears, and withdraw all my senses. I will eliminate from my thoughts all images of bodily things.' Man for Descartes is a thinking substance and our bodies are machines, machines for thinking in, things we 'possess'. 'The subject–object relationship', writes Heaton, 'becomes fundamental and with it the search for knowledge' (Heaton, 1990: 3). This is not the aim of a philosophical therapy. 'Philosophical therapy does not seek to impose rules or seek to increase knowledge but it describes. It is practice of thoughtfulness . . . so there are no advances in philosophical therapy, just changes according to the situation in which it is practised' (Heaton, 1990: 5). Søren Kierkegaard (1813–1855), with his emphasis on subjectivity and the existing subjective person, and Martin Heidegger (1889–1976) one hundred years later, writing of existence, provide important contrasts to the still powerfully thriving Cartesian tradition.

Carl Rogers has popularised a phenomenological approach to counselling and psychotherapy which has been enormously influential. He managed to reduce the phenomenological tradition to what he termed 'three core conditions', which he felt it is essential for the therapist to display: unconditional positive regard, empathy and congruence (Rogers, 1967). Through this simplification Rogers has been able to bring the complexities of phenomenological thought to a wide, particularly anglophone audience. However, we would wish to argue that such a reduction is, by definition, not phenomenological.

Similarly, in Britain, Ernesto Spinelli has taken Husserl's foundational work in modern phenomenology and reduced it to a three-step method. Step 1: *epoché*: 'to set aside our initial biases and prejudices of things, to suspend our expectations and assumptions, in short, to *bracket* all such temporarily and as far as is possible so that we can focus on the primary data of our experience'. Step 2, the rule of description: 'The essence of this rule is: "Describe, don't explain"'. Step 3, the rule of horizontalisation: 'having stuck to an immediate experience which we seek to describe, this rule further urges us to avoid placing any initial hierarchies of significance or importance upon the items of our descriptions and instead to treat each initially as having equal value or significance' (Spinelli, 1989: 17 etc.).

Spinelli's introduction to Edmund Husserl's phenomenological method provides a more easily digestible account than the original, and can be useful, but there is a danger that in its somewhat humanistic simplification, and its offer of implied understanding, it may work to diminish a sense of the complexities and inherent tensions of experience, which phenomenology sets out to uncover. It may detract from the Husserl who opened so much up for Heidegger and subsequent Continental philosophers. We therefore provide an introductory reading from Husserl himself in this section.

Notions such as *epoché* also have an ancient history. Arcesilaus (316–*c*.241 BC), according to Heaton, introduced *epoché* into Plato's academy around 272 BC. *Epoché* meant 'suspension of judgement' for the undogmatic Skeptics of the Greek Academy; in their view, since problems of knowledge were insoluble, the best course, when controversy arose over what could or could not be known, was an attitude of non-involvement, in order to gain peace of mind for daily living. This tradition of scepticism, and with it, a therapeutic phenomenology, can be seen as influencing the essayist Michel de Montaigne (1533–1592), and in the twentieth-century, Ludwig Wittgenstein (1889–1951), both with their notions of philosophy as therapy (Heaton, 1997: 81–2).

Post-modern thought has particularly flourished in France and our choice of extracts aims to reflect this. It was Emmanuel Levinas who brought Husserl's and Heidegger's ideas to France, where they were taken up after the Second World War by Maurice Merleau-Ponty, among others (Levinas's work is discussed in

Chapter 4). Phenomenology becomes 'the method of existentialism' in France; the French emphasis in phenomenology tends – to generalise – to be on the concrete manifestations and experiences of everyday living.

Thus, for Jean-Paul Sartre (1905–1980), 'Appearance does not hide the essence, it reveals it; it is the essence'. Appearance reveals. Sartre's *Being and Nothingness* (Sartre, 1956) is a 'phenomenological ontology', that is, an attempt to describe the manner of our being (Reid, 1976: 576). Sartre's notion of being can best be illustrated by reading his novels, particularly perhaps, the second volume of his projected four-volume novel *The Roads to Freedom*; his philosophising was never separate from lived experience. Sartre writes of the complexity of defining ourselves in relation to others: 'In order to get any truth about myself, I must have contact with another person'. He raises questions of choice and conscious decision; a person can decide what he is and what others are: 'let us at once announce the discovery of a world which we shall call inter-subjectivity; this is the world in which man decides what he is and what others are' (Sartre, cited in Friedman, 1964: 186). However, the way in which he does this, as with the character Mathieu in *The Reprieve* (Sartre, 2001), is far from simple; struggle is at its heart.

For Sartre 'Man is nothing but what he makes of himself'; this is a 'heroic subjectivism' (Cahoone, 1996: 259) which, however, post-modernism would reject. Does one have absolute freedom to create oneself in a world without god or nature? Is it all about personal transformation? Can one decide for oneself? In this sense Sartre's existentialism can be seen as modern, with the individual in the centre. Thus Sartre is perhaps more concerned with personal transformation, even though this transformation needs the company of others in which to take place. Levinas in contrast is more concerned with what it means to put the other first.

Simone de Beauvoir (1908–1986) brought to Western philosophy a new critique of gender (Beauvoir, 1953). She was a friend of Merleau-Ponty, and Sartre was her lover. Her major concerns were the social and cultural structures that limit individual development, particularly the oppression of women, through their being left by men in an inessential role, as only there to support men's position. She explored how women have internalised this. De Beauvoir questioned Freud, and his notion of a castration complex. Would it not be more reasonable, she wrote, to look at the social privilege and power that accompany the prestige of the penis? She was equally sceptical of a Marxist view, which would ascribe the oppression of women to class. Nothing, de Beauvoir wrote, would change in a socialist environment; there would still be the will to objectify and dominate the other (Kearney and Rainwater, 1996: 94, and see Moi, 1990).

How far are psychotherapy and its associated patriarchal institutions particularly created by men for men's advantage? What does the therapist (male or female) regard as ordinary, in terms of women's relationships, thinking and being? Male or female, it does not matter – both may have internalised the oppression of women. Phenomenology raises questions about the way we look at our experience and in so doing, it raises socio-political questions.

We now take some key writers on phenomenology and, by offering some prefatory thoughts, suggest ways of approaching the extracts. In structuring the book in this way we wish to stress the importance of reading these philosophers' original texts, rather than just commentaries on them. 'Heidegger's texts', said Derrida (Kearney, 1995: 160), ' . . . harbour a future of meaning which will ensure they are read and reread for centuries.' It is indeed impossible to read Heidegger the same way twice, and this does not reflect any shortcoming on the reader's or Heidegger's part. This impossibility is the very source of the potency and potentiality of the writing. The text invites our engagement and re-engagement; the reader–writing relationship echoes and models something for the practice of psychotherapy. What emerges between therapist and patient can similarly be seen as calling for an open, engaged, phenomenological approach, rather than a scientific or psychological one with its claims for neutrality, impartiality or objectivity. Psychotherapy can be considered to be an attempt to carry out phenomenology *à deux*.

Suggested further reading

Becker, C (1992), *Living and Relating*. London: Sage
Binswanger, L (1963), *Being-in-the-World. Selected Papers of Ludwig Binswanger*. New York: Basic Books
Boss, M (1963), *Psychoanalysis and Dasein Analysis*. New York: Basic Books
Buber, M (1958), *I and Thou*. New York: Charles Scribner's Sons
Cohn, H (1997), *Existential Thought and Therapeutic Practice*. London: Sage
Frankl, V (1973 [1967]), *Psychotherapy and Existentialism. Selected Papers on Logotherapy*. Harmondsworth: Penguin
Heaton, J (1990), 'What Is Existential Analysis?', *Journal of the Society for Existential Analysis*, No. 1
Koning, A J J and Jenner F A (1982), *Phenomenology and Psychiatry*. London: Academic Press
Laing, R D (1965 [1960]), *The Divided Self. An Existential Study in Sanity and Madness*. Harmondsworth: Penguin
May, R (ed.) (1961), *Existential Bases of Psychotherapy*. New York: Random House
Spinelli, E (1989), *The Interpreted World. An Introduction to Phenomenological Psychology*. London: Sage
Van Deurzen-Smith, E (1996), *Everyday Mysteries. Existential Dimensions of Psychotherapy*. London: Routledge
Worsley, R. (2001), *Process Work in Person-Centred Therapy. Phenomenological and Existential Perspectives*. Basingstoke: Palgrave

Kierkegaard (1813–1855)

Søren Kierkegaard was the son of a pastor. He trained for the Lutheran ministry in his native Denmark, and saw himself as religious, but was very critical of organised Christianity.

Kierkegaard insisted on his own experience and thought (and his thought about thought), and valued solitude in the face of what he saw as the threat to individuality posed by the modern world. Tragedy, he felt, was also brushed aside by modernity, whereas it is the condition of life. In becoming aware of our existence as individuals before God we necessarily experience an accompanying *dread* and suffer from it. 'Kierkegaard's preoccupation with the self and existence and the accompanying dread . . . and suffering, made him the father of modern Existentialism' (Garland and Garland, 1976: 466). His influence was, indeed, greater in the twentieth century than in the nineteenth. In encouraging an examination of one's own being, his method was, arguably, phenomenological: he was concerned never to flinch from the phenomena of experience as he apprehended them. He refused, and does not allow the reader, to take refuge behind the twin masks of 'subjectivity' and 'objectivity': his conclusions are hard to write off as merely 'subjective', and at the same time he makes no claim to have discovered 'objective' truths outside of himself.

One way of locating him in the history of ideas is to look at him in relation to Hegel. Kierkegaard criticised Hegel's dialectic: that is, Hegel's key idea that history is a progress which happens through force meeting counter-force, thesis meeting antithesis, leading to a new synthesis. Kierkegaard's critique has important implications for psychotherapy. For Kierkegaard the dialectic is a mere abstraction. Abstraction is not the right starting place. To Hegelian collective thinking he opposed his radical attention to the uniqueness of the individual. In speaking, for example, against the organised Church, he might have been speaking about over-professionalised psychotherapy, which he would similarly have understood as a way of not being aware of one's own existence and death. Hegel's 'synthesis' has no place in Kierkegaard's view of who we are. It is as if he were saying: don't fudge it. Don't accept false consolations.

In the first extract below Kierkegaard writes of despair. He is saying that the worst despair is our unwillingness to be our own despair. This unwillingness can lead people into a therapy where they look for transformation as they would through buying a new coat. What then happens is an attempt at an immediate solution rather than staying with 'immediacy', with 'what is'. It is this worst form of despair, 'wishing for a new self', that has such important implications for the practice of psychotherapy. Those therapists influenced by the implications of phenomenology are therefore unlikely to hear such wishes as something positive. Instead positive action would be an examination through description of such despair.

In the second extract ('Dread is the dizziness of freedom . . . ') Kierkegaard introduces the possibility of dread, a possibility for individual exploration in psychotherapy. When we are free we can see that we are guilty of previously closing things down. This process is something that psychology cannot explain. 'No science has explained or can explain.' Dread does not tempt us like a definite choice, but 'alarms and fascinates with its sweet anxiety'. Hence the grasping at finiteness, the positing of 'synthesis'. This is an important influence on the development of post-modernism, with its characteristic tendency to resist such closure.

Later Kierkegaard talks about being clear what 'self' means, which may be different from having understanding or knowledge of self. By starting to talk about the self Kierkegaard raises questions about the individual versus the general: '[A]lthough there have lived countless millions of such selves, no science can state what the self is.'

Perhaps the therapeutic encounter can usefully be thought of in terms of Kierkegaard's view of (the patient's)

> shut-upness unfreely revealed . . . for the shut-up is precisely the mute, and if it has to express itself, this must come about against its will when the freedom lying prone in unfreedom revolts upon coming into communication with freedom outside [the therapist's presence], and now betrays unfreedom in such a way that it is the individual who betrays himself against his will in dread.

Yet the importance of the therapist being able to stay with dread (and thus through his/her own therapy, his/her own dread) might be seen when Kierkegaard goes on to say, in the extract below, 'he who is educated by dread is educated by possibility, and only the man who is educated by possibility is educated in accordance with his infinity'. Psychotherapy could, then, be seen as an exploration of 'possibility' ('the heaviest of all categories'), through exploration of dread. Thus on emerging from such a therapy the patient 'goes out from the school of possibility, and knows more thoroughly than a child knows the alphabet that he can demand of life absolutely nothing . . . he will extol reality . . . it is far far lighter than the possibility was'.

From Kierkegaard [1848] (1954), *Fear and Trembling* and [1849] (1954) *Sickness unto Death* (trans. Lowry, W). In: Friedman, M (ed.) (1964), *The Worlds of Existentialism. A Critical Reader*, pp. 371–3 (bracketed numbers in the text are Friedman's page references to the 1954 edition from which he has selected).

> *The Despair which is Conscious of being Despair, as also it is Conscious of being a Self wherein there is after all something Eternal, and then is either in despair at not willing to be itself, or in despair at willing to be itself.* (180)

This form of despair is: despair at not willing to be oneself; or still lower, despair at not willing to be a self; or lowest of all, despair at willing to be another than himself, wishing for a new self. Properly speaking, immediacy has no self, it does not recognize itself, so neither can it recognize itself again, it terminates therefore preferably in the romantic. When immediacy despairs it possesses not even enough self to wish or to dream that it had become what it did not become. The immediate man helps himself in a different way: he wishes to be another. Of this one may easily convince oneself by observing immediate men. At the moment of despair no wish is so natural to them as the wish that they had become or might become another. In any case one can never forbear to smile at such a despairer, who, humanly speaking, although he is in despair, is so very innocent. Commonly such a despairer is infinitely comic. Think of a self (and next to God there is no thing so eternal as a self), and then that this self gets the notion of asking whether it might not let itself become or be made into another . . . than itself. And yet such a despairer, whose only wish is this most crazy of all transformations, loves to think that this change might be accomplished as easily as changing a coat. For the immediate man does not recognize his self, he recognizes himself only by his dress, he recognizes (and here again appears the infinitely comic trait) he recognizes that he has a self only by externals. There is no more ludicrous confusion, for a self is just infinitely different from externals. (186f.)

This despair is one quality deeper than the foregoing and is a sort which rarely is met with in the world. That blind door behind which there was nothing is in this case a real door, a door carefully locked to be sure, and behind it sits as it were the self and watches itself, employed in filling up time with not willing to be itself, and yet is self enough to love itself. This is what is called *introversion*. (196)

If the despairing *self* is *active*, it really is related to itself only as experimenting with whatsoever it be that it undertakes, however great it may be, however astonishing, however persistently carried out. It acknowledges no power over it, hence in the last resort it lacks seriousness and is able only to conjure up a show of seriousness when the self bestows upon its experiments its utmost attention. . . . It is so far from being true that the self succeeds more and more in becoming itself, that in fact it merely becomes more and more manifest that it is a hypothetical self. The self is its own lord and master, so it is said, absolutely its own lord, and precisely this is despair, but it also is what it regards as its pleasure and enjoyment. However, by closer inspection one easily ascertains that this ruler is a king without a country, he rules really over nothing; his condition, his dominion, is subjected to the dialectic that every instant revolution is legitimate. For in the last resort this depends arbitrarily upon the self. . . .

. . . In spite of or in defiance of the whole of . . . existence he wills to be himself with it, to take it along, almost defying his torment. For to hope in the possibility of help, not to speak of help by virtue of the absurd, that for God all things are possible – no, that he will not do. And as for seeking help from any other – no, that he will not do for all the world; rather than seek help he would prefer to be himself – with all the tortures of hell, if so it must be. . . .

But the more consciousness there is in such a sufferer who in despair is determined to be himself, all the more does despair too potentiate itself and become demoniac. (202–5)

This despair does not will to be itself with Stoic doting upon itself, nor with self-deification, willing in this way, doubtless mendaciously, yet in a certain sense in terms of its perfection; no, with hatred for existence it wills to be itself, to be itself in terms of its misery; it does not even in defiance or defiantly will to be itself, but to be itself in spite; it does not even will in defiance to tear itself free from the Power which posited it, it wills to obtrude upon this Power in spite, to hold on to it out of malice. And that is natural, a malignant objection must above all take care to hold on to that against which it is an objection. Revolting against the whole of existence, it thinks it has hold of a proof against it, against its goodness. This proof the despairer thinks he himself is, and that is what he wills to be, therefore he wills to be himself, himself with his torment, in order with this torment to protest against the whole of existence. (207)

From Kierkegaard [1848] (1944), *The Concept of Dread* (trans. Lowry, W). In: Friedman, M (ed.) (1964), *The Worlds of Existentialism. A Critical Reader*, pp. 369–71 (bracketed numbers in the text are Friedman's page references to the 1944 edition from which he has selected).

. . . Dread is the dizziness of freedom which occurs when the spirit would posit the synthesis, and freedom then gazes down into its own possibility, grasping at finiteness to sustain itself. In this dizziness freedom succumbs. Further than this psychology cannot go and will not. That very instant everything is changed, and when freedom rises again it sees that it is guilty. Between these two instants lies the leap, which no science has explained or can explain. He who becomes guilty in dread becomes as ambiguously guilty as it is possible to be. Dread is a womanish debility in which freedom swoons.
. . . In dread there is the egoistic infinity of possibility, which does not tempt like a definite choice, but alarms (*ængster*) and fascinates with its sweet anxiety (*Beængstelse*).

In the later individual dread is more reflective. This may be expressed by saying that the nothing which is the object of dread becomes, as it were, more and more a something. . . . The nothing of dread is a complex of presentiments which reflect themselves in themselves, coming nearer and nearer to the individual, notwithstanding that in dread they signify again essentially nothing, not, however, be it noted, a nothing with which the individual has nothing to do, but a nothing in lively communication with the ignorance of innocence. This reflectiveness is a predisposition which, before the individual becomes guilty, signifies essentially nothing, whereas when by the qualitative leap he becomes guilty it is the presupposition in which the individual goes beyond himself because sin presupposes itself, not of course before it is posited (that would be a predestination), but presupposes itself when it is posited. (55f.)

If one does not first make clear to oneself what 'self' means, there is not much use in saying of sin that it is selfishness. But 'self' signifies precisely the contradiction of positing the general as the particular (*Enkelte*). Only when the concept of the particular individual (*Enkelte*) is given can there be any question of the selfish. But although there have lived countless millions of such 'selves', no science can state what the self is, without stating it in perfectly general terms. The real 'self' is first posited by the qualitative leap. In the situation preceding this there can be no question of such a thing. Therefore when one would explain sin by selfishness, one becomes involved in confusions, since on the contrary it is true that by sin and in sin selfishness comes into being. (70f.)

. . . Nature's security is due to the fact that time has no significance for it. Only in the instant does history begin. . . . The instant is that ambiguous moment in which time and eternity touch one another, thereby positing *the temporal*, where time is constantly intersecting eternity and eternity constantly permeating time. (80)

The possible corresponds precisely to the future. For freedom the possible is the future; and for time the future is the possible. Corresponding to both of these in the individual life is dread. . . . Dread is the psychological state which precedes sin, comes as near as possible to it, and is as provocative as possible of dread, but without explaining sin, which breaks forth first in the qualitative leap.

The instant sin is posited, the temporal is sin. (82)

In the state of innocence freedom was not posited as freedom, its possibility appears in the dread of the individuality. In the demoniacal the situation is reversed. Freedom is posited as unfreedom, for freedom is lost. The possibility of freedom is in turn dread. The difference is absolute; for the possibility of freedom manifests itself here in relation to unfreedom, which is exactly the opposite of innocence, which is a determinant oriented towards freedom.

The demoniacal is unfreedom which would shut itself off. This, however, is an impossibility; it always maintains a relationship, and even when this has apparently disappeared it is nevertheless there, and dread manifests itself at once in the instant of contact with the good. . . . The demoniacal is *shut-upness* [*det Indesluttede*, or *Indesluttedhed*] *unfreely revealed*. These two traits denote, as they should, the same thing; for the shut-up is precisely the mute, and if it has to express itself, this must come about against its will when the freedom lying prone in unfreedom revolts upon coming into communication with freedom outside and now betrays unfreedom in such a way that it is the individual who betrays himself against his will in dread. (109f.)

He who is educated by dread is educated by possibility, and only the man who is educated by possibility is educated in accordance with his infinity. Possibility is therefore the heaviest of all categories. . . . When such a person, therefore, goes out from the school of possibility, and knows more thoroughly than a child knows the alphabet that he can demand of life absolutely nothing, and that terror, perdition, annihilation, dwell next door to every man, and has learned the profitable lesson that every dread which alarms [*ængste*] may the next instant become a fact, he will then interpret reality differently, he will extol reality, and even when it rests upon him heavily he will remember that after all it is far, far lighter than the possibility was. (139f.)

Suggested further reading

Ree, J and Chamberlain, J (eds) (1998), *Kierkegaard: A Critical Reader*. Oxford: Blackwell

Husserl (1859–1938)

Although there is a long prehistory stemming from Aristotle, Edmund Husserl is generally regarded as the founding father of phenomenology. Others might wish to start with Friedrich Hegel (1770–1831). We shall be examining Hegel more later, and here take Husserl to be the person who reawakened interest in phenomenology in the twentieth century and pointed phenomenological research in its modern directions.

Husserl was not opposed to science. He originally studied mathematics; his teacher, Wilhelm Wundt, who was a pioneer of what became the modern discipline of psychology, encouraged him to study philosophy: philosophy, in the late nineteenth century, included both metaphysics and the philosophy of mind; it studied both the spiritual and the cognitive. Husserl's project was to give science firmer philosophical foundations (see Kearney and Rainwater, 1996: 3), through a new, descriptive method. Like Kierkegaard, however, he provides an antidote to the excesses of a modern scientific world-view. In this sense Husserl can help us think about healing in a way that is different from the current dominant medical/scientific model. He invites us to think about psychotherapy in a way that is different from what has now become mainstream psychology.

Husserl (like Freud) was born in Moravia. He spent his working life in German universities until he was prevented from teaching by the Nazis, because he was Jewish. Husserl's seminal work, *Logical Investigations*, was, like Freud's *Interpretation of Dreams*, published in 1900. Both books are concerned with the nature of consciousness, and each from its different starting place changed the course of European thinking. Husserl's influence extends from Heidegger and Levinas, to Derrida.

For Husserl the notion of *intentionality* was crucial. As intentional creatures we are moved to make sense of the world, and it is how we do this through what we perceive that determines what we consider *is* our world. Husserl derived this thinking from Franz Brentano (whose lectures in Vienna in the 1870s Freud also attended). In his key work, *Psychology from an Empirical Standpoint* (1874), Brentano proposed a descriptive psychology which aimed at clarifying mental phenomena. Out of this Husserl developed his own famous rallying cry, 'to the things themselves', in a search for the essences of things, their essential quality. It was a return to human experience. He came to see, however, that one can never get back to the things themselves (which does not stop us trying): we are all caught up in the way we perceive them, and it is our own personal and cultural history that helps to determine how we perceive.

We give below an extract from Husserl's *Cartesian Meditations* (Husserl, 1960). As counsellors and psychotherapists we might consider Husserl's phenomenology, as he outlines it here, primarily to be about trying to bracket out our own biases and to be aware of the further biases involved in doing this.

> This 'phenomenological epoché' and 'parenthesizing' of the Objective world . . . does not leave us confronting nothing. On the contrary when we gain possession of something by it; and what we (or, to speak more precisely, what I, the one who is meditating) acquire by it is my pure living, with all the pure subjective processes making it up, and everything meant in them, *purely as* meant in them; the universe of "phenomena". . . . The concrete subjective processes, let us repeat, are indeed the things to which his attentive regard is directed: by the attentive Ego, qua philosophizing Ego, practises abstention with regard to what he intuits.
>
> (Husserl, 1960: 20, cited in Friedman, 1964: 77)

Thus we may, for example, be able to bracket off a response to a patient/client which is really a response to the person the client/patient person reminds us of, and thus free ourselves up to respond to the patient because they are who they are, and allow them to speak to us. Thus we may be helped to keep our observations 'free from all interpretations that read into them more than is genuinely seen' (Husserl, 1960, cited in Friedman, 1964: 78). Above all, we are encouraged to invite our patients to take their experience seriously.

Further implications of Husserlian phenomenology for practice might thus be that we encourage clients/patients to *describe* their feelings and experiences, their thoughts, doubts, wishes and dreams, rather than trying to *explain*, rationalise or justify them; that we are alert to the tendency (in ourselves and our clients/patients) to impose hierarchical systems of thought – for example, prejudging one aspect of what a client says as more important than another. This is complex. It requires an attentiveness to the *client's* hierarchy of importance, and an awareness of the therapist's point of view, which, like the client's, is affected by current cultural orderings and hierarchies of ideas. These the therapist can also be seen as representing.

Extract from Husserl [1931] (1960), *Cartesian Meditations. An Introduction to Phenomenology* (trans. Cairns, D) In: Friedman, M (ed.) (1964), *The Worlds of Existentialism. A Critical Reader* pp. 77–83 (bracketed numbers in the text are Friedman's page references to the 1960 edition from which he has selected).

. . . This 'phenomenological epoché' and 'parenthesizing' of the Objective world . . . does not leave us confronting nothing. On the contrary we gain possession of something by it; and what we (or, to speak more precisely, what I, the one who is meditating) acquire by it is my pure living, with all the pure subjective processes making this up, and everything meant in them, *purely* as meant in them: the universe of 'phenomena' . . . The concrete subjective processes, let us repeat, are indeed the things to which his attentive regard is directed: but the attentive Ego, *qua* philosophizing Ego, practices abstention with respect to what he intuits. Likewise everything *meant* in such accepting or positing processes of consciousness (the meant judgement, theory, value, end, or whatever it is) is still retained completely – but with the acceptance-modification, 'mere phenomenon' . . . The world is for me absolutely nothing else but the world existing for and accepted by me in such a conscious *cogito* . . .

Thus the being of the pure ego and his *cogitationes*, as a being that is prior in itself, is antecedent to the natural being of the world – the world of which I always speak, the one of which I *can* speak. Natural being is a realm whose existential status [*Seinsgeltung*] is secondary; it continually presupposes the realm of transcendental *epoché*, because it leads back to this realm, is called transcendental–phenomenological reduction. (20f.)

. . . There is no psychological Ego and there are no psychic phenomena in the sense proper to psychology, i.e., as components of psychophysical men . . . This world, with all its Objects . . . derives its whole sense and its existential status, which it has for me, from me myself, *from me as the transcendental Ego*, the Ego who comes to the fore only with transcendental–phenomenological epoché. (26)

If the Ego, as naturally immersed in the world, experiencingly and otherwise, is called *'interested' in the world*, then the phenomenologically altered – and, as so altered, continually maintained – attitude consists in a *splitting of the Ego*: in that the phenomenological Ego establishes himself as *'disinterested onlooker'*, above the naively interested Ego. That this takes place is then itself accessible by means of a new reflection, which, as transcendental, likewise demands the very same attitude of looking on *'disinterestedly'* – the Ego's sole remaining interest being to see and to describe adequately what he sees, purely as seen, as what is seen and seen in such and such a manner . . . That signifies restriction to the pure data of transcendental reflection, which therefore must be taken precisely as they are given in simple evidence, purely 'intuitively', and always kept free from all interpretations that read into them more than is genuinely seen . . . Consequently I, the transcendental phenomenologist, have *objects* (singly or in universal complexes) as a theme for my universal descriptions: *solely as the intentional correlates of modes of consciousness of them* . . . Or, dated more distinctly: I, the mediating phenomenologist, set myself the all-embracing task of *uncovering myself*, in my full concreteness – that is, with all the intentional correlates that are included therein. (35–8)

Consequently the world is a universal problem of egology, as is likewise the whole of conscious life, in its immanent temporality, when we direct our regard to the purely immanent. . . . Any 'Objective' object, *any object whatever* (even an immanent one), points to *a structure, within the transcendental ego, that is governed by a rule.* (53)

That the being of the world 'transcends' consciousness in this fashion (even with respect to the evidence in which the world presents itself), and that it necessarily remains transcendent, in no wise alters the fact that it is conscious life alone, wherein everything transcendent becomes constituted as something inseparable from consciousness, and which specifically, as world-consciousness, bears within itself inseparably the sense: world – and indeed: 'this actually existing' world. (62)

Since, by his *own active generating*, the Ego constitutes himself as *identical substrate of Ego-properties*, he constitutes himself also as a 'fixed and abiding' *personal Ego*. . . . Since the monadically concrete ego includes also the whole of actual and potential conscious life, it is clear that the problem of *explicating this monadic ego phenomenologically* (the problem of his constitution for himself) must include *all constitutional problems without exception*. Consequently the phenomenology of this *self-constitution* coincides with *phenomenology as a whole*. (67f.)

Thus removed from all factualness, it has become the pure '*eidos*' perception, whose '*ideal*' extension is made up of all ideally possible perceptions, as purely phantasiable processes. Analyses of perception are then '*essential*' or '*eidetic*' analyses . . . *an intuitive and apodictic consciousness of something universal*. The eidos itself is a beheld or beholdable universal, one that is pure, 'unconditioned' – that is to say: according to its own intuitional sense, a universal not conditioned by any fact. It is *prior to all 'concepts'*, in the sense of verbal significations; indeed, as pure concepts, these must be made to fit the eidos. . . . Eidetic phenomenology, accordingly, explores the universal Apriori without which neither I nor any transcendental Ego whatever is 'imaginable'; or, since every eidetic universality has the value of an unbreakable law, eidetic phenomenology explores the all-embracing laws that prescribe for every factual statement about something transcendental the possible sense (as opposed to the absurdity or inconsistency) of that statement. . . . *Along with phenomenological reduction, eidetic intuition is the fundamental form of all particular transcendental methods.* . . . Both of them determine, through and through, the legitimate sense of a transcendental phenomenology. (70–2)

Every imaginable sense, every imaginable being, whether the latter is called immanent or transcendent, falls within the domain of transcendental subjectivity, as the subjectivity that constitutes sense and being. The attempt to conceive the universe of true being as something lying outside the universe of possible consciousness, possible knowledge, possible evidence, the two being related to one another merely externally by a rigid law, is nonsensical. They belong together essentially; and, as belonging together essentially, they are also concretely one, one in the only absolute concretion: transcendental subjectivity. . . . Genuine theory of knowledge is accordingly possible [*sinnvoll*] only as a transcendental–phenomenological theory, which, instead of operating within consistent inferences leading from a supposed immanency to a supposed transcendency (that of no matter what 'thing in itself', which is alleged to be essentially unknowable), has to do exclusively with systematic clarification of the knowledge performance, a clarification in which this must become thoroughly understandable as an intentional performance. . . . *The proof of this idealism is therefore phenomenology itself.* (84–6)

First of all, my 'transcendental clue' is the experienced Other, given to me in straightforward consciousness and as I immerse myself in examining the noematic–ontic content belonging to him (purely as correlate of my cogito, the particular structure of which is yet to be uncovered). . . . As 'psychophysical' Objects, they are *'in' the world*. On the other hand, I experience them at the same time as *subjects for this world*, as experiencing it (this same world that I experience) and, in so doing, experiencing me too, even as I experience the world and others in it. (90f.)

Accordingly *the intrinsically first other* (the first 'non-Ego') *is the other Ego*. And the other Ego makes constitutionally possible a new infinite domain of what is 'other': an *Objective Nature* and a whole Objective world, to which all other Egos and I myself belong. . . . An *Ego-community*, which includes me, becomes constituted (in my sphere of ownness, naturally) as a community of Egos existing with each other and for each other – *ultimately a community of monads*, which, moreover, (in its communalized intentionality) constitutes the *one identical world. In this world* all Egos again present themselves, but *in an Objectivating apperception* with the sense *'men'* or 'psychophysical men as worldly Objects' . . . I can recognize that the

Objective world does not, in the proper sense, *transcend* that sphere or that sphere's own intersubjective essence, but rather inheres in it as an 'immanent' transcendency. Stated more precisely: The Objective world as an *idea* – the ideal correlate of an intersubjective (intersubjectively communalized) experience, which ideally can be and is carried on as constantly harmonious – is essentially related to intersubjectivity (itself constituted as having the ideality of endless openness), whose component particular subjects are equipped with mutually corresponding and harmonious constitute systems. Consequently, *the constitution of the world essentially involves a 'harmony' of the monads*. (107f.)

. . . *Ego* and *alter ego* are always and necessarily given *in an original 'pairing'*. . . . We find, more particularly, a living mutual awakening and an overlaying of each with the objective sense of the other . . . the limiting case being that of complete 'likeness'. As the result of this overlaying, there takes place in the paired data a mutual transfer of sense. (112f.)

But, since the other body there enters into a pairing association with my body here and, being given perceptually, becomes the core of an appresentation, the care of my experience of a coexisting ego, that ego, according to the whole sense-giving course of the association, must be appresented as *an ego now coexisting in the mode There*, 'such as I should be if I were there'. My own ego however, the ego given in constant self-perception, is actual now with the content belonging to his Here. Therefore an ego is *appresented*, as *other* than mine. . . . It is quite comprehensible that, *as a further consequence*, an 'empathizing' of definite contents belonging to the '*higher psychic sphere*' arises. Such contents too are indicated somatically and in the conduct of the organism toward the outside world – for example: as the outward conduct of someone who is angry or cheerful, which I easily understand from my own conduct under similar circumstances. (119f.)

. . . Since every pairing association is reciprocal, every such understanding uncovers my own psychic life in its similarity and difference and, by bringing new features into prominence, makes It fruitful for new associations. . . .

The first thing constituted in the form of community, and *the foundation for all other intersubjectively common things*, is the *commonness of Nature*, along with that of the *Other's organism* and his *psychophysical Ego*, as paired with *my own psychophysical Ego*. (120)

If that body functions appresentatively, then, in union with it, the other Ego becomes an object of my consciousness – and primarily the other Ego with his organism, as given to him in the manner of appearance pertaining to his 'absolute Here'. (121)

The only conceivable manner in which others can have for me the sense and status of existent others, thus and so determined, consists in their being constituted *in me* as others . . . as monads existing for themselves precisely as I exist for myself, yet existing also in communion, therefore (I emphasize the expression already used earlier) *in connexion with me* qua concrete ego, qua monad. . . . *Something that exists is in intentional communion with something else that exists.* It is an essentially *unique connectedness*, an actual community and precisely the one that makes transcendentally possible the being of a world, a world of men and things. . . . In the sense of *a community of men* and in that of *man* – who, even as solitary, has the sense: member of a community – there is implicit a mutual being for one another, which entails an *Objectivating equalization* of my existence with that of all others – consequently: I or anyone else, as a man among other men. If, with my understanding of someone else, I penetrate more deeply into him, into his horizon of ownness, I shall soon run into the fact that just as his animate bodily organism lies in my field of perception, so my animate organism lies in his field of perception and that, in general, he experiences me forthwith as an Other for him, just as I experience him as *my* Other. Likewise I shall find that, in the case of a plurality of Others, they are experienced also by one another as Others, and consequently that I can experience any given Other not only as himself an Other but also as related in turn to *his* Others and perhaps – with a mediatedness that may be conceived as reiterable – related at the same time to me. . . . Openly endless Nature itself then becomes a Nature that includes an open plurality of men (conceived more generally: animalia), distributed one knows not how in infinite space, as subjects of possible intercommunion. To this community there naturally corresponds, in transcendental concreteness, a similarly open community of monads, which we designate as *transcendental intersubjectivity*. We need hardly say that, as existing for me, it is constituted purely within me, the meditating ego, purely by virtue of sources belonging to my intentionality; nevertheless it is constituted thus as a community constituted also in every other monad (who, in turn, is constituted with the modification: 'other') as the same community – only with a different subjective mode of appearance – and as necessarily bearing within itself the same Objective world. (128–30)

Our monadological results are *metaphysical*, if it be true that ultimate cognitions of being should be called metaphysical. On the other hand, what we have here is *anything but metaphysics in the customary sense*: a historically degenerate metaphysics, which by no means conforms to the sense with which metaphysics, as 'first philosophy', was instituted originally. Phenomenology's purely intuitive, concrete, and also apodictic mode of demonstration excludes all 'metaphysical adventure', all speculative excesses. (139)

For the first time, the problem of empathy has been given its true sense, and the true method for its solution has been furnished, by constitutional phenomenology. . . . It has never been recognized that the otherness of 'someone else' becomes extended to the whole world, as its 'Objectivity', giving it this sense in the first place. (147)

I must first explicate *my own as such, in order to understand that, within my own, what is not my own likewise receives existential sense* – and does so as something appresented analogically. . . . The *illusion* of a solipsism is dissolved, even though the proposition that everything existing for me must derive its existential sense exclusively from me myself, from my sphere of consciousness, retains its validity and fundamental importance. . . . *Monadology* . . . draws its content purely from phenomenological explication of the transcendental experience laid open by transcendental reduction, accordingly from the most ordinary evidence, wherein all conceivable evidences must be grounded. . . . Phenomenological explication does nothing but *explicate the sense this world has for us all, prior to any philosophizing*, and obviously gets solely from our experience – *a sense which philosophy can uncover but never alter.* (150f.)

Science – as a system of *phenomenological* disciplines, which treat correlative themes and are ultimately grounded, not on an axiom, ego cogito, but on an *all-embracing   self-investigation.* . . . Philosophical   knowledge . . . is necessarily the path of universal self-knowledge – first of all monadic, and then intermonadic. . . . Positive science is a science lost in the world. I must lose the world by epoché, in order to regain it by a universal self-examination. (156f.)

Suggested further reading

Moran, D. (2000), *Introduction to Phenomenology*. London: Routledge (in particular chapters 2 to 5).

Heidegger (1889–1976)

To paraphrase, with Derrida, the pre-Socratic philosopher Heraclitus's famous dictum about stepping into a river (Russell, 1961: 63), reading the challenging and difficult work of Martin Heidegger is never the same twice.

Heidegger drew from Kierkegaard's writings on existence, and above all from Husserl's researches into essences, in his major work *Being and Time* (*Sein und Zeit*, 1927). His influence on twentieth century thinking is considerable, in fields as diverse as theology and literary criticism. A controversial figure, he was appointed Rector of Freiburg University in 1933 when the Nazis came to power, taking over from Husserl who had been his teacher.

Heidegger's notion of being contrasts starkly with certain prevailing notions modelled on science and technology. This is, arguably, what is most important to psychotherapy about his thinking. By saying, as he does in the extract that follows, that we must make the enquirer transparent in his own being, he lends force to the view that therapists need to be in therapy themselves. Similarly, the patient's 'essential character' will also emerge 'from what is enquired about – namely, Being'. This enquiry into the nature of their being is an essential part of their being. 'Enquiring' . . . is 'one of the possibilities of . . . Being.'

This is part of what Heidegger denotes by the term 'Dasein' (*da – sein*: there – being). 'Understanding of being is itself a definite characteristic of Dasein's being.' Such enquiry, being part of being, is always the starting point: the 'fundamental ontology from which alone all other ontologies can take their rise must be sought in the existential analytic of Dasein' (Heidegger, 1963: 32–4). The *way* in which we enquire is part of our being. It is not just what is told, but is in the telling. This 'being' is how the patient is with us.

It is vital to psychotherapy that the work of helping our patients with 'the question of the meaning of Being' (everything our patients bring can be seen as part of this question) 'must be carried through by explicating Dasein beforehand in its temporality and historicality'. Thus *time* is always a standpoint, and this is part of Heidegger's major contribution to Husserl's project: what is spoken of will also always be in a specific temporal and historical context, the cultural context – *this* place and time – of the therapist and client, the condition for their both being there.

'Dasein simultaneously falls prey to the tradition of which it has more or less explicitly taken hold.' We are so much *in* time and history that it is hard to see where we are. Thus one of the problematics of psychotherapy which emerges with clarity through a reading of Heidegger is that what the therapeutic process '"transmits" is made so inaccessible . . . that it rather becomes concealed'.

From this extract two further important suggestions for psychotherapy can be derived. The first is that 'only as phenomenology is ontology possible'. Heidegger insists that 'the question of the meaning of Being . . . must be treated phenomenologically'. This is where we see Heidegger developing Husserl's notion of 'to the things themselves'. To start with phenomenology means 'to let that which shows itself be seen from itself in the way in which it shows itself from itself'. In order to study being you need to start with what *is* – not with abstract speculation. This is important for both patient and therapist.

The second point is the way Heidegger seems to underline the importance of interpretation in psychotherapy. 'The meaning of phenomenological description as a method lies in *interpretation*. . . . Being and the structure of Being lie beyond every entity and every possible character which an entity may possess.' Thus for the patient to enquire into the nature of his or her own being, another needs to be there to provide interpretation. You cannot see yourself on your own.

Before we turn to the extract, we reproduce two translator's notes from Friedman (1964) – to whom we are indebted for all the extracts in this chapter – which we have found to be of help in our own encounters with Heidegger.

The first is on *Dasein*:

> The word 'Dasein' plays so important a role in this work and is already so familiar . . . that it seems simpler to leave it untranslated except in the . . . passages in which Heidegger himself breaks it up with a hyphen ('Da-sein') to show its etymological construction: literally 'Being-there'. Though in traditional German philosophy it may be used quite generally to stand for almost any kind of Being or 'existence' which we can say that something has . . . in everyday usage it tends to be used more narrowly to stand for the kind of Being that belongs to persons. Heidegger . . . often uses it to stand for any person who has such Being . . .
>
> (Cited in Friedman, 1964: 95n)

The second spells out a tricky distinction: 'Ontological inquiry is concerned primarily with Being; ontical inquiry is concerned primarily with entities and the facts about them' (cited in Friedman, 1964: 97n).

From Heidegger (1927), *Being and Time* (trans. Macquarrie, J and Robinson, E). In: Friedman, M (ed.) (1964), *The Worlds of Existentialism. A Critical Reader*, pp. 94–100 (bracketed numbers in the text are Friedman's page references to the 1963 edition from which he has selected).

> To work out the question of Being adequately, we must make an entity – the inquirer – transparent in his own Being. The very asking of this question is an entity's mode of *Being*; and as such it gets its essential character from what is inquired about – namely Being. This entity which each of us is himself and which includes inquiring as one of the possibilities of its Being, we shall denote by the term '*Dasein*'. (27) . . . *understanding of being is itself a definite characteristic of Dasein's being. Dasein is ontically distinctive in that it* is ontological. . . . By 'existentiality' we understand the state of Being that is constitutive for those entities that exist. But in the idea of such a constitutive state of Being, the idea of Being is already included. And thus even the possibility of carrying through the analytic of Dasein depends on working out beforehand the question about the meaning of Being in general. . . . Thus Dasein's understanding of Being pertains with equal primordiality both to an understanding of something like a 'world', and to the understanding of the Being of those entities which become accessible within the world. . . . Therefore *fundamental ontology*, from which alone all other ontologies can take their rise, must be sought in the *existential analytic of Dasein*. (32–4)

> Whenever Dasein tacitly understands and interprets something like Being, it does so with *time* as its standpoint. Time must be brought to light – and

genuinely conceived – as the horizon for all understanding of Being and for any way of interpreting it. (39) . . . The question of the meaning of Being must be carried through by explicating Dasein beforehand in its temporality and historicality . . . Dasein simultaneously falls prey to the tradition of which it has more or less explicitly taken hold. . . . When tradition thus becomes master, it does so in such a way that what it 'transmits' is made so inaccessible, proximally and for the most part, that it rather becomes concealed. (42f.)

With the question of the meaning of Being, our investigation comes up against the fundamental question of philosophy. This is one that must be treated *phenomenologically.* . . . The term 'phenomenology' expresses a maxim which can be formulated as 'To the things themselves!' It is opposed to all free-floating constructions and accidental findings; it is opposed to taking over any conceptions which only seem to have been demonstrated; it is opposed to those pseudo-questions which parade themselves as 'problems', often for generations at a time. . . . The expression *'phenomenon'* signifies that *which shows itself in itself,* the manifest. Accordingly the 'phenomena' are the totality of what lies in the light of day or can be brought to the light – what the Greeks sometimes identified simply with entities. (49–51)

Thus 'phenomenology' means to let that which shows itself be seen from itself in the very way in which it shows itself from itself . . . 'Phenomenology' neither designates the object of its researches, nor characterizes the subject-matter thus comprised. The word merely informs us of the '*how*' with which *what* is to be treated in this science gets exhibited and handled. To have a science 'of' phenomena means to grasp its objects *in such a way* that everything about them which is up for discussion must be treated by exhibiting it directly and demonstrating it directly. . . . That which remains *hidden* in an egregious sense, or which relapses and gets *covered up* again, or which shows itself only '*in disguise*', is not just this entity or that, but rather the *being* of entities. This Being can be covered up so extensively that it becomes forgotten and no question arises about it or about its meaning. Thus that which demands that it become a phenomenon, and which demands this in a distinctive sense and in terms of its own-most content as a thing, is what phenomenology has taken into its grasp thematically as its object. . . . *Only as phenomenology, is ontology possible.* In the phenomenological conception of 'phenomenon' what one has in mind as that which shows itself is the Being of entities, its meaning, its modifications and derivatives.
    . . . Least of all can the Being of entities ever be anything such that 'behind it' stands something else 'which does not appear'. . . . And just because the phenomena are proximally and for the most part *not* given, there is need for phenomenology. Covered-up-ness is the counter-concept to 'phenomenon'.
    . . . Because phenomena, as understood phenomenologically, are never anything but what goes to make up Being, while Being is in every case the

Being of some entity, we must first bring forward the entities themselves if it is our aim that Being should be laid bare; and we must do this in the right way. These entities must likewise show themselves with the kind of access which genuinely belongs to them. . . . With regard to its subject-matter, phenomenology is the science of the Being of entities – ontology. . . . Our investigation itself will show that the meaning of phenomenological description as a method lies in *interpretation*. . . . Being and the structure of Being lie beyond every entity and every possible character which an entity may possess. *Being is the* transcendens *pure and simple*. And the transcendence of Dasein's Being is distinctive in that it implies the possibility and the necessity of the most radical *individuation*. Every disclosure of Being as the *transcendens* is *transcendental knowledge*. *Phenomenological truth (the disclosedness of Being) is* veritas transcendentalis.

. . . Philosophy is universal phenomenological ontology, and takes its departure from the hermeneutic of Dasein, which, as an analytic of *existence*, has made fast the guiding-line for all philosophical inquiry at the point where it *arises* and to which it *returns*. (58–62)

. . . If we are to Interpret this entity *ontologically*, the problematic of its Being must be developed from the existentiality of its existence. . . . It is particularly important that Dasein should not be Interpreted with the differentiated character of some definite way of existing, but that it should be uncovered in the undifferentiated character which it has proximally and for the most part. . . . We call this everyday undifferentiated character of Dasein '*averageness*'. (69)

. . . Descartes, who is credited with providing the point of departure for modern philosophical inquiry by his discovery of the '*cogito sum*', . . . investigates the '*cogitare*' of the '*ego*', at least within certain limits. On the other hand, he leaves the '*sum*' completely undiscussed, even though it is regarded as no less primordial than the *cogito*. Our analytic raises the ontological question of the Being of the '*sum*'. Not until the nature of this Being has been determined can we grasp the kind of Being which belongs to *cogitationes*. (71) . . . Over and above the attempt to determine the essence of 'man' as an entity, the question of his Being has remained forgotten. This Being is rather conceived as something obvious or 'self-evident' in the sense of *Being-present-at-hand* of other created Things. . . . But since even the *cogitationes* are either left ontologically undetermined, or get tacitly assumed as something 'self-evidently' 'given' whose 'Being' is not to be questioned, the decisive ontological foundations of anthropological problematics remain undetermined. (75)

Taking up relationships towards the world is possible only *because* Dasein, as Being-in-the-world, is as it is. This state of Being does not arise just because some other entity is present-at-hand outside of Dasein and meets up with it. Such an entity can 'meet up with' Dasein only in so far as it can, of its own accord, show itself within a *world*. (84) . . . If Being-in-the-world is a basic state of Dasein, and one in which Dasein operates not only in general but pre-eminently in the mode of everydayness, then it must also be something which has always been experienced ontically. (86) . . . And furthermore, the perceiving of what is known is not a process of returning with one's booty to the 'cabinet' of consciousness after one has gone out and grasped it; even in perceiving, retaining, and preserving, the Dasein which knows remains outside, and it does so as Dasein. . . . A *'commercium'* of the subject with a world does not get *created* for the first time by knowing, nor does it *arise* from some way in which the world acts upon a subject. Knowing is a mode of Dasein founded upon Being-in-the-world. Thus Being-in-the-world, as a basic state, must be Interpreted *beforehand*. . . . Even the forgetting of something, in which every relationship of Being towards what one formerly knew has seemingly been obliterated, must be conceived *as a modification of the primordial Being-in*; and this holds for every delusion and for every error. (89f.)

'Worldhood' is an ontological concept, and stands for the structure of one of the constitutive items of Being-in-the-world. But we know Being-in-the-world as a way in which Dasein's character is defined existentially. Thus worldhood itself is an *existentiale*. . . . Ontologically, 'world' is not a way of characterizing those entities which Dasein essentially is not; it is rather a characteristic of Dasein itself. (92) . . . *Dasein, in its familiarity with significance, is the ontical condition for the possibility of discovering entities which are encountered in a world with involvement (readiness-to-hand) as their kind of being, and which can thus make themselves known as they are in themselves.* Dasein as such is always something of this sort; along with its Being, a context of the ready-to-hand is already essentially discovered: Dasein, in so far as it *is*, has always submitted itself already to a 'world' which it encounters, and this *submission* belongs essentially to its Being. But in significance itself, with which Dasein is always familiar, there lurks the ontological condition which makes it possible for Dasein, as something which understands and interprets, to disclose such things as 'significations'; upon these, in turn, is founded the Being of words and of language. (120f.)

. . . Even the positive Interpretation of Dasein which we have so far given, already forbids us to start with the formal givenness of the 'I', if our purpose is to answer the question of the 'who' in a way which is phenomenally adequate. In clarifying Being-in-the-world we have shown that a bare subject without a world never 'is' proximally, nor is it ever given. And so in the end an isolated 'I' without Others is just as far from being proximally given. If, however, 'the Others' already *are there with us* in Being-in-the-world, and if this is ascertained phenomenally, even this should not mislead us into supposing that the *ontological* structure of what is thus 'given' is obvious, requiring no investigation. Our task is to make visible phenomenally the species to which this Dasein-with in closest everydayness belongs, and to Interpret it in a way which is ontologically appropriate. . . . *If the 'I' is an essential characteristic of Dasein, then it is one which must be interpreted existentially.* In that case the 'Who?' is to be answered only by exhibiting phenomenally a definite kind of Being which Dasein possesses. If in each case Dasein is its Self only in *existing*, then the constancy of the Self no less than the possibility of its 'failure to stand by itself' requires that we formulate the question existentially and ontologically as the sole appropriate way of access to its problematic. (152f.)

A state-of-mind not only discloses Dasein in its thrownness and its submission to that world which is already disclosed with its own Being; it is itself the existential kind of Being in which Dasein constantly surrenders itself to the 'world' and lets the 'world' 'matter' to it in such a way that somehow Dasein evades its very self. . . . A state-of-mind is a basic existential way in which Dasein is its 'there'. It not only characterizes Dasein ontologically, but, because of what it discloses, it is at the same time methodologically significant in principle for the existential analytic. Like any ontological Interpretation whatsoever, this analytic can only, so to speak, 'listen in' to some previously disclosed entity as regards its Being. And it will attach itself to Dasein's distinctive and most far-reaching possibilities of disclosure, in order to get information about this entity from these. Phenomenological Interpretation must make it possible for Dasein itself to disclose things primordially; it must, as it were, let Dasein interpret itself. Such Interpretation takes part in this disclosure only in order to raise to a conceptual level the phenomenal content of what has been disclosed, and to do so existentially. (178f.)

Even where the issue is not only one of ontical experience, but also one of ontological understanding, the interpretation of Being takes its orientation in the first instance from the Being of entities within-the-world. Thereby the Being of what is proximally ready-to-hand gets passed over, and entities are first conceived as a context of Things which are present-at-hand. '*Being*' acquires the meaning of '*reality*'. Substantiality becomes the basic characteristic of Being. . . . Like any other entity, *Dasein* too is *present-at-hand as real*. In this way '*Being in general*' acquires the meaning of '*reality*'. Accordingly the concept of Reality has a peculiar priority in the ontological problematic. By this priority the route to a genuine existential analytic of Dasein gets diverted, and so too does our view of the Being of what is proximally ready-to-hand within-the-world. (245)

Suggested further reading

Collins, J (2000), *Heidegger and the Nazis*. Duxford, Cambridge: Icon
Heidegger, M (1947), 'Letter on Humanism', in Heidegger, M (1993), *Martin Heidegger. Basic Writings* (ed. Krell, D F). London: Routledge
—— (2001) *The Zollikon Seminars* (ed. Boss, M). Evanston, IL: Northwestern University Press
McCall, R J (1983), *Phenomenological Psychology. An Introduction, with a glossary of some key Heideggerian terms*. Madison: University of Wisconsin Press

Merleau-Ponty (1908–1961)

Maurice Merleau-Ponty drew on Husserl, and on Heidegger, to formulate an elegant rejection of Cartesian dualism, Descartes's mind–body split. He was opposed both to extreme empiricism, and to subjectivism: he might help us, for example, both to be critical of narrow notions of 'evidence-based practice', and to be wary of the naïve subjectivity of those who meet any personal challenge by appealing to the inviolability of their personal experience. Merleau-Ponty developed a 'phenomenology of perception', and a notion of the 'body–subject': he insisted on the fact of our being embodied as fundamental to our being in the world. We occupy, he wrote, a dual position, as both subject and object, seers and seen, both visible and invisible to ourselves, literally as well as metaphorically (Merleau-Ponty, 1964: 16–18 etc; Matthews, 1996: 92 etc). It follows, logically, that Merleau-Ponty, both visible and invisible to himself, could make no claim to offering a definitive account, to having a 360-degree vision. He abhorred 'absolutes and conclusions, regarding his philosophy as more a vision of reality than as a system' (Reid, 1976: 407). Furthermore, consciousness for Merleau-Ponty could, by definition, never be fully explained. Since it is always an embodied consciousness, and since we exist in a world of other bodies, consciousness is by definition inter-subjective: we are in a world with and *of* others.

Reading Merleau-Ponty can remind us of the importance of what emerges in the in-between, in psychotherapy, in the present relationship with the other. Merleau-Ponty himself wrote more or less directly about the implications of his phenomenology for psychotherapy (see Friedman, 1964: 200–1, 385); what is important, he wrote, is the exploration of past material in the present in the way it is relived with the psychotherapist. '[M]y thought and his are interwoven into a single fabric' (Merleau-Ponty, in Friedman, 1964: 200); this is Merleau-Ponty's way of describing the therapeutic process. Once this idea is grasped it is that much harder to conceptualise the other as merely a bit of behaviour, to be studied.

In addressing the question 'what is phenomenology?' (in the extract below), Merleau-Ponty takes Heidegger's 'Being-in-the-world' towards notions of embodiment, ambiguity, and a sense of wonder. For those interested in seeing phenomenology as the basis for psychotherapy in the post-modern world it is important to note that Merleau-Ponty considered phenomenology 'as laborious as the work of Balzac, or of Proust, or of Valéry or of Cézanne, because of the same type of attention and wonder'. For Merleau-Ponty, and this is of vital importance for psychotherapists, 'the world and reason are no problem. They are mysterious, but mystery defines them. There is no question of dissipating the mystery by some solution. . . . Our fate is in our own hands. We become responsible for our history by reflection, but also by a decision in which we commit our life. In each case the act is violent and is verified only in actual exercise.'

There are no transcendent values; yet we are subject to something – language. Merleau-Ponty's emphasis on language in his later work points towards post-modern decentring and the post-modern turn to language. Language is that to which we as speakers are subject: neither speaker in a dialogue is the creator of the language. Nor is language ever neutral or transparent. Language has a certain autonomy, beyond mere expression of the speaker's or the writer's thought. It is 'never the mere clothing of a thought which otherwise possesses itself in full clarity'. It has the ability to capture 'a meaning which until then had never been objectified' (Merleau-Ponty, in Matthews, 1996: 104). We use it to express our involvement with reality; it does not function merely to reflect an objective reality, but grows out of that involvement. In the words of Merleau-Ponty's excellent commentator Eric Matthews, poets (or counsellors, psychotherapists and clients and patients) make use of given meanings to 'change our involvement with our world, and with each other, through language' (Matthews, 1996: 106).

Merleau-Ponty's vision, in Matthews's words, 'is of human beings finding themselves in a pre-existing situation, whose meaning and structure are neither objectively there, waiting to be discovered, nor simply imposed on objects by our consciousness, but emerge out of the interaction between our purposes and the external world' (Matthews, 1996: 101).

What then does Merleau-Ponty's 'search for essences' mean? It is a search for what meaning emerges for the individual at any particular moment, from moment to moment. 'The core of philosophy', he wrote, 'is no longer an autonomous transcendental subjectivity, to be found everywhere and nowhere: it lies in the perpetual beginning of reflection, at the point where an individual life begins to reflect on itself' (Merleau-Ponty, 1994: 62): we are 'condemned to meaning'. It is implicit in our experience of reality. It is not a search for generalisation, even if behind it may be a longing for generalisation. In that way Merleau-Ponty builds on Husserl's notion that we need to describe rather than explain, and, while he is saying that this way of description rather than explanation is an 'exact science', it is against the notion of science as causality. It would be wrong to think we are determined or explained by science; it would equally be wrong to ignore science, because it is part of our world. 'To turn back to the things themselves is to return to that world prior to knowledge of which knowledge speaks, and with regard to which every scientific determination is abstracted, dependent and a sign; it is like the relationship of geography to the countryside'. It is about what comes to one. It is worth pondering what relationship scientific psychology has to our patients. One does not need a knowledge of geography to be with Van Gogh in his cornfield or with Cézanne in front of his mountain. In this sense, perception is not a science.

From 'What Is Phenomenology?', preface to Merleau-Ponty (1945), *Phénoménologie de la perception* (trans. Bannan, J F), *Cross Currents*, Vol. VI, No. 1 (Sept. 1956). In: Friedman, M (ed.) (1964), *The Worlds of Existentialism. A Critical Reader*, pp. 83–7 (bracketed numbers in the text are Friedman's page references to the 1956 publication from which he has selected).

Phenomenology is the study of essences and accordingly its treatment of every problem is an attempt to define an essence, the essence of perception, or the essence of consciousness, for example. But phenomenology is also a philosophy which replaces essences in existence, and does not believe that man and the world can be understood save on the basis of their state of fact. It is a transcendental philosophy which suspends our spontaneous natural affirmations in order to understand them, but it is also a philosophy for which the world is always 'already there' as an inalienable presence which precedes reflection. The whole effort of phenomenology is to recover this naive contact with the world and to give it, at last, a philosophical status. It is a philosophy intent upon being an 'exact science', but it is also an account of space, time, and the world 'as lived' . . .

It is a question of description, and not of explanation or analysis. That first command which Husserl gave to the new phenomenology, that it be a 'descriptive psychology' or that it return 'to the things themselves' is above all a disavowal of science. I am not the result of the intersection of a multiplicity of causal influences which determine my body and my 'psychism'. I cannot think of myself as a part of the world, the simple object of biology, psychology and sociology, nor can I shut myself out of the universe of science. Everything that I know of the world, even through science, I know on the basis of a view which is my own, or an experience of the world without which the symbols of science would be meaningless. The entire universe of science is constructed upon the world as lived, and if we wish to think about science itself rigorously, appreciating its meaning and scope exactly, we must first of all reawaken that experience of the world of which science is an inferior expression. Science has not and will never have the same sense of being that the world as perceived has, for the simple reason that it is a determination or explanation of that world.

I am not a 'living being' or even a 'man' or even a 'consciousness' with all the characteristics which zoology, social anatomy or inductive psychology attributes to these products of nature or history. I am the absolute source. My existence does not come from my antecedents or my physical and social entourage, but rather goes toward them and sustains them. For it is I that make exist for myself (and hence 'be' in the only sense that the word can have for me) that tradition which I chose to adopt or that horizon whose distance from me tends to disappear, since it would have no such property as distance were I not there to view it. Scientific views according to which I am an event in the world are always naive and hypocritical because, without mentioning the fact, they sustain themselves on that other view, that consciousness by which, initially, a world is disposed around me and begins to exist for me. To turn back to the things themselves is to return to that world prior to knowledge of which knowledge speaks, and with regard to which every scientific determination is abstractive, dependent and a sign; it is like the relationship of geography to the countryside where we first learned what a forest, a prairie or a river was. This movement is absolutely distinct from the idealist turning upon consciousness, and the demands of pure description exclude both the procedure of reflective analysis and that of scientific explanation . . .

Perception is not a science of the world, nor even an act, a deliberate taking up of a position. It is the basis from which every act issues and it is presupposed by them. The world is not an object the law of whose constitution I possess. It is the natural milieu and the field of all my thoughts and of all my explicit perceptions. Truth does not 'dwell' only in the 'interior man' for there is no interior man. Man is before himself in the world and it is in the world that he knows himself. . . .

If the other person is in his own right, and not merely for me, and if we are for each other, and are not merely one and another for God, we must appear to one another. He must have an exterior and so must I. Beyond the *Pour Soi* perspective – my view of myself and his view of himself – there must be a *Pour Autrui* perspective – my view of him and his view of me. . . . I must be my exterior and he his body. This paradox and the dialectic of the Ego and the Alter-Ego are only possible if each is defined by his situation and not freed of all inherence. They are only possible if philosophy does not attain its completion in the return to the self, and if I discover by reflection not only my presence to myself but also . . . an internal weakness which prevents me from being absolutely individual, exposing me to the regard of others as a man among men or at least a consciousness among consciousnesses. . . .

The world that I distinguished from myself as a sum of things or of causally connected processes is re-discovered 'in me' as the permanent horizon of all my thinking and as a dimension in relation to which I never cease to situate myself. The genuine Cogito does not define the existence of the subject by the thought that it has of existing. It does not convert the certitude of the world into certitude of the world as thought, nor does it replace the world by the signification world. On the contrary it recognizes my thought as an inalienable fact and it eliminates every type of idealism in discovering me as presence to a world. . . .

Here, reflection does not retreat from the world toward the unity of a consciousness upon which the world is founded. It withdraws in order to see the transcendences stand forth clearly. It distends the intentional ties which bind us to the world in order to make them appear. It alone is consciousness of the world because it reveals it as strange and paradoxical. . . . Precisely in order to see the world and to seize it as a paradox, it is necessary to disrupt our familiarity with it, and that disruption can teach us nothing save the unmotivated surging forth of the world. The greatest lesson of the reduction is the impossibility of a complete reduction. . . . Far from being, as one might think, the formula for an idealist philosophy, the phenomenological reduction is that of an existentialist philosophy: The 'In-der-Welt-Sein' of Heidegger only appears on the basis of the phenomenological reduction. . . .

The fact that essences are instrumental in reflection does not mean that philosophy takes them as its object, but rather that our existence is too strictly caught up in the world to know itself as such at the moment when it is thrown forth upon the world, and that it needs the idea in order to recognize and conquer its state of fact. . . . It is the function of language to make essences exist in a separation, which is actually only apparent since they still repose on the antepredicative life of consciousness. . . . Seeking the essence of consciousness . . . means recovering my effective presence to myself. (65)

The eidetic reduction . . . is the resolution to make the world appear as it is prior to all turning upon ourselves. It is the ambition to make reflection equal to the nonreflective life of consciousness. . . . For if I can speak of 'dreams' and of 'reality', and pose for myself the question of the imaginary and the real, and if I can doubt the real, it is because that distinction is already made for me prior to the analysis, and because I have an experience of the real as well as of the imaginary. . . .

We must not wonder, then, if we really perceive a world. Rather, we must say that the world is that which we perceive. . . . To look for the essence of perception is to declare, not that perception is presumed to be truth, but that it is defined for us as access to truth. . . . The evidence of perception is not an adequate thought nor apodictic evidence. The world is not what I think, but that which I live. I open out upon the world. Unquestionably I communicate with it, but I do not take possession of it. It is inexhaustible. 'There is a world', or rather, 'there is the world': this is a constant theme of my life which I can never completely think through. . . .

Whether it is a case of something perceived, or a historical event or doctrine, 'to understand' means to seize again the total intention. . . . Seizing the total intention means grasping the unique manner of existing which is expressed in the properties of the pebble, the glass or the piece of wax, in all the facts of a revolution, in all the thoughts of a philosopher. In each civilization the Idea must be found . . . the formula of a unique behaviour with regard to others, nature, time and death. . . . In relation to them, no single word nor human gesture, however habitual or distracted, is without meaning. . . . The chance happenings compensate each other, and that dust of facts forms an agglomeration. There appears the outline of a way of facing the human situation, an event whose contours are defined and of which one can speak. . . .

The most important acquisition of phenomenology is undoubtedly to have joined extreme subjectivism and extreme objectivism in its notion of world or of rationality. Rationality is exactly measured out in the experiences in which it reveals itself. There is rationality, that is, perspectives overlap, perceptions confirm one another, and a meaning appears. But it cannot be set apart and transformed into either absolute Spirit or world in the realist sense. The phenomenological world is not pure being, but the meaning which appears at the intersection of my experiences and at the intersection of my experiences with those of others by the enmeshing of one with the other. Thus it is inseparable from the subjectivity and from the intersubjectivity which form their unity by taking up my past experiences in my present experiences and the experience of others in my own. . . . The phenomenological world is not a more primary being rendered explicit, but the foundation of being. Philosophy is not the reflection of a more original truth but the art of making a truth real. . . .

The world and reason are no problem. They are mysterious, but mystery defines them. There is no question of dissipating the mystery by some solution, for they are prior to solutions. Genuine philosophy is re-learning to see the world, and in this sense a story recounted can signify the world with as much 'depth' as a treatise in philosophy. Our fate is in our own hands. We become responsible for our history by reflection, but also by a decision in which we commit our life. In each case the act is violent and is verified only in actual exercise. . . .

It is not accidental that phenomenology was a movement before being a doctrine or a system. It is as laborious as the work of Balzac, or of Proust or of Valéry or of Cézanne, because of the same type of attention and wonder, the same demands of consciousness, the same will to seize the meaning of the world or of history in its state of genesis. In this regard it fuses with modern thought. (59–70)

Suggested further reading

Hoeller, K (ed.) (1993), *Merleau-Ponty and Psychology*. Atlantic Highlands, NJ: Humanities Press.

Chapter 3

Other roots

Hegel, Marx, Nietzsche, Freud, Saussure

Introduction

In this chapter we first introduce some basic Hegelian and Marxist ideas which have been important in the development of post-modern thinking. Hegel and Marx also point to another current in European philosophy, to the body of thought known as Critical Theory and to the work of the Frankfurt School and of those around it: Walter Benjamin, Hannah Arendt, Herbert Marcuse, Max Horkheimer, Theodor Adorno and Jürgen Habermas. The constraints of this volume do not allow us to begin to do justice to this current (although we shall note some of Habermas's critiques of post-modernism in Chapter 5), nor to other important post-Marxist thinkers such as Louis Althusser, with his post-structural re-reading of Marx. We do, however, provide some key references at the end of this chapter.

We also consider the equally powerful influence of Nietzsche, and then of Freud. Psychoanalysis is a vital ingredient of post-modern thought, thanks in particular to the notion, as developed by Freud and continued by key post-Freudians such as Klein, Winnicott and Lacan, that we are subject to that of which we are not conscious. The final part of this chapter draws attention to Saussure, the founder of structural linguistics and semiology, the study of signs. Once again space only permits us to provide bibliographic references to important developments within this field, in particular the work of Roman Jakobson on linguistic structure, Claude Lévi-Strauss on kinship, exchange and ritual, and the later (post-structuralist) thinking of Roland Barthes and Umberto Eco.

The process of compiling these 'roots' chapters leads us to reflect on the education of psychotherapists in the UK and elsewhere. Phenomenology may seem more familiar and palatable (we have found it easier to stay with), perhaps because it can be seen to be more to do with the individual. Some of the areas on which we are now touching are more questioning of socialising processes themselves, and are more likely to threaten a political status quo, which is in turn less likely to encourage education in this arena.

Perhaps, furthermore, it is harder than ever to see phenomenology as consistent with its own theory. Because of the pioneering work of Saussure, and the 'turn to language' in the 1960s, anticipated by Merleau-Ponty, we must now reconsider what we understand by description, and situate it in the arena of language and politics.

Some may be more comfortable using psychoanalysis to link the individual and the social. Many people trained as psychotherapists, and licensed to call themselves such, will not have read any Freud. Those who have read Freud may favour those aspects of his work that support an individualistic point of view; they are likely to have had very little in the way of education in sociology or cultural studies, and, schooled in a more individualistic approach, will find that Freudian concepts provide sufficient explanation of social forces. Frosh (1987) offers a more rigorous commentary on the relationship of psychoanalysis and politics and society. He writes about how psychoanalysis 'contains the possibilities for an approach that analyses the mechanisms by which the social world enters into the experience of each individual, constructing the human "subject" and reproducing itself through the perpetuation of particular patterns of ideology', and about how 'psychoanalysis offers insights into the mechanisms by which individuality becomes constructed within a social context' (Frosh, 1987: 11). Frosh's is a radical view from within psychoanalysis; arguably, however, University English, modern language, or cultural studies departments may be the places in which to find psychoanalysis used to offer the most radical critiques of the status quo.

Perhaps psychotherapists rarely have another standpoint from which to look at Freud. Because of frequent limitations in the training of therapists there is less likelihood of their being able to have a conversation about changes in cultural practices. There is a history and a tradition in continental Europe which would regard philosophy as an essential basis for education, in all kinds of disciplines and occupations, and we hope we may contribute towards providing such a basis in this chapter.

Suggested further reading

Althusser, L (with Balibar, E) (1970), *Reading Capital*. London: New Left Books

Arendt, H (1961), *Between Past and Future*. New York: Viking

Barthes, R (1977), *Image/Music/Text*. London: Fontana

Benjamin W (1973), *Illuminations*. London: Fontana

Eagleton, T (2000), *The Idea of Culture*. Oxford: Blackwell

Eco, U (1984), *Semiotics and the Philosophy of Language*. London: Macmillan

Habermas, J (1987), *The Philosophical Discourse of Modernity*. Cambridge, MA: MIT Press

Horkheimer, M and Adorno, T (1979), *Dialectic of Enlightenment*. London: Verso

Jakobson, R (1980), *Selected Writings – III. The Poetry of Grammar and the Grammar of Poetry*. The Hague and Paris: Mouton

Lévi-Strauss, C (1963 [1958]), *Structural Anthropology*. New York: Basic Books

Marcuse, H (1955), *Eros and Civilization*. London: Allen Lane

Payne, M (ed.) (1998), *A Dictionary of Cultural and Critical Theory*. Oxford: Blackwell

Hegel (1770–1831)

Georg Wilhelm Friedrich Hegel has been described as 'the last Romantic idealist' (Garland and Garland, 1976: 352) in German philosophy. He was an 'idealist' because he believed in progress towards a state in which material reality and spirit might finally be apprehended as one: this he called the Absolute, or Absolute Spirit. He was a profound influence on Marx, and, through the teachings of Alexandre Kojève (Kojève, 1980) in the twentieth century, on Lacan.

Kant, the pre-eminent philosopher of the later Enlightenment, claimed in his critique of knowledge that what humans can know is only 'appearance'; the 'thing in itself' remains unknowable. For Hegel, in contrast, appearance and essence belong together: 'the innermost structure of reality corresponds with that of the self-knowing human spirit' (Bottomore, 1983: 198). Thus God (the Absolute) is a product of human knowledge.

Hegel 'sought to devise a concept of logic which is not based on empirical cause and effect, but on a dialectical process' (Garland and Garland, 1976: 351–2); this is the process he discerned to be behind all historical development. History is 'progress in the consciousness of freedom' (Hegel, cited in Bottomore, 1983: 198), and this consciousness leads to the variety of forms of social organisation across history. Hence 'consciousness determines being' (Bottomore, 1983: 198); Kant's categories of thought, ways of thinking inherent in humans, are thus for Hegel also forms of Being. Logic *is* ontology. Being and thought are identified in a single principle, the *idea*, which develops in the three moments of the famous dialectic: thesis meets antithesis and gives birth to synthesis, which in turn becomes a new thesis.

In terms of method, Hegel conceived the dialectic, in *The Science of Logic* (1812–16), as 'the grasping of opposites in their unity or of the positive in the negative' (Hegel, cited in Bottomore, 1983: 122). The dialectic enables the observer to follow the process by which forms of consciousness emerge out of each other to become more inclusive forms. Error thus lies in one-sidedness and partiality, since truth is the whole, the Absolute towards which consciousness strives. Error, for Hegel, is recognisable through the contradictions it generates. One can begin to see how fundamentally important Hegel is for Derrida and deconstruction.

The dialectic can cut both ways: it is a way of keeping things open, but it also acknowledges the human wish for synthesis and closure. It is this first aspect that is of importance for post-modern thinking and for a practice of therapy in which the patient is open to being more, rather than less, destabilised.

Hegel's principle of *sublation* also has resonance for such a practice: 'as the dialectic unfolds no partial insight is ever lost . . . the Hegelian dialectic progresses in two basic ways: by bringing out what is implicit, but not explicitly articulated . . . or by repairing some want, lack or inadequacy . . . there is always a tension, latent irony or incipient surprise between any form and what is in the process of becoming' (Bottomore, 1983: 122).

If consciousness determines Being, one of Hegel's fundamental questions is, what is it to be conscious of oneself? In the paraphrase of one modern commentator, what is that 'something' that reflects consciousness back on itself? (Sarup, 1993: 12) (it is on this Hegelian notion of reflection that Lacan drew in his use of the metaphor of the mirror). Identity, for Hegel, finally depends on recognition by the other: 'consciousness cannot grasp itself without recognition by others'. This is the theme of Hegel's story of the Master and the Slave, the famous Master–Slave dialectic, in which the master's own recognition of his identity and desire depend on the existence and the recognition of the slave, who must as a slave suppress his own desires and instincts. The slave thus 'negates' and 'overcomes' himself; and, moreover, through his work, he educates himself, thus transforming himself and finding his freedom from slavery, or at least moving from a worse to a better slavery. For Hegel history is 'the progressive negation of Slavery by the Slave' (Sarup, 1993: 13).

For 'in his nascent state, man is never simply man. He is always, necessarily, and essentially, either Master or Slave' (Kojève, 1980: 8). By suggesting that one's identity depends on recognition of the other, Hegel provides what might be considered compelling arguments for psychotherapy. The anxiety this dependency can cause can lead us to want to reduce the other to an instrumental mirror. Then one is only recognised through making the other one's slave rather than being dependent as another (Sarup, 1993: 13). Through Hegel one might see therapy as being over when the patient recognises their slavery, no longer tends to avoid this by striving for mastery, and, as Freud said, becomes free to work. The process might be described as one of the patient moving from attempts at mastery to the position of a slave who is negating slavery by in part undertaking an 'auto-creative act' (therapy). Perhaps not just the world's but one's own 'future and history hence belong not to the warlike Master, but to the working Slave' (Sarup, 1993: 18).

Through Hegelian spectacles psychotherapy can be seen as an effective form of education by 'overcoming the given in favour of what does not (yet) exist' (Sarup, 1993: 19). For example, in Freudian terms, through a reduction in id impulses, one has to undermine one's own identity and through this 'negation' lead a better life. A patient, therefore, might '"overcome" . . . himself while preserving and sublimating himself' (Sarup, 1993: 19).

Hegel can also be helpful for psychotherapists with his notions of particularity and universality. This is another fundamental opposition. 'It is only in and by the universal recognition of human particularity that individuality realises and manifests itself.' Are there dangers that the psychotherapist wrongly encourages a short cut to individuality? For example, by attempting to validate a person's individuality without overcoming himself or recognising the 'individuality' of others? As individuality is always produced dialectically it is a process of constant struggle.

In the passage that follows, questions are raised as to how consciousness is valued. Our interpretations as therapists will come from somewhere, according to how we value consciousness. Rational, Enlightenment, thinking might give us the idea that consciousness is value-free or neutral. It 'finds its notion in utility . . .

the Useful was directly nothing else but the self of consciousness and this latter was thereby in possession of it'. Yet through this 'being for self' we might be led to 'being for another'.

If therapy is about opening up consciousness, then it might lead to a recognition that its being-in-itself is essentially being-for-another. Therapy can assist in that movement. So while Hegel in some ways seems to go along with the idea of enlightenment leading to self-understanding, he is also pointing out that underlying this idea of Enlightened consciousness is the danger of using others – they become one's objects. The French Revolution, he pointed out, executed 40,000 people in the 1790s in the name of the Republic (Cahoone, 1996: 83). The human spirit, Hegel seems to argue, has to pass through a phase of believing its consciousness is neutral, before developing further, towards Absolute Spirit. True freedom has really to take place in the context of a community, with its institutions of law and morality.

How much, for therapy, is the other merely an object? How do you hear the patient? Do you frustrate your patient as much as possible? Is the notion of analytic 'working through' just a way of avoiding the inevitability of the Master–Slave dialectic? For to some extent we will always remain nasty people – it is an illusion that we can ever be completely free of that dialectic, in our search for recognition and validation.

From Hegel (1977), *Phenomenology of Spirit*, pp. 335 *et seq.*

Consciousness had found its Notion in Utility. But it is partly still an *object*, and partly, for that very reason, still an *End* to be attained, which consciousness does not find itself to possess immediately. Utility is still a predicate of the object, not itself a subject for the immediate and sole *actuality* of the object. It is the same thing that appeared before, when being-for-self had not yet shown itself to be the substance of the other moments, a demonstration which would have meant that the Useful was directly nothing else but the self of consciousness and that this latter was thereby in possession of it. This withdrawal from the form of objectivity of the Useful has, however, already taken place in principle and from this inner revolution there emerges the actual revolution of the actual world, the new shape of consciousness, *absolute freedom*.

In fact, what we have here is no more than an empty show of objectivity separating self-consciousness from possession. For, partly, all existence and validity of the specific members of the organization of the actual world and the work of faith have, in general, returned into this simple determination as into their ground and spiritual principle; partly, however, this simple determination no longer possesses anything of its own, it is rather pure metaphysic, pure Notion, or a pure knowing by self-consciousness. That is to say, of the *being-in-and-for-itself* of the Useful *qua* object, consciousness recognizes that its *being-in-itself*, is essentially a *being-for-an-other*; being-in-itself, as *devoid of self*, is in truth a passive self, or that which is a self for another self. The object, however, exists for consciousness in this abstract form of pure being-in-itself, for consciousness is pure insight whose distinctions are in the pure form of Notions. But the *being-for-self* into which being-for-an-other returns, i.e. the self, is not a self belonging exclusively to what is called object and distinct from the "I"; for consciousness, *qua* pure insight, is not a *single* self which could be confronted by the object as equally having a self of its own, but is pure Notion, the gazing of the self into the self, the absolute seeing of *itself* doubled; the certainty of itself is the universal Subject, and its conscious Notion is the essence of all actuality. If, then, the Useful was merely the alternation of the moments, an alternation which did not return into its own *unity*, and hence was still an object for knowing, it now ceases to be this. For knowing is itself the movement of those abstract moments, it is the universal self, the self of itself as well as of the object and, as universal, is the self-returning unity of this movement.

Spirit thus comes before us as *absolute freedom*. It is self-consciousness which grasps the fact that its certainty of itself is the essence of all the spiritual 'masses', or spheres, of the real as well as of the supersensible world, or conversely, that essence and actuality and consciousness's knowledge of *itself*. It is conscious of its pure personality and therein of all spiritual reality, and all reality is solely spiritual; the world is for it simply its own will, and this is a general will. And what is more, this will is not the empty thought of will which consists in silent assent, or assent by a representative, but a real general will, the will of all *individuals* as such. For will is in itself the consciousness of personality, or of each, and it is as this genuine actual will that it ought to be, as the *self-conscious* essence of each and every personality, so that each, undivided from the whole, always does everything, and what appears as done by the whole is the direct and conscious deed of each.

This undivided Substance of absolute freedom ascends the throne of the world without any power being able to resist it. For since, in truth, consciousness alone is the element in which the spiritual beings or powers have their substance, their entire system which is organized and maintained by division into 'masses' or spheres has collapsed, now that the individual consciousness conceives the object as having no other essence than self-consciousness itself, or as being absolutely Notion. What made the Notion into an existent *object* was its diremption into separate *subsistent* spheres, but when the object becomes a Notion, there is no longer anything in it with a continuing existence; negativity had permeated all its moments. It comes into existence in such a way that each individual consciousness raises itself out of its allotted sphere, no longer finds its essence and its work in this particular sphere, but grasps itself as the *Notion* of will, grasps all spheres as the essence of this will, and therefore can only realize itself in a work which is a work on the whole. In this absolute freedom, therefore, all social groups or classes which are the spiritual spheres into which the whole is articulated are abolished; the individual consciousness that belonged to any such sphere, and willed and fulfilled itself in it, has put aside its limitation; its purpose is the general purpose, its language universal law, its work the universal work.

The object and the [moment of] *difference* have here lost the meaning of *utility*, which was the predicate of all real being; consciousness does not begin its movement in the object as if this were something *alien* from which it first had to return into itself; on the contrary, the object is for it consciousness itself. The antithesis consists, therefore, solely in the difference between the *individual* and the *universal* consciousness; but the individual consciousness itself is directly in its own eyes that which had only the *semblance* of an antithesis; it is universal consciousness and will. The *beyond* of this, its actual existence, hovers over the corpse of the vanished independence of real being, or the being of fate, merely as the exhalation of a stale gas, of the vacuous *Être suprême*.

After the various spiritual spheres and the restricted life of the individual have been done away with, as well as his two worlds, all that remains, therefore, is the immanent movement of universal self-consciousness as a reciprocity of self-consciousness in the form of *universality* and of *personal* consciousness: the universal will goes *into itself* and is a *single, individual* will to which universal law and work stand opposed. But this *individual* consciousness is no less directly conscious of itself as universal will; it is aware that its object is a law given by that will and a work accomplished by it; therefore, in passing over into action and in creating objectivity, it is doing nothing individual, but carrying out the laws and functions of the state.

This movement is thus the interaction of consciousness with itself in which it lets nothing break loose to become a *free object* standing over against it. It follows from this that it cannot achieve anything positive, either universal works of language or of reality, either of laws and general institutions of *conscious* freedom, or of deeds and works of a freedom that *wills* them. The work which *conscious* freedom might accomplish would consist in that freedom, *qua universal* substance, making itself into an *object* and into an *enduring being*. This otherness would be the moment of difference in it whereby it divided itself into stable spiritual 'masses' or spheres and into the members of various powers. These spheres would be partly the 'thought-things' of a power that is separated into legislative, judicial, and executive powers; but partly, they would be the *real essences* we found in the real world of culture, and, looking more closely at the content of universal action, they would be the particular spheres of labour which would be further distinguished as more specific 'estates' or classes. Universal freedom, which would have separated itself in this way into its constituent parts and by the very fact of doing so would have made itself into an *existent* Substance, would thereby be free from *particular* individuality, and would apportion the *plurality* of individuals to its various constituent parts. This, however, would restrict the activity and the being of the personality to a branch of the whole, to one kind of activity and being; when placed in the element of *being*, personality would have the significance of a specific personality; it would cease to be in truth universal self-consciousness. Neither by the mere idea of obedience to *self-given* laws which would assign to it only a part of the whole, nor by its being *represented* in law-making and universal action, does self-consciousness let itself be cheated out of *reality*, the reality of *itself* making the law and accomplishing, not a particular work, but the universal work itself. For where the self is merely *represented* and is present only as an idea, there it is not *actual*; where it is represented by proxy, it is *not*.

Just as the individual self-consciousness does not find itself in this *universal work* of absolute freedom *qua* existent Substance, so little does it find itself in the *deeds* proper and *individual* actions of the will of this freedom. Before the universal can perform a deed it must concentrate itself into the One of individuality and put at the head an individual self-consciousness; for the universal will is only an *actual* will in a self, which is a One. But thereby all other individuals are excluded from the entirety of this deed and have only a limited share in it, so that the deed would not be a deed of the *actual universal* self-consciousness. Universal freedom, therefore, can produce neither a positive work nor a deed; there is left for it only *negative* action; it is merely the *fury* of destruction.

But the supreme reality and the reality which stands in the greatest antithesis to universal freedom, or rather the sole object that will still exist for that freedom, is the freedom and individuality of actual self-consciousness itself. For that universality which does not let itself advance to the reality of an organic articulation, and whose aim is to maintain itself in an unbroken continuity, at the same time creates a distinction within itself, because it is movement or consciousness in general. And, moreover, by virtue of its own abstraction, it divides itself into extremes equally abstract, into a simple, inflexible cold universality, and into the discrete, absolute hard rigidity and self-willed atomism of actual self-consciousness. Now that it has completed the destruction of the actual organization of the world, and exists now just for itself, this is its sole object, an object that no longer has any content, possession, existence, or outer extension, but is merely this knowledge of itself as an absolutely pure and free individual self. All that remains of the object by which it can be laid hold of is solely its *abstract* existence as such. The relation, then, of these two, since each exists indivisibly and absolutely for itself, and thus cannot dispose of a middle term which would link them together, is one of wholly *unmediated* pure negation, a negation, moreover, of the individual as a being existing in the universal. The sole work and deed of universal freedom is therefore *death*, a death too which has no inner significance or filling, for what is negated is the empty point of the absolutely free self. It is thus the coldest and meanest of all deaths, with no more significance than cutting off a head of cabbage or swallowing a mouthful of water.

In this flat, commonplace monosyllable is contained the wisdom of the government, the abstract intelligence of the universal will, in the fulfilling of itself. The government is itself nothing else but the self-established focus, or the individuality, of the universal will. The government, which wills and executes its will from a single point, at the same time wills and executes a specific order and action. On the one hand, it excludes all other individuals from its act, and on the other hand, it thereby constitutes itself a government that is a specific will, and so stands opposed to the universal will; consequently, it is absolutely impossible for it to exhibit itself as anything else but a *faction*. What is called government is merely the *victorious* faction, and in the very fact of its being a faction lies the direct necessity of its overthrow; and its being government makes it, conversely, into a faction, and [so] guilty. When the universal will maintains that what the government has actually done is a crime committed against it, the government, for its part, has nothing specific and outwardly apparent by which the guilt of the will opposed to it could be demonstrated; for what stands opposed to it as the actual universal will is only an unreal pure will, *intention*. *Being suspected*, therefore, takes the place, or has the significance and effect, of *being guilty*, and the external reaction against this reality that lies in the simple inwardness of intention, consists in the cold, matter-of-fact annihilation of this existent self, from which nothing else can be taken away but its mere being.

In this its characteristic *work*, absolute freedom becomes explicitly objective to itself, and self-consciousness learns what absolute freedom in effect is. *In itself*, it is just this *abstract self-consciousness*, which effaces all distinction and all continuance of distinction within it. It is as such that it is objective to itself, the *terror* of death is the vision of this negative nature of itself. But absolutely free self-consciousness finds this its reality quite different from what its own Notion of itself was, viz. that the universal will is merely the *positive* essence of personality, and that this latter knows itself in it only positively, or as preserved therein. Here, however, this self-consciousness which, as pure insight, completely separates its positive and its negative nature – completely separates the predicateless Absolute as pure *Thought* and as pure *Matter* – is confronted with the absolute transition of the one into the other as a present reality. The universal will, *qua* absolutely *positive*, actual self-consciousness, because it is this self-conscious reality heightened to the level of *pure* thought or of *abstract* matter, changes round into its negative nature and shows itself to be equally that which *puts an end to the thinking of oneself*, or to self-consciousness.

Suggested further reading

Kojève, A (1980), *Introduction to the Reading of Hegel* (trans. Nichols, J). Ithaca, NY: Cornell University Press

Marx (1818–1883)

> [T]he nature of individuals depends on the material conditions determining their production.
>
> (Marx, cited in Bottomore, 1983: 303)

Marx replaced Hegel's 'Spirit' with 'Economy' (Sarup, 1993: 92); what Marx takes in particular from Hegel is the conviction that humanity makes progress over the course of history (Bottomore, 1983: 200–1).

The French communist and philosopher Louis Althusser, who was responsible for inviting Jacques Lacan to hold his seminars at the Ecole Normale in Paris in 1963, tried to rethink Marx without any reference to Hegel's Absolute Spirit; Althusser saw Lacan trying to rethink psychoanalysis without any reference to a unified conception of self or ego (Sarup, 1993: 5). The influence of Marxism on the development of post-modernism stems partly from the involvement of French philosophers in the political upheavals of the 1960s in France. The students' and workers' revolts of 1968 saw a confluence of Marxist critiques of capitalist modes of production and social relations, with notions of personal and sexual liberation (release of id impulses, etc.) ultimately deriving from Freud. For many now interested in Lacan and psychoanalysis this important link with Marxism seems forgotten. In the wider culture, words such as 'ideology' and 'class', which were very much part of intellectual discourse in the 1960s, '70s and '80s, are less frequently heard, at least in anglophone academia. In most counselling, psychotherapy, and psychology trainings, they barely feature.

Whilst Marx argued for economic determinism, most of psychotherapy seems hardly to allow for it at all. To what extent might this mean that psychotherapy, as many of its critics on the left (e.g. Timpanaro, 1976) have claimed, is fundamentally about the maintenance of the dominant order, whilst sometimes pretending otherwise? It might be argued that psychotherapy provides frameworks for the generation of ideologies. This can be thought about in terms of the negative definition of ideology given by Marx and Engels, as that which distorts, misrepresents and covers over contradictions (Bottomore, 1983: 220). For Marx, philosophy (we might substitute 'psychotherapy') is 'a material force' which affects 'the common sense' of an age. Perhaps Marx's 'common sense' is akin to what the British Marxist cultural historian Raymond Williams called a 'structure of feeling', the structure within which certain thoughts and feelings are available to be commonly thought and felt, at any particular historical juncture (Williams, 1965: 64–88). To follow the Italian Marxist Antonio Gramsci, psychotherapy as a kind of philosophical practice 'must be placed in historical perspective, in the sense that it cannot be criticised simply at an abstract level but must be related to the ideologies which it helps various social forces to generate' (Bottomore, 1983: 195).

A person's therapy, it can be argued, is paid for by the surplus value produced by the labour of others, for example, in the Third World. Yet this economic underpinning of psychotherapy is unlikely to be examined in the therapeutic encounter (for an extended wrestle with such issues, see Samuels, 2000); if such concerns are raised, it is likely to be in terms of personal or family dynamics. Therapy can thus be seen as a bourgeois activity, bourgeois in the sense of an ideology of settled, independent citizens (Williams, 1976: 39). Psychotherapists, furthermore, have a vested interest in not raising these issues. Yet it is hardly difficult to see how economics so frequently and obviously determines social relations, not excluding those around the practice of psychotherapy.

Who has the money to train as a psychotherapist? One generally needs to be in a privileged position to do so. The patient pays the psychotherapist. These factors might seem inevitably to lead to an innate conservatism within the institutions of psychotherapy. Historically, Freud's first 'analytic' patients were among the richest women in Europe (Forrester and Appignanese, 1992).

In *The Communist Manifesto*, an extract from which appears below, obvious key terms are oppressor and oppressed. In the case of the psychotherapist and patient, will there be a 'revolutionary reconstitution' of the power in the relationship? In analytic psychotherapy at least, although many humanists would think differently, it is a relatively fixed power relationship; perhaps the fact that there is something fixed about the place of the therapist, how ever it is called into question by the therapist, echoes something about the nature of oppression in capitalist society. It is not a relationship of equality. Only by accepting his or her place as patient will the therapy begin to work. It is not our intention necessarily to question this; but the therapeutic relationship could help us think about how relations and inter-subjectivities in society are constituted. Conversely, how much might the practice of psychotherapy mirror the status quo and insidiously reinforce oppression?

To turn to the extract: 'Each step of the development of the bourgeoisie was accompanied by a corresponding political advance of that class'. What is the place of psychotherapy in the political advance and development of the bourgeoisie? If feudalism 'bound man to his natural superiors', and psychotherapy is a way of freeing up people from their parents, is it helping or hindering with a moving away from 'the icy water of egotistical calculation'? Was Freud's popularity in the first half of the twentieth century a product of the middle-class need to move to the next phase of development? 'Emancipation', or 'alienation' from our roots – how much are we as therapists caught up in this process while appearing to do something else?

'The bourgeoisie has torn away from the family its sentimental veil and . . . reduced it to mere money relations . . . the bourgeoisie cannot exist without constantly revolutionising the instruments of production, and thereby the relations of production, and with them the whole relations of society . . . All that is solid melts into air, all that is holy is profaned, and man is at last compelled to face with sober senses, his real conditions of life, and his relations with his kind.' Can we come to our senses? Is psychotherapy, from a Marxist point of view, at best a kind of Custer's Last Stand – a way of finally looking at our relations with our kind, or appearing to? Can we really do this if we are not looking at the economic underpinning? If we ignore this, are we not inevitably engaged in a way of maintaining capitalism, rather than looking with sober senses at other ways of being with each other? Psychotherapy can stop us doing it in the name of doing it. A diminishing of mutuality has significant effects on what can be regarded as common-sense relationships in the consulting room.

'Unconsciable' means 'not conformable to conscience'. Is psychotherapy's role to free people up so they can trade better? Levinas (see p. 150 *et seq*, below) talks of ethics as practice; but Levinas is not questioning the economic order. For a Marxist, psychotherapy could be viewed as providing an illusion, beneath which to maintain an exploitation which would otherwise be in danger of being uncovered. Its historic aim, in this view, would be to take bourgeois class interests forward.

From Marx and Engels (1848), *Manifesto of the Communist Party*, in Tucker (ed.) (1978), *The Marx–Engels Reader*, pp. 473–83

Bourgeois and Proletarians

The history of all hitherto existing society is the history of class struggles.

Freeman and slave, patrician and plebeian, lord and serf, guild-master and journeyman, in a word, oppressor and oppressed, stood in constant opposition to one another, carried on an uninterrupted, now hidden, now open fight, a fight that each time ended, either in a revolutionary re-constitution of society at large, or in the common ruin of the contending classes.

In the earlier epochs of history, we find almost everywhere a complicated arrangement of society into various orders, a manifold gradation of social rank. In ancient Rome we have patricians, knights, plebeians, slaves; in the Middle Ages, feudal lords, vassals, guild-masters, journeymen, apprentices, serfs; in almost all of these classes, again, subordinate gradations.

The modern bourgeois society that has sprouted from the ruins of feudal society has not done away with class antagonisms. It has but established new classes, new conditions of oppression, new forms of struggle in place of the old ones.

Our epoch, the epoch of the bourgeoisie, possesses, however, this distinctive feature: it has simplified the class antagonisms: Society as a whole is more and more splitting up into two great hostile camps, into two great classes directly facing each other: Bourgeoisie and Proletariat.

From the serfs of the Middle Ages sprang the chartered burghers of the earliest towns. From these burgesses the first elements of the bourgeoisie were developed.

The discovery of America, the rounding of the Cape, opened up fresh ground for the rising bourgeoisie. The East-Indian and Chinese markets, the colonisation of America, trade with the colonies, the increase in the means of exchange and in commodities generally, gave to commerce, to navigation, to industry, an impulse never before known, and thereby, to the revolutionary element in the tottering feudal society, a rapid development.

The feudal system of industry, under which industrial production was monopolised by closed guilds, now no longer sufficed for the growing wants of the new markets. The manufacturing system took its place. The guild-masters were pushed on one side by the manufacturing middle class; division of labour between the different corporate guilds vanished in the face of division of labour in each single workshop.

Meantime the markets kept ever growing, the demand ever rising. Even manufacture no longer sufficed. Thereupon, steam and machinery revolutionised industrial production. The place of manufacture was taken by the giant, Modern Industry, the place of the industrial middle class, by industrial millionaires, the leaders of whole industrial armies, the modern bourgeois.

Modern industry has established the world-market, for which the discovery of America paved the way. This market has given an immense development to commerce, to navigation, to communication by land. This development has, in its turn, reacted on the extension of industry; and in proportion as industry, commerce, navigation, railways extended, in the same proportion the bourgeoisie developed, increased its capital and pushed into the background, every class handed down from the Middle Ages.

We see, therefore, how the modern bourgeoisie is itself the product of a long course of development, of a series of revolutions in the modes of production and of exchange.

Each step in the development of the bourgeoisie was accompanied by a corresponding political advance of that class. An oppressed class under the sway of the feudal nobility, an armed and self-governing association in the mediaeval commune, here independent urban republic (as in Italy and Germany), there taxable 'third estate' of the monarchy (as in France), afterwards, in the period of manufacture proper, serving either the semi-feudal or the absolute monarchy as a counterpoise against the nobility, and, in fact, corner-stone of the great monarchies in general, the bourgeoisie has at last, since the establishment of Modern Industry and of the world-market, conquered for itself, in the modern representative State, exclusive political sway. The executive of the modern State is but a committee for managing the common affairs of the whole bourgeoisie.

The bourgeoisie, historically, has played a most revolutionary part.

The bourgeoisie, wherever it has got the upper hand, has put an end to all feudal, patriarchal, idyllic relations. It has pitilessly torn asunder the motley feudal ties that bound man to his 'natural superiors', and has left remaining no other nexus between man and man than naked self-interest, than callous 'cash payment'. It has drowned the most heavenly ecstasies of religious fervour, of chivalrous enthusiasm, of philistine sentimentalism, in the icy water of egotistical calculation. It has resolved personal worth into exchange value, and in place of the numberless indefeasible chartered freedoms, has set up that single, unconscionable freedom – Free Trade. In one word, for exploitation, veiled by religious and political illusions, it has substituted naked, shameless, direct, brutal exploitation.

The bourgeoisie has stripped of its halo every occupation hitherto honoured and looked up to with reverent awe. It has converted the physician, the lawyer, the priest, the poet, the man of science, into its paid wage-labourers.

The bourgeoisie has torn away from the family its sentimental veil, and has reduced the family relation to a mere money relation.

The bourgeoisie has disclosed how it came to pass that the brutal display of vigour in the Middle Ages, which Reactionists so much admire, found its fitting complement in the most slothful indolence. It has been the first to show what man's activity can bring about. It has accomplished wonders far surpassing Egyptian pyramids, Roman aqueducts, and Gothic cathedrals; it has conducted expeditions that put in the shade all former Exoduses of nations and crusades.

The bourgeoisie cannot exist without constantly revolutionising the instruments of production, and thereby the relations of production, and with them the whole relations of society. Conservation of the old modes of production in unaltered form, was, on the contrary, the first condition of existence for all earlier industrial classes. Constant revolutionising of production, uninterrupted disturbance of all social conditions, everlasting uncertainty and agitation distinguish the bourgeois epoch from all earlier ones. All fixed, fast-frozen relations, with their train of ancient and venerable prejudices and opinions, are swept away, all new-formed ones become antiquated before they can ossify. All that is solid melts into air, all that is holy is profaned, and man is at last compelled to face with sober senses, his real conditions of life, and his relations with his kind.

Suggested further reading

Althusser, L (with Balibar, E) (1970), *Reading Capital*. London: New Left Books
Timpanaro, S (1976), *The Freudian Slip*. London: New Left Books
Wolfenstein, E V (1993), *Psychoanalytic Marxism. Groundwork*. London: Free Association Books

Nietzsche (1844–1900)

> Nietzsche's madness – that is, the dissolution of his thought – is that by which
> his thought opens out onto the modern world.
>
> (Foucault, 1971a: 288)

Friedrich Nietzsche's distrust of systems, his questioning of all values and morals, his all-pervading reflexivity, qualify him as the grandfather of post-modernism. Newcomers to his writing can hardly fail to be impressed by the radical open-mindedness of his thinking, and by the rigour and energy he brought to overturning preconception and received wisdom. He took scepticism and a 'scientific' curiosity to their nth degree – perhaps to the madness in which he ended his days. Here he is in perhaps the most vehement and nihilistic of his works, the aphoristic, five-volume *The Gay Science* (1886). '*Let us beware!* . . . Let us beware of presupposing that something so orderly as the cyclical motions of our planetary neighbours are the general and universal case: even a glance at the Milky Way gives rise to doubt whether there may not there exist far more crude and contradictory motions, likewise stars with eternally straight trajectories, and the like. The astral order in which we live is an exception . . . '.

There is an undeniable sense of wonder about this; yet Nietzsche was writing about a universe that was also meaningless and chaotic: it contained no God ('God is dead') and no other ordering principle. 'The astral order in which we live is an exception; this order and the apparent permanence which is conditional upon it is in its turn made possible by the exception of exceptions: the formation of the organic. The total nature of the world is, on the other hand, to all eternity chaos . . . ' (Nietzsche, cited in Hollingdale, 1969: 15). *The Gay Science* is often taken to mark a crisis in his thinking; this was resolved in *Thus Spake Zarathustra*, which is a sustained hymn to yes-saying and to the famous 'will to power'.

Nietzsche's questioning of established values – especially moral ones – and his deliberate courting of confusion were undertaken in the search for his own truth. This is what he urged upon his readers, and it was probably for this reason above all others that he was a huge influence on avant-garde European artists of the early modernist period. 'Live dangerously!', he exhorted (Hollingdale, 1969: 29). 'I tell you: one must still have chaos in one to give birth to a dancing star . . . '. For the enemy was the encroaching uniformity and mediocrity of the modern age, and here he echoes Kierkegaard: 'Alas! There cometh the time when man will no longer give birth to any star. Alas! There cometh the time of the most despicable man, who can no longer despise himself' (Nietzsche, 1892, in Friedman, 1964: 64).

Nietzsche's Will to Power is what replaces God; it is an inner, elevating quality, and it involves a kind of Hegelian 'self-overcoming'; this could entail unconscious as well as conscious processes, for Nietzsche, not surprisingly, questioned the primacy of consciousness. This direction in his thinking led to his most famous or – thanks to its distortion by the Nazis – infamous concept, that of the Superman, he who is master of himself, and has realised his full humanness. The Superman has found the greatest amount of the power needed to turn life's chaos into self-overcoming and joy – joy requires no justification, it is its own reward (Hollingdale, 1969: 27). The Superman wills the Eternal Recurrence of the Same: that is, he wills to eternity, in a final joyous acceptance of the wholeness and connectedness of things. Implied is an overcoming of, or a coming to terms with, the past, and with one's own history, so that we are, in the words of Žižek, no longer constrained by the 'inertia' of the past. 'The Eternal recurrence of the Same ultimately means that there is no longer any traumatic kernel resisting its recollection, that the subject can fully assume his/her past, projecting it into the future as willing its recurrence' (Žižek, 2001: 367).

We always have an uneasy relationship with our history. To love one's fate would be the Nietzschian ideal. If we do not forget the past we cannot grow up, so we need to study history and forget it. For Nietzsche there is no single reality or meaning beyond our interpretations; we search for our own truth, yet at the same time we cannot escape language – we are always trapped within it and its concepts, and can only express ourselves within the concepts that trap us. (For a discussion of psychoanalytic thinking on memory, trauma and false memory, see Scott, 1996.)

'What, therefore, is truth? A mobile army of metaphors, metonymies, anthropomorphisms; truths are illusions of which one has forgotten that they are illusions. . . . Coins which have their obverse effaced and are now no longer of account as coins but merely as metal' (Nietzsche, in Sarup, 1993: 46).

But we can (as therapists and patients) reverse our perspectives as much as possible – seek out the opposites of the concepts in which we are trapped. For Nietzsche, 'thinking is always inseparably bound to the rhetorical devices that support it' (Sarup, 1993: 46), and it is on the strength of insight such as this that Nietzsche looms as a formidably powerful presence behind post-modern thinking.

From Nietzsche (1974), *The Gay Science*, pp. 181–2, and (1989), *Beyond Good and Evil*, pp. 97–9

'The Madman'

Have you not heard of that madman who lit a lantern in the bright morning hours, ran to the market place, and cried incessantly: "I seek God! I seek God!" – As many of those who did not believe in God were standing around just then, he provoked much laughter. Has he got lost? asked one. Did he lose his way like a child? asked another. Or is he hiding? Is he afraid of us? Has he gone on a voyage? Emigrated? – Thus they yelled and laughed.

The madman jumped into their midst and pierced them with his eyes. "Whither is God" he cried; "I will tell you. *We have killed him* – you and I.

All of us are his murderers. But how did we do this? How could we drink up the sea? Who gave us the sponge to wipe away the entire horizon? What were we doing when we unchained this earth from its sun? Whither is it moving now? Whither are we moving? Away from all suns? Are we not plunging continually? Backward, sideward, forward, in all directions? Is there still any up or down? Are we not straying as through an infinite nothing? Do we not feel the breath of empty space? Has it not become colder? Is not night continually closing in on us? Do we not need to light lanterns in the morning? Do we hear nothing as yet of the noise of the gravediggers who are burying God? Do we smell nothing as yet of the divine decomposition? Gods, too, decompose. God is dead. God remains dead. And we have killed him.

"How shall we comfort ourselves, the murderers of all murderers? What was holiest and mightiest of all that the world has yet owned has bled to death under our knives: who will wipe this blood off us? What water is there for us to clean ourselves? What festivals of atonement, what sacred games shall we have to invent? Is not the greatness of this deed too great for us? Must we ourselves not become gods simply to appear worthy of it? There has never been a greater deed; and whoever is born after us – for the sake of this deed he will belong to a higher history than all history hitherto."

Here the madman fell silent and looked again at his listeners; and they, too, were silent and stared at him in astonishment. At last he threw his lantern on the ground, and it broke into pieces and went out. "I have come too early", he said then; "my time is not yet. This tremendous event is still on its way, still wandering; it has not yet reached the ears of men. Lightning and thunder require time; the light of the stars requires time; deeds, though done, still require time to be seen and heard. This deed is still more distant from them than the most distant stars – *and yet they have done it themselves.*"

It has been related further that on the same day the madman forced his way into several churches and there struck up his *requiem aeternam deo*. Led out and called to account, he is said always to have replied nothing but: "What after all are these churches now if they are not the tombs and sepulchers of God?"

From Nietzsche, F. (1989), 'The Natural History of Morals', *Beyond God and Evil*, pp. 97–9.

186

The moral sentiment in Europe today is as refined, old, diverse, irritable, and subtle, as the "science of morals" that accompanies it is still young, raw, clumsy, and butterfingered – an attractive contrast that occasionally even becomes visible and incarnate in the person of a moralist. Even the term "science of morals" is much too arrogant considering what it designates, and offends *good* taste – which always prefers more modest terms.

One should own up in all strictness to what is still necessary here for a long time to come, to what alone is justified so far: to collect material, to conceptualize and arrange a vast realm of subtle feelings of value and differences of value which are alive, grow, beget, and perish – and perhaps attempts to present vividly some of the more frequent and recurring forms of such living crystallizations – all to prepare a *typology* of morals.

To be sure, so far one has not been so modest. With a stiff seriousness that inspires laughter, all our philosophers demanded something far more exalted, presumptuous, and solemn from themselves as soon as they approached the study of morality: they wanted to supply a *rational foundation* for morality – and every philosopher so far has believed that he has provided such a foundation. Morality itself, however, was accepted as "given". How remote from their clumsy pride was that task which they considered insignificant and left in dust and must – the task of description – although the subtlest fingers and senses can scarcely be subtle enough for it.

Just because our moral philosophers knew the facts of morality only very approximately in arbitrary extracts or in accidental epitomes – for example, as the morality of their environment, their class, their church, the spirit of their time, their climate and part of the world – just because they were poorly informed and not even very curious about different peoples, times, and past ages – they never laid eyes on the real problems of morality; for these emerge only when we compare *many* moralities. In all "science of morals" so far one thing was *lacking*, strange as it may sound: the problem of morality itself, what was lacking was any suspicion that there was something problematic here. What the philosophers called "a rational foundation for morality" and tried to supply was, seen in the right light, merely a scholarly variation of the common *faith* in the prevalent morality; a new means of *expression* for this faith; and thus just another fact within particular morality; indeed, in the last analysis a kind of denial that this morality might ever be considered problematic – certainly the very opposite of an examination, analysis, questioning, and vivisection of this very faith.

Listen, for example, with what almost venerable innocence Schopenhauer still described his task, and then draw your conclusions about the scientific standing of a "science" whose ultimate masters still talk like children and little old women: "The principle," he says (p. 136 of *Grundprobleme der Moral*), "the fundamental proposition on whose contents all moral philosophers are *really* agreed – *neminem laede, immo omnes, quantum potes, juva*[1] – that is *really* the proposition for which all moralists endeavor to find the rational foundation . . . the *real* basis of ethics for which one has been looking for thousands of years as for the philosopher's stone."

---

[1]   'Hurt no one; rather, help all as much as you can.'

The difficulty of providing a rational foundation for the principle cited may indeed be great – as is well known, Schopenhauer did not succeed either – and whoever has once felt deeply how insipidly false and sentimental this principle is in a world whose essence is will to power, may allow himself to be reminded that Schopenhauer, though a pessimist, *really* – played the flute. Every day, after dinner: one should read his biography on that. And incidentally: a pessimist, one who denies God and the world but *comes to a stop* before morality – who affirms morality and plays the flute – the *laede neminem* morality – what? is that really – a pessimist?

187

Even apart from the value of such claims as "there is a categorical imperative in us", one can still always ask: what does such a claim tell us about the man who makes it? There are moralities which are meant to justify their creator before others. Other moralities are meant to calm him and lead him to be satisfied with himself. With yet others he wants to crucify himself and humiliate himself. With others he wants to wreak revenge, with others conceal himself, with others transfigure himself and place himself way up, at a distance. This morality is used by its creator to forget, that one to have others forget him or something about him. Some moralists want to vent their power and creative whims on humanity; some others, perhaps including Kant, suggest with their morality: "What deserves respect in me is that I can obey – and you ought not to be different from me." – In short, moralities are also merely a *sign language of the affects*.

Suggested further reading

Magnus, B and Higgins, K M (eds) (1996), *The Cambridge Companion to Nietzsche*. Cambridge: Cambridge University Press
Nietzsche, F (1977), *A Nietzsche Reader* (ed. Rieu, E V). Harmondsworth: Penguin
Robinson, D (1999), *Nietzsche and Postmodernism*. Duxford, Cambs.: Icon

Freud (1856–1939)

Sigmund Freud's thinking had a profound impact on the twentieth century; this is uncontestable. Yet he does not appear in many anthologies of post-modern thinking, even as a precursor. This is very strange, since almost all the post-modern thinkers who feature in this volume have engaged with his work in one way or another. Freud might be considered a quintessentially post-modern thinker himself, in the sense that he constantly reminds us that we are subject to something – unconscious forces – over which we have little or no control. Ambivalence (a key Freudian term; see Laplanche and Pontalis, 1988: 26–9) seems to come unavoidably into play in this recognition.

His work is certainly, in the early twenty-first century, still controversial – in fact it seems to be becoming more, rather than less, so. Attacks upon psychoanalysis, especially since the early 1980s, have charged it with being unscientific or even fraudulent, individualistic, élitist, expensive, and with having the hallmarks of a dubious religious sect (for a more detailed summary of such criticisms, see Frosh, 1987: 6–10 etc.). Its defenders point to its explanatory power, its efficacy as therapy, and its grasp – like that of great literature – of the complexity of what it is to be flawed and human. It has been seen as a continuation of the Enlightenment project (see for example Habermas, 1972), which, in extending the reach of rationality, also confronts us with the terrifying limits of reason. It was hailed, not least by Freud himself, as a new Copernican revolution, *the* major intellectual upheaval of the twentieth century. If Copernicus determined that the earth was not the centre of the universe, and Darwin, in the nineteenth century, that humans were not the god-given pinnacles of creation, directly created by God, Freud decentred us in another way: conscious, reasoning ego is 'not even master in its own house' (Freud, 1916–17: 285). Outside the realms of psychotherapy, psychoanalysis continues to have tremendous influence on other fields, from literature and media studies to sociology.

The notion of an unconscious was not invented by Freud – it has a prehistory extending at least as far back as Galen (*c*. AD 130–200) (Whyte, 1979: 78–9). The more rigorous study Freud made of it derives first of all from the work of the French physician Charcot with patients diagnosed as hysterical. Charcot demonstrated, famously, that hysterical symptoms can be produced by suggestion; Freud's discovery, with his colleague Breuer, was that they can also be understood as unconscious *communications*.

He found further evidence for the existence and power of the unconscious in dreams, jokes, mistakes and slips of the tongue – that is, in phenomena of the everyday world (the *Psychopathology of Everyday Life*). Freud's early writings are indeed influenced by phenomenology; he attended Franz Brentano's lectures in 1874–6, the only philosophy courses he took during his medical training (Moran, 2000: 24).

Nowhere are these phenomena manifest more than in dreams. Yet, as Freud wrote, 'Waking thought pushes dream thoughts aside as alien'. In other words we have a limited capacity for staying with the products of the unconscious; it is too much for us; we must (to use Lacan's term) foreclose on it. Perhaps it is inevitable that we reify it as 'the unconscious', that is, speak of it as if it were a thing – in a vain attempt to reassert our mastery.

Freud himself was not immune to this difficulty of 'staying with' unconscious phenomena, as a 'pure' phenomenologist might seek to do. As the French philosopher and psychoanalyst Jean Laplanche has argued (Laplanche, 1996), there is a tension in Freud's work between Freud the phenomenologist and writer, and Freud the ambitious scientist, who wanted to synthesise his observations and experiences into something generalisable, to construct grand theories and universal laws (the most notable being the Oedipus complex). In awakening us to dreams Freud points up the limits of generalisation. It is, however, one thing to say that dreams have meaning, and another to generalise further, along the lines of 'dream book' explanations (for example, water always equals sex). The 'method' of psychoanalysis, free association, can open onto what is frightening, awesome, mythic and demonic in human experience, all that Enlightenment rationality sought to distance. (This is the aspect of the Freudian enquiry that C. G. Jung particularly developed. See also, below, Kristeva, who privileges madness, holiness and poetry over a reductionist, modern world-view.) Freud needed to be a phenomenologist in order not to dismiss the demonic and mythic. '[T]o my great astonishment', he wrote, ' . . . the view of dreams that came closest to the truth was not the medical but the popular one', with, however, the additional comment: ' . . . half involved though it still was in superstition' (Freud, 1901, in Gay, 1995: 143). He was open to mystery; yet he also felt he needed to recover this view of dreams for science. Thus, he had, characteristically, to talk in the *first* place about 'psychical significance . . . the relation of dreams to other mental processes' etc., and only in the *second* place about dreams and meaning.

Free association can open us up to new meanings; but this is not the same as saying it leads us necessarily to a lucid understanding of what is going on, or of how our meanings are determined. In *The Interpretation of Dreams* (1900) Freud provided a kind of key for decoding (condensation, displacement, repression, etc.) which certainly opened new possibilities for thinking about dream phenomena. The danger, however, is of a slippage, into a technical language, with claims to final explanation, as, for example, when Freud asserted that all dreams are the fulfilment of repressed wishes. Free association is a method of investigation into the unconscious meanings, for the therapeutic couple, of words, actions and the products of fantasy. This is something different in kind from a psychotherapeutic method which systematically interprets resistance, transference and desire – something which, arguably, a computer could do.

Thus Freud had a foot in two camps, the scientific and something closer to the phenomenological, and the tension can be felt throughout his work. The case studies, used to come up with scientific 'truths', are also great literature and biography. Freud has kept alive a sense of the sacred and of the unknown in an increasingly scientific, materialist world, and the free associative method has had a massive impact on literature, art, and culture in general (particularly through the work of the Surrealists, of whom Freud did not approve) from the 1920s onwards.

In helping to institute the modern 'talking cure', Freud demonstrated afresh the potency of words; he gave back to secular thinking a sense of the potency of the word that had perhaps been lost since the late seventeenth century, in rationalistic, post-Reformation Europe. Along with other precursors of the post-modern 'turn to language', he paved the way to a new recognition of how much speech and language are worthy of study. He showed that the sense we appear to make of things is always something else: he points towards a post-modern notion that meaning and sense are always horizonal, just out of reach. What words work both to reveal and to veil, as Freud and Breuer found from the very start, is the sexual; the Freudian enterprise ensured that questions of sex and sexual development, of sexuality and gender, were at centre stage for most of the twentieth century. No contemporary debate on these matters can ignore the impact of Freud and his followers: they map out the very terrain on which the debate must take place.

The work of Freud's followers has taken many directions, from American ego psychology, with its 'modernist' aim to increase ego strength and adaptive functioning; to the contributions of Melanie Klein and her followers, with their emphasis on the deep unconscious (R. D. Laing called Klein 'a natural empirical phenomenologist', although, he added, she would not have known the meaning of the word – Grosskurth, 1987: 447); to British object-relations theory and the work of Winnicott and Fairbairn; to Lacan.

The text we have selected is 'The Unconscious'. Freud's English editors wrote that the essay 'may perhaps be regarded as the most important of all Freud's theoretical writings' (Freud, 1915). Mental events, wrote Freud, are like pearls on an invisible chain; his rhetorical starting point is a grievance against philosophers, who equate mind with consciousness. In this paper Freud also sought to demonstrate that the mind is ruled by inexorable laws (Gay, 1995: 572); the paper takes us through a typography of mind. It reflects both Freud the phenomenologist, and Freud the systematiser.

Freud wrote: 'We have learned from psychoanalysis that the essence of repression lies, not in putting an end to, in annihilating, the idea which represents an instinct, but in preventing it from becoming conscious.' What is unconscious can 'produce effects', regardless of whether or not they become conscious. 'Repression' is certainly used as a part of a technical vocabulary; the paper might lend itself to a modernist or literal reading, such as Roudinesco and Plon (1997: 490) seem to give it, when they write of the patient coming to 'know' the contents of his unconscious.

Another way of thinking about this might be as follows. Through the process of psychoanalysis we can be more open to that which we can never know – a knowledge that we shall never have the knowledge – thus perhaps becoming more appropriately able to stay with the 'id', where the life is. Through a process of psychoanalysis we can be helped with what is appropriate for us. We are all dysfunctional, caught up with all manner of anxieties. Let us imagine, for example, a patient whose mother suddenly left her in childhood: she has felt frozen ever since. Coming to 'know', in this sense, might mean her feeling freer to go with the flow, more open to the unknown, that which she most fears, out of terror that she will expose herself to further loss.

What is therapeutic about psychotherapy is the process gone through. It is not something like dental treatment, a repair after the damage has been done, but rather a new experience of life in itself. This is not about strengthening the ego; it is not humanist in the sense of reinforcing an idea that the patient can now decide who he or she wants to be. Rather, the hope is that he or she may be able to find out a bit more who s/he *is*, and breathe more easily. Freud led to the professionalisation of psychotherapy, but he also opened up something else, and held it for us: dark forces, our greatest fears and traumata. One could perhaps say that his scientific bias not only legitimised his quest, it also had the function, in the context of the culture of his, and our, times, of holding it for us. Of helping to do the impossible and stay with what is, with what is beyond our current, cultural, ability to describe.

From Freud (1915), 'The Unconscious', *The Standard Edition of the Complete Psychological Works of Sigmund Freud*, Vol. XIV, pp. 166 *et seq*.

THE UNCONSCIOUS

We have learnt from psycho-analysis that the essence of the process of repression lies, not in putting an end to, in annihilating, the idea which represents an instinct, but in preventing it from becoming conscious. When this happens we say of the idea that it is in a state of being 'unconscious', and we can produce good evidence to show that even when it is unconscious it can produce effects, even including some which finally reach consciousness. Everything that is repressed must remain unconscious; but let us state at the very outset that the repressed does not cover everything that is unconscious. The unconscious has the wider compass: the repressed is a part of the unconscious.

How are we to arrive at a knowledge of the unconscious? It is of course only as something conscious that we know it, after it has undergone transformation or translation into something conscious. Psycho-analytic work shows us every day that translation of this kind is possible. In order that this should come about, the person under analysis must overcome certain resistances – the same resistances as those which, earlier, made the material concerned into something repressed by rejecting it from the conscious.

1. Justification for the Concept of the Unconscious

Our right to assume the existence of something mental that is unconscious and to employ that assumption for the purposes of scientific work is disputed in many quarters. To this we can reply that our assumption of the unconscious is *necessary* and *legitimate*, and that we possess numerous proofs of its existence.

It is *necessary* because the data of consciousness have a very large number of gaps in them; both in healthy and in sick people psychical acts often occur which can be explained only by presupposing other acts, of which, nevertheless, consciousness affords no evidence. These not only include parapraxes and dreams in healthy people, and everything described as a psychical symptom or an obsession in the sick; our most personal daily experience acquaints us with ideas that come into our head we do not know from where, and with intellectual conclusions arrived at we do not know how.

All these conscious acts remain disconnected and unintelligible if we insist upon claiming that every mental act that occurs in us must also necessarily be experienced by us through consciousness; on the other hand, they fall into a demonstrable connection if we interpolate between them the unconscious acts which we have inferred. A gain in meaning is perfectly justifiable ground for going beyond the limits of direct experience. When, in addition, it turns out that the assumption of there being an unconscious enables us to construct a successful procedure by which we can exert an effective influence upon the course of conscious processes, this success will have given us an incontrovertible proof of the existence of what we have assumed. This being so, we must adopt the position that to require that whatever goes on in the mind must also be known to consciousness is to make an untenable claim.

We can go further and argue, in support of there being an unconscious psychical state, that at any given moment consciousness includes only a small content, so that the greater part of what we call conscious knowledge must in any case be for very considerable periods of time in a state of latency, that is to say, of being psychically unconscious. When all our latent memories are taken into consideration it becomes totally incomprehensible how the existence of the unconscious can be denied. But here we encounter the objection that these latent recollections can no longer be described as psychical, but that they correspond to residues of somatic processes from which what is psychical can once more arise. The obvious answer to this is that a latent memory is, on the contrary, an unquestionable residuum of a *psychical* process. But it is more important to realize clearly that this objection is based on the equation – not, it is true, explicitly stated but taken as axiomatic – of what is conscious with what is mental. This equation is either a *petitio principii* which begs the question whether everything that is psychical is also necessarily conscious; or else it is a matter of convention, of nomenclature. In this latter case it is, of course, like any other convention, not open to refutation. The question remains, however, whether the convention is so expedient that we are bound to adopt it. To this we may reply that the conventional equation of the psychical with the conscious is totally inexpedient. It disrupts psychical continuities, plunges us into the insoluble difficulties of psycho-physical parallelism, is open to the reproach that for no obvious reason it over-estimates the part played by consciousness, and that it forces us prematurely to abandon the field of psychological research without being able to offer us any compensation from other fields.

It is clear in any case that this question – whether the latent states of mental life, whose existence is undeniable, are to be conceived of as conscious mental states or as physical ones – threatens to resolve itself into a verbal dispute. We shall therefore be better advised to focus our attention on what we know with certainty of the nature of these debatable states. As far as their physical characteristics are concerned, they are totally inaccessible to us: no physiological concept or chemical process can give us any notion of their nature. On the other hand, we know for certain that they have abundant points of contact with conscious mental processes; with the help of a certain amount of work they can be transformed into, or replaced by, conscious mental processes, and all the categories which we employ to describe conscious mental acts, such as ideas, purposes, resolutions and so on, can be applied to them. Indeed, we are obliged to say of some of these latent states that the only respect in which they differ from conscious ones is precisely in the absence of consciousness. Thus we shall not hesitate to treat them as objects of psychological research, and to deal with them in the most intimate connection with conscious mental acts.

The stubborn denial of a psychical character to latent mental acts is accounted for by the circumstance that most of the phenomena concerned have not been the subject of study outside psycho-analysis. Anyone who is ignorant of pathological facts, who regards the parapraxes of normal people as accidental, and who is content with the old saw that dreams are froth ['*Träume sind Schäume*'] has only to ignore a few more problems of the psychology of consciousness in order to spare himself any need to assume an unconscious mental activity. Incidentally, even before the time of psycho-analysis, hypnotic experiments, and especially post-hypnotic suggestion, had tangibly demonstrated the existence and mode of operation of the mental unconscious.

The assumption of an unconscious is, moreover, a perfectly *legitimate* one, inasmuch as in postulating it we are not departing a single step from our customary and generally accepted mode of thinking. Consciousness makes each of us aware only of his own states of mind; that other people, too, possess a consciousness is an inference which we draw by analogy from their observable utterances and actions, in order to make this behaviour of theirs intelligible to us. (It would no doubt be psychologically more correct to put it in this way: that without any special reflection we attribute to everyone else our own constitution and therefore our consciousness as well, and that this identification is a *sine qua non* of our understanding.) This inference (or this identification) was formerly extended by the ego to other human beings, to animals, plants, inanimate objects and to the world at large, and proved serviceable so long as their similarity to the individual ego was overwhelmingly great; but it became more untrustworthy in proportion as the difference between the ego and these 'others' widened. Today, our critical judgement is already in doubt on the question of consciousness in animals; we refuse to admit it in plants and we regard the assumption of its existence in inanimate matter as mysticism. But even where the original inclination to identification has withstood criticism – that is, when the 'others' are our fellow-men – the assumption of a consciousness in them rests upon an inference and cannot share the immediate certainty which we have of our own consciousness.

Psycho-analysis demands nothing more than that we should apply this process of inference to ourselves also – a proceeding to which, it is true, we are not constitutionally inclined. If we do this, we must say: all the acts and manifestations which I notice in myself and do not know how to link up with the rest of my mental life must be judged as if they belonged to someone else: they are to be explained by a mental life ascribed to this other person. Furthermore, experience shows that we understand very well how to interpret in other people (that is, how to fit into their chain of mental events) the same acts which we refuse to acknowledge as being mental in ourselves. Here some special hindrance evidently deflects our investigations from our own self and prevents our obtaining a true knowledge of it.

This process of inference, when applied to oneself in spite of internal opposition, does not, however, lead to the disclosure of an unconscious; it leads logically to the assumption of another, second consciousness which is united in one's self with the consciousness one knows. But at this point, certain criticisms may fairly be made. In the first place, a consciousness of which its own possessor knows nothing is something very different from a consciousness belonging to another person, and it is questionable whether such a consciousness, lacking, as it does, its most important characteristic, deserves any discussion at all. Those who have resisted the assumption of an unconscious *psychical* are not likely to be ready to exchange it for an unconscious *consciousness*. In the second place, analysis shows that the different latent mental processes inferred by us enjoy a high degree of mutual independence, as though they had no connection with one another, and knew nothing of one another. We must be prepared, if so, to assume the existence in us not only of a second consciousness, but of a third, fourth, perhaps of an unlimited number of states of consciousness, all unknown to us and to one another. In the third place – and this is the most weighty argument of all – we have to take into account the fact that analytic investigation reveals some of these latent processes as having characteristics and peculiarities which seem alien to us, or even incredible, and which run directly counter to the attributes of consciousness with which we are familiar. Thus we have grounds for modifying our inference about ourselves and saying that what is proved is not the existence of a second consciousness in us, but the existence of psychical acts which lack consciousness. We shall also be right in rejecting the term 'subconsciousness' as incorrect and misleading. The well-known cases of 'double conscience' (splitting of consciousness) prove nothing against our view. We may most aptly describe them as cases of a splitting of the mental activities into two groups, and say that the same consciousness turns to one or the other of these groups alternately.

In psycho-analysis there is no choice for us but to assert that mental processes are in themselves unconscious, and to liken the perception of them by means of consciousness to the perception of the external world by means of the sense-organs. We can even hope to gain fresh knowledge from the comparison. The psycho-analytic assumption of unconscious mental activity appears to us, on the one hand, as a further expansion of the primitive animism which caused us to see copies of our own consciousness all around us, and, on the other hand, as an extension of the corrections undertaken by Kant of our views on external perception. Just as Kant warned us not to overlook the fact that our perceptions are subjectively conditioned and must not be regarded as identical with what is perceived though unknowable, so psycho-analysis warns us not to equate perceptions by means of consciousness with the unconscious mental processes which are their object. Like the physical, the psychical is not necessarily in reality what it appears to us to be. We shall be glad to learn, however, that the correction of internal perception will turn out not to offer such great difficulties as the correction of external perception – that internal objects are less unknowable than the external world.

Suggested further reading

Elliott, A, and Spezzano, C (eds) (2000), *Psychoanalysis at its Limits. Navigating the Postmodern Turn*. London: Free Association Books

Frosh, S (1987), *The Politics of Psychoanalysis. An Introduction to Freudian and Post-Freudian Theory*. New Haven, CT and London: Yale University Press

Gay, P (1995), *The Freud Reader*. New York: Vintage

Klein, M (1975 [1946]), 'Notes on some Schizoid Mechanisms', *The Writings of Melanie Klein*, Vol II. London: The Hogarth Press and the Institute of Psycho-Analysis

Sass, L A (1992), 'The Epic of Disbelief: The Postmodernist Turn in Contemporary Psychoanalysis', in Kvale (1992)

Winnicott, D W (1958 [1951]), 'Transitional Objects and Transitional Phenomena', *Through Paediatrics to Psychoanalysis. Collected Papers*. London: Tavistock

Saussure (1857–1913)

The importance of the Swiss linguist Ferdinand de Saussure is incalculable. He influenced twentieth-century thinking across a huge cultural field, and his work is still of direct use in helping us think about psychotherapy. Saussure's life's work was the study of language. He studied what most would argue is the very basis of psychotherapy, and certainly of that branch of it that stems from Freud and Breuer's 'talking cure'.

Saussure's *Course in General Linguistics*, which consisted of notes from his lectures in Geneva and Paris, only became available as a book in English in 1959. His resulting theory of language, known as *semiology*, the 'science of signs', influenced French thought earlier, from around 1916. Saussure effected a shift in the study of language, from the attempt to delineate its history and origins, which had been the general direction previous scholars had taken, to a study of its present configuration. What Saussure determined to be most important is the *structure* of language. For Saussure, an individual element in language (a word, or a sound) is without intrinsic or 'natural' meaning. It has no meaning outside convention. It has to be seen in relation to the structure, which he saw as a system, or set of systems, of relations between elements.

There is no intrinsic value to the word used to point to something. Saussure used the analogy of a chess piece, which one could replace with a button, or any other suitable object; what matters is that one knows its relationship to the other chess pieces. For Saussure, language is a system of *signs*, and each sign is composed of both a *signifier*, and a *signified*: the signifier is a word, or sound pattern, and the signified is the concept to which it relates. There is an autonomy of language in relation to reality; the relation of the signifier to the signified is not fixed, but ultimately arbitrary. What is fundamental for the generation and sharing of meaning is that language is a *structure of differences*. It is this insight that is crucial to the development of Continental structuralist and – with the added stress that this structure of differences is itself always shifting – post-structuralist thinking, from Lévi-Strauss to Barthes, Eco, Lacan, Foucault, Derrida and Kristeva.

What is particularly important for psychotherapy is Saussure's insight that the basic structure of language cannot be revealed by etymology – the story of the development of a word. Saussure opens the way to a search for meaning not in roots or sources, but in present usage, in how the patient's language itself states change. It would be misguided only to look at history and development – as therapists we need to listen to the whole context of the particular patient's utterances, and to how the patient structures their meanings and experiences. Lacan, indeed, through his reading of Saussure, shifted the emphasis in psychoanalysis to an almost exclusive focus on its linguistic aspects, famously claiming that the unconscious itself is 'structured like a language' (Lacan, 1993: 167).

Saussure developed the concepts of *langue* and *parole* as a way of distinguishing language as a structure, the totality of an abstract system, governed by rules (*langue*), from individual speech acts (*parole*). From this he argued that we (our patients/clients) are as much shaped by language as shapers of language; *langue* subsumes *parole*. Language is fundamentally a social institution, it precedes us, we are born into it; a merely individualistic approach to it would be inadequate. Words, in other words, also speak us. Thus there is always a tension between *langue* and *parole*, and the relations between the two – between part and whole – need to be understood not only by means of an examination of the content of the individual (patient's) utterances, but also through attention to structural form.

This opens up questions of direct and immediate relevance to psychotherapeutic practice. Only in paying attention to the *how* rather than just the *what* of speech is the therapist in a position to ask: what sort of place, in speaking, does the patient, the speaking subject, take up in the world (how does their *parole* relate to *langue*?). What sort of place, in attempting to speak to my patient about this, am I as a therapist then taking up, in relation to my patient and to the world, and in relation to my patient's relation to the world? A broader question also follows: how far does Saussure's emphasis on structure allow for individual freedom? Can there be a society of free individuals 'where freedom would be the result of a social life understood as a structure of differences'? (Lechte, 1994: 152)

In the extract that follows Saussure starts with a criticism of the notion that language is only a naming process. 'The linguistic sign unites, not a thing and a name, but a concept and a sound-image.' Crucially, it has an acoustic aspect. The linguistic sign has two characteristics which Saussure states as basic principles, namely the arbitrary nature of the sign, and the linear nature of the signifier: 'the signifier, being auditory, is unfolded solely in time'. For psychotherapists, there is not only the question of the arbitrary nature of the sign in terms of its meaning in our culture at a particular moment in time; there is also the meaning that the sign has for our patients/clients within such a culture. It may have some similarity, but will also always have a different meaning for us as people who are psychotherapists, one which unfolds over time. 'In language, as in any semiological system, whatever distinguishes one sign from the others constitutes it.' 'Language is a form, not a substance'; the precise ways in which language forms us are fundamental concerns of psychotherapy.

From Saussure (1966 [1916]), *Course in General Linguistics*, pp. 65–70 and 120–2

Sign, Signified, Signifier

Some people regard language, when reduced to its elements, as a naming-process only – a list of words, each corresponding to the thing that it names. For example [see Figure 1].

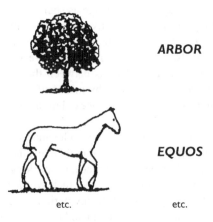

ARBOR

EQUOS

etc.   etc.

Figure 1 Arbor/equos

This conception is open to criticism at several points. It assumes that ready-made ideas exist before words; it does not tell us whether a name is vocal or psychological in nature (*arbor*, for instance, can be considered from either viewpoint); finally, it lets us assume that the linking of a name and a thing is a very simple operation – an assumption that is anything but true. But this rather naive approach can bring us near the truth by showing us that the linguistic unit is a double entity, one formed by the associating of two terms.

We have seen in considering the speaking-circuit that both terms involved in the linguistic sign are psychological and are united in the brain by an associative bond. This point must be emphasized.

The linguistic sign unites, not a thing and a name, but a concept and a sound-image. The latter is not the material sound, a purely physical thing, but the psychological imprint of the sound, the impression that it makes on our senses. The sound-image is sensory, and if I happen to call it 'material', it is only in that sense, and by way of opposing it to the other term of the association, the concept, which is generally more abstract.

The psychological character of our sound-images becomes apparent when we observe our own speech. Without moving our lips or tongue, we can talk to ourselves or recite mentally a selection of verse. Because we regard the words of our language as sound-images, we must avoid speaking of the 'phonemes' that make up the words. This term, which suggests vocal activity, is applicable to the spoken word only, to the realization of the inner image in discourse. We can avoid that misunderstanding by speaking of the *sounds* and *syllables* of a word provided we remember that the names refer to the sound-image.

The linguistic sign is then a two-sided psychological entity that can be represented by the drawing [in Figure 2].

The two elements are intimately united, and each recalls the other. Whether we try to find the meaning of the Latin word *arbor* or the word that Latin uses to designate the concept 'tree', it is clear that only the associations sanctioned by that language appear to us to conform to reality, and we disregard whatever others might be imagined.

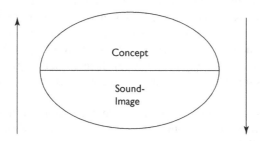

Figure 2 Concept/sound image

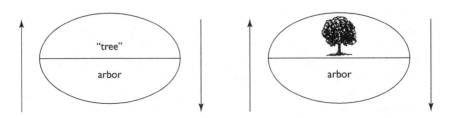

Figure 3 Arbor

Our definition of the linguistic sign poses an important question of terminology. I call the combination of a concept and a sound-image a *sign*, but
in current usage the term generally designates only a sound-image, a word,
for example (*arbor*, etc.). One tends to forget that arbor is called a sign only
because it carries the concept 'tree', with the result that the idea of the sensory
part implies the idea of the whole [Figure 3].

Ambiguity would disappear if the three notions involved here were
designated by three names, each suggesting and opposing the others. I propose
to retain the word *sign* [*signe*] to designate the whole and to replace *concept*
and *sound image* respectively by *signified* and *signifier*; the last two terms
have the advantage of indicating the opposition that separates them from
each other and from the whole of which they are parts. As regards *sign*, if
I am satisfied with it, this is simply because I do not know of any word to
replace it, the ordinary language suggesting no other.

The linguistic sign, as defined, has two primordial characteristics. In
enunciating them I am also positing the basic principles of any study of this
type.

Principle I: The Arbitrary Nature of the Sign

The bond between the signifier and the signified is arbitrary. Since I mean by
sign the whole that results from the associating of the signifier with the
signified, I can simply say: *the linguistic sign is arbitrary*.

The idea of 'sister' is not linked by any inner relationship to the succession
of sounds *s-ö-r* which serves as its signifier in French, that it could be
represented equally by just any other sequence is proved by differences among
languages and by the very existence of different languages: the signified
'ox' has as its signifier *b-ö-f* on one side of the border and *O-k-s (Ochs)* on the
other.

No one disputes the principle of the arbitrary nature of the sign, but it is
often easier to discover a truth than to assign to it its proper place. Principle
I dominates all the linguistics of language, its consequences are numberless.
It is true that not all of them are equally obvious at first glance, only after many

detours does one discover them, and with them the primordial importance of the principle.

One remark in passing: when semiology becomes organized as a science, the question will arise whether or not it properly includes modes of expression based on completely natural signs, such as pantomime. Supposing that the new science welcomes them, its main concern will still be the whole group of systems grounded on the arbitrariness of the sign. In fact, every means of expression used in society is based, in principle, on collective behavior or – what amounts to the same thing – on convention. Polite formulas, for instance, though often imbued with a certain natural expressiveness (as in the case of a Chinese who greets his emperor by bowing down to the ground nine times), are nonetheless fixed by rule; it is this rule and not the intrinsic value of the gestures that obliges one to use them. Signs that are wholly arbitrary realize better than the others the ideal of the semiological process; that is why language, the most complex and universal of all systems of expression, is also the most characteristic; in this sense linguistics can become the master-pattern for all branches of semiology although language is only one particular semiological system.

The word *symbol* has been used to designate the linguistic sign, or more specifically, what is here called the signifier. Principle I in particular weighs against the use of this term. One characteristic of the symbol is that it is never wholly arbitrary, it is not empty, for there is the rudiment of a natural bond between the signifier and the signified. The symbol of justice, a pair of scales, could not be replaced by just any other symbol, such as a chariot.

The word *arbitrary* also calls for comment. The term should not imply that the choice of the signifier is left entirely to the speaker (we shall see below that the individual does not have the power to change a sign in any way once it has become established in the linguistic community); I mean that it is unmotivated, i.e. arbitrary in that it actually has no natural connection with the signified.

. . .

Principle II: The Linear Nature of the Signifier

The signifier, being auditory, is unfolded solely in time from which it gets the following characteristics: (a) it represents a span, and (b) the span is measurable in a single dimension; it is a line.

While Principle II is obvious, apparently linguists have always neglected to state it, doubtless because they found it too simple; nevertheless, it is fundamental, and its consequences are incalculable. Its importance equals that of Principle I; the whole mechanism of language depends upon it. In contrast to visual signifiers (nautical signals, etc.) which can offer simultaneous groupings in several dimensions, auditory signifiers have at their command only the dimension of time. Their elements are presented in succession; they form a chain. This feature becomes readily apparent when they are represented in writing and the spatial line of graphic marks is substituted for succession in time.

Sometimes the linear nature of the signifier is not obvious. When I accent a syllable, for instance, it seems that I am concentrating more than one significant element on the same point. But this is an illusion, the syllable and its accent constitute only one phonational act. There is no duality within the act but only different oppositions to what precedes and what follows.

The Sign Considered in Its Totality

Everything that has been said up to this point boils down to this: in language there are only differences. Even more important: a difference generally implies positive terms between which the difference is set up; but in language there are only differences *without positive terms*. Whether we take the signified or the signifier, language has neither ideas nor sounds that existed before the linguistic system but only conceptual and phonic differences that have issued from the system. The idea or phonic substance that a sign contains is of less importance than the other signs that surround it. Proof of this is that the value of a term may be modified without either its meaning or its sound being affected, solely because a neighboring term has been modified.

But the statement that everything in language is negative is true only if the signified and the signifier are considered separately; when we consider the sign in its totality, we have something that is positive in its own class. A linguistic system is a series of differences of sound combined with a series of differences of ideas; but the pairing of a certain number of acoustical signs with as many cuts made from the mass of thought engenders a system of values; and this system serves as the effective link between the phonic and psychological elements within each sign. Although both the signified and the signifier are purely differential and negative when considered separately, their combination is a positive fact; it is even the sole type of facts that language has, for maintaining the parallelism between the two classes of differences is the distinctive function of the linguistic institution.

Certain diachronic facts are typical in this respect. Take the countless instances where alteration of the signifier occasions a conceptual change and where it is obvious that the sum of the ideas distinguished corresponds in principle to the sum of the distinctive signs. When two words are confused through phonetic alteration (e.g. French *décrépit* from *dēcrepitus* and *décrépi* from *crispus*), the ideas that they express will also tend to become confused if only they have something in common. Or a word may have different forms (cf. *chaise* "chair" and *chaire* "desk"). Any nascent difference will tend invariably to become significant but without always succeeding or being successful on the first trial. Conversely, any conceptual difference perceived by the mind seeks to find expression through a distinct signifier, and two ideas that are no longer distinct in the mind tend to merge into the same signifier.

When we compare signs – positive terms – with each other, we can no longer speak of difference; the expression would not be fitting, for it applies only to the comparing of two sound-images, e.g. *father* and *mother*, or two ideas, e.g. the idea 'father' and the idea 'mother'; two signs, each having a signified and signifier, are not different but only distinct. Between them there is only *opposition*. The entire mechanism of language, with which we shall be concerned later, is based on oppositions of this kind and on the phonic and conceptual differences that they imply.

What is true of value is true also of the unit. A unit is a segment of the spoken chain that corresponds to a certain concept; both are by nature purely differential.

Applied to units, the principle of differentiation can be stated in this way: the characteristics of the unit blend with the unit itself. In language, as in any semiological system, whatever distinguishes one sign from the others constitutes it. Difference makes character just as it makes value and the unit.

Another rather paradoxical consequence of the same principle is this: in the last analysis what is commonly referred to as a 'grammatical fact' fits the definition of the unit, for it always expresses an opposition of terms; it differs only in that the opposition is particularly significant (e.g. the formation of German plurals of the type *Nacht: Nächte*). Each term present in the grammatical fact (the singular without umlaut or final e in opposition to the plural with umlaut and e) consists of the interplay of a number of oppositions within the system. When isolated, neither *Nacht* nor *Nächte* is anything: thus everything is opposition. Putting it another way, the *Nacht: Nächte* relation can be expressed by an algebraic formula a/b in which a and b are not simple terms but result from a set of relations. Language, in a manner of speaking, is a type of algebra consisting solely of complex terms. Some of its oppositions are more significant than others; but units and grammatical facts are only different names for designating diverse aspects of the same general fact: the functioning of linguistic oppositions. This statement is so true that we might very well approach the problem of units by starting from grammatical facts. Taking an opposition like *Nacht: Nächte*, we might ask what are the units involved in it. Are they only the two words, the whole series of similar words, a and ä, or all singulars and plurals, etc.?

Units and grammatical facts would not be confused if linguistic signs were made up of something besides differences. But language being what it is, we shall find nothing simple in it regardless of our approach; everywhere and always there is the same complex equilibrium of terms that mutually condition each other. Putting it another way, *language is a form and not a substance*. This truth could not be overstressed, for all the mistakes in our terminology, all our incorrect ways of naming things that pertain to language, stem from the involuntary supposition that the linguistic phenomenon must have substance.

Suggested further reading

Culler, J (1986), *Ferdinand de Saussure*. Ithaca, NY: Cornell University Press

Chapter 4

Post-modern Continental philosophers

Introduction

Post-modernism questions notions of universality and truth, and this seems to us mandatory, in spite of the accusations of relativism that post-modern thinkers have often had levelled at them. Post-modern questioning can help us be more open to our patients' truths, to be more alert to how what is true in one moment may not be the next, and to how what is true for one patient may not be for another. Post-modernism raises questions about authorship: to what extent are we authors of our own lives? Psychotherapy has the potential to open us up to the unknown (Levinas), and to the excitement of living, which, perhaps by definition, means giving up the illusion that we can ever be fully in charge of our own destinies. This view could be contrasted with that of therapies with a more modernistic bias, which tacitly or explicitly foster the hope that one can become the person one would like to be (in this connection, see Kierkegaard, on despair at being who one *is*). The Lacanian notion of getting in touch with one's desire may sound as if it belongs to this way of thinking; Lacanian desire, however, is about something very different indeed, something which might be extremely disruptive of the destiny one thinks one has chosen for oneself.

All this is not to say therapy does not have a part to play in helping with a sense of direction, in helping people find some relief from torment – on the contrary. Post-modernism might enable us, through re-examination or deconstruction of psychotherapy's definitions and assumptions, to return to a notion of 'soul', as an alternative to a prevalent scientific or medical conception of the mind. It might help us towards 're-enchantment', towards reversing the process of 'disenchantment' that was, for Max Weber, the necessary accompaniment to the development of rationalist modernism (Weber, 1974: 155). Post-modern thinking might help us to question whether a rationalist and reductive conception of mind means a mind closed by definition, while 'soul' might stand more chance of being open. We might then move from a notion of 'soul' which by-passes religious dogmatism and leads to a keener alertness to otherness and to difference.

To some extent the distinction between modernism and post-modernism in psychotherapy might be seen in terms of Lacan's mirror, in that those who mainly reflect back to the patient/client the view they think the client wants to be seen, might be crudely classified as modern. Refusal necessarily to reflect the response asked for might be more post-modern (as well as consistent with usual psychodynamic practice). However, practitioners who do not meet such demands from the patient/client, but nevertheless work from a universalised theoretical place, might be considered distinctly modern, particularly if they are expecting the patient finally to arrive at a pre-ordained healthy or normative place. Perhaps the Jungian idea of working through your complexes, or Klein's 'depressive position', for all its elegance as metaphor, and precisely *because* of its persuasiveness, invites the practioner to reify it as such an end-point. It would be unfair, moreover, to single out psychoanalytic thinking as the only kind of thinking that might lend itself in this way. For example, to deduce, following the ethical example of Levinas, that when the patient can put the other first then he or she is ready to leave therapy, would also be to pre-ordain an approved outcome. The emphasis of the post-modern is on what emerges rather than 'what I make emerge'. It is not that, as a therapist, one does not have a place in what emerges; it is that one is only to a limited extent in charge of what emerges.

In writing about something called 'post-modernism' we may give the impression that we are discussing something monolithic; in fact, as we hope will be clear from this chapter, post-modernism is an umbrella term for a diverse collection of voices, very often in lively dialogue and debate with one another. It might, nevertheless, also be helpful here if we try to open up another general and rather blurry distinction, that between post-modernism and post-structuralism. The terms are often used in juxtaposition, or interchangeably. Structuralists, for example, the French anthropologist Claude Lévi-Strauss (b. 1908) or the post-Marxist philosopher Louis Althusser (1918–1990), would question the view that it is enough to say that humans are free, reasoning, autonomous and coherent; they would claim that we are who we are by virtue of our rituals, practices, customs, and our notions and methods of exchange. Structuralists would also oppose the view that there are patterns in history, and, following Saussure, they would insist on the conventionality and arbitrariness of language.

Post-structuralists – like most of those who follow in our next chapter – would go along with this and take it further, in particular by bringing together notions of subjecthood, gender and language: we are structured by, and find our places within, language. The post-modern/post-structural turn to language is most obvious in its insistence on attending to how things are said, and acceptance that language is not simply a neutral, value-free tool. It also involves a recognition of language as that to which we are subject in our relations to one another individually, and collectively. It structures our differences as well as our commonalities. For Lacan the unconscious is structured like a language; for Derrida we are caught in an endless *deferral* of meaning and a chain of *differences*.

Post-structuralists would also stress that truth, or meaning, lies not 'behind', or 'in', a text (or the patient's utterances), but, as we have suggested above, emerges in between, as a result of the reading activity of the reader (therapist), who thus becomes a co-producer. Post-structuralism tends to reduce the role of explanation, preferring in this way to let difference and discontinuity stand, rather than attempting to link and subsume them within an overarching system, be it evolutionary, political, or psychological (see Sarup, 1993: 59). This is where post-structuralism shows its phenomenological roots, the historical and ethical importance of which we have sought to explore in the preceding chapter.

'How is it', asks a recent commentator, 'that students and intellectuals from New York to Tokyo, Belgrade to Pretoria, are able to use the work of Derrida as the foundation for a sane, critical interpretation of the contemporary world?' (Roudinensco, 1999: 245). Post-modern/post-structural thinking can alert us to the complexity and the lack of fixity of the kinds of personal and political issues facing us. As therapists we have a part to play in staying open to changes in cultural practices, which affect who and how we are, and what is thought of currently as psychotherapy. We contrast this with a modernist ethic of certainty and coherence; post-modernism might critique this in terms, for example, of relations between knowledge and power. Foucault would ask: whose certainty, whose coherence, in whose interest, and how articulated?

What is the evidence of successful therapy? How do we know when it is completed? A post-modern answer to this modernist question might involve the Kierkegaardian notion of being open to possibility, which is what Lacan and other post-modern writers seem to encourage in the reader through the very 'openness' of their writing.

Is deconstructing psychotherapy as a modernist project finally of any real help to our clients/patients? In exploring this question perhaps we could start with a provisional conclusion: post-modernism enables psychotherapy usefully to open up an acceptance of difference, through both practice and research. The main limitation, for research, is the difficulty of making a case for the impossibility of generalisation, while at the same time considering, as these post-modern thinkers all do, that something important can indeed still be communicated. The question of generalisation may concern us less in the therapeutic relationship if we consider that psychotherapy needs to be re-invented with each client.

Suggested further reading

Anderson, W T (ed.) (1996), *The Fontana Postmodern Reader*. London: Fontana

Appignanesi, L (ed.) (1989), *Postmodernism: ICA Documents*. London: Free Association Books

Best, S and Kellner, D (1997), *The Postmodern Turn*. New York: Guilford Press

Cahoone, L (ed.) (1996), *From Modernism to Postmodernism*. Oxford: Blackwell

Connor, S (1989), *Postmodernist Culture: An Introduction to Theories of the Contemporary*. Oxford: Blackwell

Docherty, T (ed.) (1993), *Postmodernism: A Reader*. New York: Columbia University Press

Elliott, A (1999), *Social Theory and Psychoanalysis in Transition. Self and Society from Freud to Kristeva*. London: Free Association Books

Featherston, M (ed.) (1988), *Postmodernism*. London: Sage

Foster, H (ed.) (1985), *Post-Modern Culture*. London: Pluto

Gutting, G (2001), *French Philosophy in the Twentieth Century*. Cambridge: Cambridge University Press

Harvey, D (1989), *The Condition of Postmodernity*. Oxford: Blackwell

Jencks, C (ed.) (1992), *The Postmodern Reader*. London: Academy Editions

—— (1996), *What Is Post-Modernism?* New York: Wiley

Kearney, R (1995), *States of Mind. Dialogues with Contemporary Thinkers on the European Mind*. Manchester: Manchester University Press

Kearney, R and Rainwater, M (1996), *The Continental Philosophy Reader*. London: Routledge

Kvale, S (1992), *Psychology and Postmodernism*. London: Sage

Lechte, J (1994) *Fifty Key Thinkers*. London: Routledge

Moi, T (1987), *French Feminist Thought. A Reader*. Oxford: Blackwell

Rosenau, P (1991), *Post-Modernism and the Social Sciences*. Princeton, NJ: Princeton University Press

Sarup, M. (1993) *An Introductory Guide to Post-Structuralism and Postmodernism*. Hemel Hempstead: Harvester

Sim, S (ed.) (1998), *The Critical Dictionary of Postmodern Thought*. Cambridge: Icon Books

West, D (1998), *An Introduction to Continental Philosophy*. Oxford: Polity Press

Williams, C (2001), *Contemporary French Philosophy. Modernity and the Persistence of the Subject*. London: The Athlone Press

Wright, E (1998) *Psychoanalytic Criticism* (2nd edn). Cambridge: Polity Press

Young, R (ed.) (1981), *Untying the Text: A Post-Structuralist Reader*. London: Routledge

Lyotard (1924–1998)

> I will use the term modern to designate any science that legitimates itself with reference to a meta-discourse. . . . I define post-modernism as incredulity towards meta-narratives.
>
> (Lyotard, 1984: xxiv)

Jean-François Lyotard was one of the leading figures in the post-modern debate. It has been claimed that he invented the term post-modern itself. He was born in Versailles, and studied philosophy under the mentorship of Merleau-Ponty. Heidegger and Levinas are among other phenomenological thinkers who particularly influenced him. He also drew from Wittgenstein, from whom he borrowed the term 'language games'. He was, like many of his contemporaries in the 1950s, involved in the Marxist left. His main concerns, however, became the inter-relationships between the post-modern condition, narrative, science, knowledge, language games and feminism. Lyotard's thinking has raised questions for branches of enquiry from architecture to anthropology to literary and cultural studies.

For Lyotard one of the defining features of post-modernism was that it needs no legitimation 'beyond expediency and "performativity"' (Cahoone, 1996: 481), as against modernist notions of justification residing in scientific proof. Through Lyotard one might question the purpose of psychotherapy. Is the therapist's task to help people with their expediency and performativity? And in so doing to hear the patient as, possibly, being appropriate if they seem to be speaking in a way that seems discontinuous, or paralogous (reaching logically unjustifiable conclusions)? All of this holds up if one is no longer in a culture underpinned by science with its ideas of unity and proof. We might also, through Lyotard, become more incredulous about our clients'/patients' own 'grand narratives', the stories they tell about and to themselves as if they were the only stories around; in other words, more open to shifting and multiple narrative possibilities.

Lyotard enables a fundamental questioning of the nature of psychotherapeutic knowledge, and potentially opens up a more radical notion of it. Knowledge, for Lyotard, is developed by vested interests such as professional bodies to maintain their position. This, if one accepts it, must be true for psychotherapists and their legitimising organisations; thus any notion of truth and justice in the consulting room must always become at best secondary to the primary purpose of theory, which is to maintain the privilege of the therapist. These implications of Lyotard's work for psychotherapy can be drawn from the extract from *The Postmodern Condition* which follows.

> Science . . . is obliged to legitimate the rules of its own game. It then produces a discourse of legitimation with respect to its own status, a discourse called philosophy. I will use the term modern to designate any science that legitimates itself with reference to a meta-discourse making an explicit appeal to some grand narrative . . . For example, the rule of consensus between a sender and addressee of a statement with truth-value is deemed acceptable if it is cast in terms of a possible unanimity between rational minds: this is the Enlightenment narrative, in which the hero of knowledge works towards a good ethico-political end – universal peace. As can be seen from this example, if meta-narrative implying a philosophy of history is used to legitimate knowledge, questions are raised concerning the validity of the institutions governing the social bond: these must be legitimated as well. Thus justice is consigned to the grand narrative in the same way as truth.
>
> (Lyotard, 1984: xxiii)

In his definitions of modernism and post-modernism Lyotard is referring to the Enlightenment project (see Foucault, below) with its rational faith that one day science will know. Here he is on the Enlightenment quest for knowledge, which he links to ancient history, a masculine discourse, and to colonising moves:

> Philosophy is the West's madness, and never ceases to underwrite its quest for knowledge and politics in the name of Truth and the Good . . . By specifically considering the *question* of men's relationship to women,

philosophy . . . sends us in the direction of an *answer* . . . What matters is that the question . . . can be posed only in the *meta-language* . . . of philosophy. For such a meta-language is already the language of masculinity in the Western, and particularly Greek, sense . . . In fact, where do we actually see meta-language founded? In those communities of free men who speak a Hellenic language, carry arms, worship the same gods, and submit themselves to the law of equal political rights for all. These are the communities . . . at the heart of feudal Greek society. Women are excluded at the outset from such groups (along with children, foreigners, half-breeds, slaves) . . . But if the women's movement has an immense impact equal to that of slaves, colonised peoples, and other under-developed groups, it is that this movement solicits and destroys the (masculine) belief in meta-statements independent of ordinary statements . . . If 'reality' lies, it follows that men in all their claims to construct meaning, to speak the Truth, are themselves only a minority in a *patchwork* where it becomes impossible to establish and validly determine any major order.

(Lyotard, 1989: 118–20)

Enlightenment-derived meta-narratives (meta-psychology, master theory) lead to psychotherapeutically totalising moves, to attempts to know, rather than to accept who we are (see Loewenthal and Snell, 2001) – that is, parts of a patchwork. Such thinking has enormous importance for how we train students of counselling and psychotherapy. (And for the authors, for the way in which they examine the implications of the literature of phenomenology, existentialism, psychoanalysis and post-modernism with their students.) We would encourage incredulity.

We could, for example, ask in relation to the extract: Is psychotherapy a science? Should it be? To what extent is psychotherapy a (male) hero working towards the good ethico-political end, universal peace? Is psychotherapy about converting those who don't appear to be so rational? What are the institutions governing the social bond in psychotherapy? A possible answer would be, at one end, institutions such as church, state, marriage, family, and, at the other, the specialist institutions representing psychiatry, psychotherapy, psychoanalysis, counselling and psychology. Are notions of justice and truth, in terms of what the client/patient is speaking about, the relationship to the therapist, and how the therapist then talks about their work, merely consigned to the particular therapeutic theory? This could be contrasted to the Levinasian notion of justice in the moment with another. The grand theory legitimises the institution from which the therapist comes, so justice and truth are also enslaved to the theory, the grand narrative. If, for example, the notion were to be accepted that there is no court of appeal higher than the everyday – if 'ordinary statements' were to be valued over psychologising 'meta-statements' – where would these therapeutic institutions be?

Is it possible for counsellors and psychotherapists, however well intentioned they are, to do any more than shore each others' authority, in the name of Truth and the Good as universalised from their position, in such a way that those that appear to be helped are at best colonised?

Lyotard's later work, on technology and the inhuman, takes a bleak view. He points up the inhumanity of our technological thinking, which goes towards ensuring our survival rather than the quality of our lives. Such consciousness of the inhuman has filtered into our daily lives, through the encroachment of technological thinking into, for example, medicine, or into psychology through the growth of Artificial Intelligence as a university discipline. Lyotard describes a move from living with technology to being subordinate to it. He talks about such rationalism as endemic to capitalism (Sim, 2001). How far has such thinking already infiltrated its way into psychotherapy, through, for example, the increasingly dominant notion of evidence-based practice? Other examples might include interest among psychoanalysts and analytic therapists in neurology, in so far as such interest takes us away from the particular human experience. It is a question of the *place* of technology and technical thinking, and of the danger of this thinking surreptitiously coming to rule us, rather than helping us to improve the quality of our lives.

From Lyotard (1984), *The Post-Modern Condition: A Report on Knowledge*, pp. xxiii–xxv, 31–2, 37–8, 40–1

The object of this study is the condition of knowledge in the most highly developed societies. I have decided to use the word *postmodern* to describe that condition. The word is in current use on the American continent among sociologists and critics; it designates the state of our culture following the transformations which, since the end of the nineteenth century, have altered the game rules for science, literature, and the arts. The present study will place these transformations in the context of the crisis of narratives.

Science has always been in conflict with narratives. Judged by the yardstick of science, the majority of them prove to be fables. But to the extent that science does not restrict itself to stating useful regularities and seeks the truth, it is obliged to legitimate the rules of its own game. It then produces a discourse of legitimation with respect to its own status, a discourse called philosophy. I will use the term *modern* to designate any science that legitimates itself with reference to a metadiscourse of this kind making an explicit appeal to some grand narrative, such as the dialectics of Spirit, the hermeneutics of meaning, the emancipation of the rational or working subject, or the creation of wealth. For example, the rule of consensus between the sender and addressee of a statement with truth-value is deemed acceptable if it is cast in terms of a possible unanimity between rational minds: this is the Enlightenment narrative, in which the hero of knowledge works toward a good ethico-political end – universal peace. As can be seen from this example, if a metanarrative implying a philosophy of history is used to legitimate knowledge, questions are raised concerning the validity of the institutions governing the social bond: these must be legitimated as well. Thus justice is consigned to the grand narrative in the same way as truth.

Simplifying to the extreme, I define *postmodern* as incredulity toward metanarratives. This incredulity is undoubtedly a product of progress in the sciences: but that progress in turn presupposes it. To the obsolescence of the metanarrative apparatus of legitimation corresponds, most notably, the crisis of metaphysical philosophy and of the university institution which in the past relied on it. The narrative function is losing its functors, its great hero, its great dangers, its great voyages, its great goal. It is being dispersed in clouds of narrative language elements – narrative, but also denotative, prescriptive, descriptive, and so on. Conveyed within each cloud are pragmatic valencies specific to its kind. Each of us lives at the intersection of many of these. However, we do not necessarily establish stable language combinations, and the properties of the ones we do establish are not necessarily communicable.

Thus the society of the future falls less within the province of a Newtonian anthropology (such as stucturalism or systems theory) than a pragmatics of language particles. There are many different language games – a heterogeneity of elements. They only give rise to institutions in patches – local determinism.

The decision makers, however, attempt to manage these clouds of sociality according to input/output matrices, following a logic which implies that their elements are commensurable and that the whole is determinable. They allocate our lives for the growth of power. In matters of social justice and of scientific truth alike, the legitimation of that power is based on its optimizing the system's performance – efficiency. The application of this criterion to all of our games necessarily entails a certain level of terror, whether soft or hard: be operational (that is, commensurable) or disappear.

The logic of maximum performance is no doubt inconsistent in many ways, particularly with respect to contradiction in the socio-economic field: it demands both less work (to lower production costs) and more (to lessen the social burden of the idle population). But our incredulity is now such that we no longer expect salvation to rise from these inconsistencies, as did Marx.

Still, the postmodern condition is as much a stranger to disenchantment as it is to the blind positivity of delegitimation. Where, after the metanarratives, can legitimacy reside? The operativity criterion is technological; it has no relevance for judging what is true or just. Is legitimacy to be found in consensus obtained through discussion, as Jürgen Habermas thinks? Such consensus does violence to the heterogeneity of language games. And invention is always born of dissension. Postmodern knowledge is not simply a tool of the authorities, it refines our sensitivity to differences and reinforces our ability to tolerate the incommensurable. Its principle is not the expert's homology, but the inventor's paralogy.

Here is the question: is a legitimation of the social bond, a just society, feasible in terms of a paradox analogous to that of scientific activity? What would such a paradox be? . . .

9. Narratives of the Legitimation of Knowledge

We shall examine two major versions of the narrative of legitimation. One is more political, the other more philosophical, both are of great importance in modern history, in particular in the history of knowledge and its institutions.

The subject of the first of these versions is humanity as the hero of liberty. All peoples have a right to science. If the social subject is not already the subject of scientific knowledge, it is because that has been forbidden by priests and tyrants. The right to science must be reconquered. It is understandable that this narrative would be directed more toward a politics of primary education, rather than of universities and high schools. The educational policy of the French Third Republic powerfully illustrates these presuppositions.

It seems that this narrative finds it necessary to de-emphasize higher education. Accordingly, the measures adopted by Napoleon regarding higher education are generally considered to have been motivated by the desire to produce the administrative and professional skills necessary for the stability of the State. This overlooks the fact that in the context of the narrative of freedom, the State receives its legitimacy not from itself but from the people. So even if imperial politics designated the institutions of higher education as a breeding ground for the officers of the State and secondarily, for the managers of civil society, it did so because the nation as a whole was supposed to win its freedom through the spread of new domains of knowledge to the population, a process to be effected through agencies and professions within which those cadres would fulfill their functions. The same reasoning is a fortiori valid for the foundation of properly scientific institutions. The State resorts to the narrative of freedom every time it assumes direct control over the training of the 'people', under the name of the 'nation', in order to point them down the path of progress.

With the second narrative of legitimation, the relation between science, the nation, and the State develops quite differently. It first appears with the founding, between 1807 and 1810, of the University of Berlin, whose influence on the organization of higher education in the young countries of the world was to be considerable in the nineteenth and twentieth centuries.

. . .

10. Delegitimation

In contemporary society and culture – postindustrial society, postmodern culture – the question of the legitimation of knowledge is formulated in different terms. The grand narrative has lost its credibility, regardless of what mode of unification it uses, regardless of whether it is a speculative narrative or a narrative of emancipation.

The decline of narrative can be seen as an effect of the blossoming of techniques and technologies since the Second World War, which has shifted emphasis from the ends of action to its means; it can also be seen as an effect of the redeployment of advanced liberal capitalism after its retreat under the protection of Keynesianism during the period 1930–60, a renewal that has eliminated the communist alternative and valorized the individual enjoyment of goods and services.

Anytime we go searching for causes in this way we are bound to be disappointed. Even if we adopted one or the other of these hypotheses, we would still have to detail the correlation between the tendencies mentioned and the decline of the unifying and legitimating power of the grand narratives of speculation and emancipation.

It is, of course, understandable that both capitalist renewal and prosperity and the disorienting upsurge of technology would have an impact on the status of knowledge. But in order to understand how contemporary science could have been susceptible to those effects long before they took place, we must first locate the seeds of 'delegitimation' and nihilism that were inherent in the grand narratives of the nineteenth century.

First of all, the speculative apparatus maintains an ambitious relation to knowledge. It shows that knowledge is only worthy of that name to the extent that it reduplicates itself ('lifts itself up', *hebt sich auf*; is sublated) by citing its own statements in a second-level discourse (autonymy) that functions to legitimate them. This is as much as to say that, in its immediacy, denotative discourse bearing on a certain referent (a living organism, a chemical property, a physical phenomenon, etc.) does not really know what it thinks it knows. Positive science is not a form of knowledge. And speculation feeds on its suppression. The Hegelian speculative narrative thus harbors a certain skepticism toward positive learning, as Hegel himself admits.

A science that has not legitimated itself is not a true science, if the discourse that was meant to legitimate it seems to belong to a prescientific form of knowledge, like a 'vulgar' narrative, it is demoted to the lowest rank, that of an ideology or instrument of power. And this always happens if the rules of the science game that discourse denounces as empirical are applied to science itself.

. . .

If this 'delegitimation' is pursued in the slightest and if its scope is widened (as Wittgenstein does in his own way, and thinkers such as Martin Buber and

Emmanuel Levinas in theirs) the road is then open for an important current of postmodernity: science plays its own game; it is incapable of legitimating the other language games. The game of prescription, for example, escapes it. But above all, it is incapable of legitimating itself, as speculation assumed it could.

The social subject itself seems to dissolve in this dissemination of language games. The social bond is linguistic, but is not woven with a single thread. It is a fabric formed by the intersection of at least two (and in reality an indeterminate number) of language games, obeying different rules. Wittgenstein writes: 'Our language can be seen as an ancient city: a maze of little streets and squares, of old and new houses, and of houses with additions from various periods; and this surrounded by a multitude of new boroughs with straight regular streets and uniform houses.' And to drive home that the principle of unitotality – or synthesis under the authority of a metadiscourse of knowledge – is inapplicable, he subjects the 'town' of language to the old sorites paradox by asking: 'how many houses or streets does it take before a town begins to be a town?'

New languages are added to the old ones, forming suburbs of the old town: 'the symbolism of chemistry and the notation of the infinitesimal calculus'. Thirty-five years later we can add to the list: machine languages, the matrices of game theory, new systems of musical notation, systems of notation for nondenotative forms of logic (temporal logics, deontic logics, modal logics), the language of the genetic code, graphs of phonological structures, and so on.

We may form a pessimistic impression of this splintering: nobody speaks all of those languages, they have no universal metalanguage, the project of the system-subject is a failure, the goal of emancipation has nothing to do with science, we are all stuck in the positivism of this or that discipline of learning, the learned scholars have turned into scientists, the diminished tasks of research have become compartmentalized and no one can master them all. Speculative or humanistic philosophy is forced to relinquish its legitimation duties, which explains why philosophy is facing a crisis wherever it persists in arrogating such functions and is reduced to the study of systems of logic or the history of ideas where it has been realistic enough to surrender them.

Turn-of-the-century Vienna was weaned on this pessimism: not just artists such as Musil, Kraus, Hofmannsthal, Loos, Schönberg, and Broch, but also the philosophers Mach and Wittgenstein. They carried awareness of and theoretical and artistic responsibility for delegitimation as far as it could be taken. We can say today that the mourning process has been completed. There is no need to start all over again. Wittgenstein's strength is that he did not opt for the positivism that was being developed by the Vienna circle, but outlined in his investigation of language games a kind of legitimation not based on performativity. That is what the postmodern world is all about. Most people have lost the nostalgia for the lost narrative. It in no way follows that they are reduced to barbarity. What saves them from it is their knowledge that legitimation can only spring from their own linguistic practice and communicational interaction. Science 'smiling into its beard' at every other belief has taught them the harsh austerity of realism.

Suggested further reading

Lyotard, J-F (1989), *The Lyotard Reader* (ed. Benjam, A E). Oxford: Blackwell
—— (1991 [1988]), *The Inhuman: Reflections on Time*. Blackwell: Oxford, 1991
—— (1992), *The Postmodern Explained to Children. Correspondence, 1982–1983*. Sydney: Power Institute of Fine Arts
Lyotard, J-F and Thébaud, J-L (1979), *Just Gaming*. Minneapolis: University of Minnesota Press
Steuerman, E (2000), *The Bounds of Reason: Habermas, Lyotard, and Melanie Klein on Rationality*. London: Routledge

Baudrillard (b. 1929)

Jean Baudrillard's thinking helps us consider psychotherapy in relation to other cultural practices. He is interested in 'commodity as sign', in surface and seduction, in the media and the masses (he has written on TV and video, art and architecture). 'Discursive' and 'figural' are two key terms in his argumentation. The discursive–figural distinction is akin to Freud's distinction between secondary and primary process (the process of dream and the unconscious): in secondary 'discursive' process, words have priority over image, ego over id; this equates for Baudrillard with 'modernist' rationality, as against a 'figural', primary-process-like, post-modern emphasis, which is less on what things *mean* rationally than what they *do* (see Sarup, 1993: 169).

Baudrillard was born in 1929 in Reims, although he prefers to be silent about his background (Lechte, 1994: 233): why, he might be asking, should we concern ourselves with biographical so-called 'facts', as if they would reveal some hidden depth or truth about the subject, or had some special value in themselves over and above other facts? Baudrillard considers that in the post-modern, electronic and media-saturated age what he calls 'hyper-reality' has taken over – the world has become a world of excess and surface – and he can appear to celebrate this. Sign (in the broadly Saussarian sense) has primacy. Baudrillard began his intellectual career as a Marxist. In *The Mirror of Production* (Baudrillard, 1975) he came to view his earlier Marxism as merely symbolic of the culture. His view since the 1980s has been close to Marshall McLuhan's of the 1960s, that 'the medium is the message/massage' (McLuhan and Fiore 1967) – we live in an obscene 'ecstasy of communication', in which it is the ecstasy not the content which counts; and that consumption, not production, has come to be the main underpinning of the social order.

As Sarup sums it up, the object consumed has its effect when it transfers its meaning to the individual consumer, and it is the infinite play of signs thus instituted which structures and orders society (Sarup, 1993: 161). Think of brands and labels; we might also think of psychotherapy as something that is consumed: 'being in therapy' or 'being a therapist' coming to have independent and powerful existences as cultural signifiers, over and above what may actually go on in therapy. The individual, meanwhile, retains an illusory sense of freedom. In fact, for Baudrillard, 'there is no self-contained individual, there are only ways of using social systems, particularly those of language, goods and kinship, to relate people differently to the social order and thus to construct a sense of the individual' (Sarup, 1993: 161).

For Baudrillard there is no original reality or truth; no Platonic *Idea* (the ideal templates, in Plato's philosophy, of which perceived reality is the imperfect copy). There are only perfect copies, infinitely substitutable signs in an endless interplay. These are what he calls *simulacra*. 'The new postmodern universe tends to make everything a simulacrum. By this Baudrillard means a world in which all we have are *simulations*, there being no real external to them, no 'original' that is being copied. There is no longer a realm of the 'real' versus that of 'imitation' or 'mimicry', but rather a level in which there are only simulations' (Sarup, 1993: 164). One could see the dissolution of the transference as a way to minimise simulation, although perhaps all that can happen is that the quality of the simulation can change – there can never be a 'real me' to get back to, only another simulation.

Probably Baudrillard's most notorious pronouncement was that the Gulf War of 1990 never happened, except as a TV event. The simulacrum can, for Baudrillard, most clearly be seen on TV, and particularly TV news, which he characterises as just a collage of images, forgotten the next day. How often do we hear something similar in the speech of our patients? Baudrillard does not proclaim the end of history (as did Fukuyama, 1992), but he does propose a historical sequence. In early modernity, the individual's social place is clear; there is a strict hierarchy of unequivocal signs, trangressed at peril. In modernity, industrial production, and then social production, are the ordering principles. The post-modern era, the third order of simulacra, is the era of models, communication and information technology. It is governed not by the need for striving and ambition, which the modernist Freud pictured, in *Group Psychology and the Analysis of the Ego* (Freud, 1921), as the sons' struggles against the Father, but by narcissistic processes and 'constant surface change' (Sarup, 1993: 164). How much does this thinking provide a context for the kinds of distress, the vague unease, the sense of directionlessness and disinterest in the emotional life, that some practitioners report finding so prevalent among their early twenty-first-century clients?

Reading between the lines of Baudrillard's writings, one might consider, as Sarup has done, that he is nostalgic for face-to-face communication, and this of course might be of interest to psychotherapists. For Sarup, however, this nostalgia is 'conservative', in that it leaves out of account the potentials of different means of communication and mediation (Sarup, 1993: 167). Reading Baudrillard might help open up questions about e-mail as a medium for psychotherapy.

In the extract that follows Baudrillard writes of 'the structural revolution of value', in which 'nothing is produced, everything is deduced'. It invites thought about personal relations, which in this understanding are no longer determined by the social. The *consumption* aspects of the personal are valued: we consume each other. In therapy one purchases a relationship: does this lead one to meet people in a new way or to reproduce current cultural values? What is the relation between simulation and psychotherapy: do we resimulate our relation with the therapist with people outside? If it is a system of production, after a process of reproducibility, does therapy help us to develop an ability for enjoyment of the signs of 'guilt, despair, violence and death'?

However, for Baudrillard, our capacity for enjoyment of the signs is now replaced by simulation of these signs themselves, which 'abolishes cause and effect, origin and end'; thus 'the simulation principle dominates the reality principle as well as the pleasure principle'. Are we learning to be better simulators through therapy, to better simulate being with those around us? How do we then think about relations with past significant others? Is Freud's 'afterwardsness' – *Nachträgichkeit* – just a way in which cultural simulations are reproduced?

'[H]uman relations tend to be consumed (*consommer*) (in the double sense of the word: to be "fulfilled", and to be "annulled") in and through objects, which become the necessary mediation and, rapidly, the substitutive sign, the *alibi*, of the relation' (Baudrillard, 1988: 22). The question is raised in psychotherapy as to whether psychotherapy itself and the relations that the patient talks of with others are about consumption or about consummation. If people come to therapy as something to be consumed, it can only lead to annulment of the other, and through that annulment of oneself. It could mean that we have therapy instead of having relationships. Is therapy not only an alibi as regards relations with others but also as regards the relation with the therapist? Is anything else possible?

'We can see that what is consumed are not objects but the relation itself – signified and absent, included and excluded at the same time – it is *the idea of the relation* that is consumed in the series of objects which manifests it' (Baudrillard, 1988: 22).

No depths, only surfaces: Baudrillard offers an overt critique of psychoanalysis as well as of Marxism. Just as there is no superstructure with underlying economic forces (Marxism), there is nothing latent 'behind' the manifest (Freudianism). Most challenging for therapists is Baudrillard's work on seduction, and on psychoanalysis's own seductions. 'Seduction', he writes, 'is that which extracts meaning from discourse and detracts it from its truth.' While psychoanalysis, with its interest in interpretation (the discursive), attempts to break through the more obvious seduction of appearances, for Baudrillard it is still trapped.

The worst thing for psychoanalysis . . . is in fact that the unconscious seduces.

It seduces with dreams. It seduces by its concept. It seduces when 'the id speaks' and when it desires to speak. Everywhere there is a double structure in place. Everywhere there is a parallel structure in which signs from the unconscious connive with their exchange – a conniving that devours the other, the 'work' of the unconscious and the pure and simple processes of transference and countertransference. The whole edifice of psychoanalysis is crumbling from having seduced itself and seducing others in the process.

(Baudrillard, 1988: 149–51)

Baudrillard argues that Freud's dropping of seduction theory is highly significant.

Seduction is not simply dismissed as a secondary element in comparison to more significant ones, such as infant sexuality, repression, the Oedipus complex, etc. It is rather denounced as a dangerous form, which could potentially be fatal to the development and coherence of the future system . . . We cannot return to what has been destroyed. *And forgetting the original murder is part of the logical and triumphant development of a science* [our italics]. All of the energy of mourning and of the dead object will be transferred to a simulated resurrection in the activities of the living. . . . It is 're-enacted in the course of every cure'.

(Baudrillard, 1988: 151–2)

Seduction returns, like the repressed or the 'living dead', to re-emerge in the cure and in the conflictual and schismatic history of psychoanalysis itself.

For some, Baudrillard's anti-idealism, and his insistence that 'there is no appeal beyond the structures of representation', no difference between the fictive and other kinds of discourse, is relativistic to the point of nihilism (Sarup, 1993: 168; Norris, 1992). For others, he is *the* thinker of the moment. His large internet following has been swollen by the work of Arthur and Marilouise Kroker, ultra-hip Canadian commentators of the 1980s and 1990s, among whose many publications the *Panic Encyclopaedia* (Kroker *et al.*, 1994) includes contributions by Baudrillard himself.

From Baudrillard (1993), *Symbolic Exchange and Death*, pp. 8–9, 10–12, 50, 73–6

The Structural Revolution of Value

. . . The end of labour. The end of production. The end of political economy. The end of the signifier/signified dialectic which facilitates the accumulation of knowledge and meaning, the linear syntagma of cumulative discourse.

And at the same time, the end of the exchange-value/use-value dialectic which is the only thing that makes accumulation and social production possible. The end of the linear dimension of discourse. The end of the linear dimension of the commodity. The end of the classical era of the sign. The end of the era of production.

It is not *the* revolution which puts an end to all this, it is *capital itself* which abolishes the determination of the social according to the means of production, substitutes the structural form for the commodity form of value, and currently controls every aspect of the system's strategy.

This historical and social mutation is legible at every level. In this way the era of simulation is announced everywhere by the commutability of formerly contradictory or dialectically opposed terms. Everywhere we see the same 'genesis of simulacra': the commutability of the beautiful and the ugly in fashion, of the left and the right in politics, of the true and the false, in every media message, the useful and the useless at the level of objects, nature and culture at every level of signification. All the great humanist criteria of value, the whole civilisation of moral, aesthetic and practical judgement are effaced in our system of images and signs. Everything becomes undecidable, the characteristic effect of the domination of the code, which everywhere rests on the principle of neutralisation, of indifference. This is the generalised brothel of capital, a brothel not for prostitution, but for substitution and commutation.

This process, which has for a long time been at work in culture, art, politics, and even in sexuality (in the so-called 'superstructural' domains), today affects the economy itself, the whole so-called 'infrastructural' field. Here the same indeterminacy holds sway. And, of course, with the loss of determination of the economic, we also lose any possibility of conceiving it as the determinant agency.

Since for two centuries historical determination has been built up around the economic (since Marx in any case), it is there that it is important to grasp the interruption of the code.

The End of Production

. . .

The structural revolution of value eliminated the basis of the 'Revolution'. The loss of reference fatally affected first the revolutionary systems of reference, which can no longer be found in any social substance of production, nor in the certainty of a reversal in any truth of labour power. This is because labour is not a *power*, it has become one *sign* amongst many. Like every other sign, it produces and consumes itself. It is exchanged against non-labour, leisure, in accordance with a total equivalance, it is commutable with every other sector of everyday life. No more or less 'alienated', it is no longer a unique, historical 'praxis' giving rise to unique social relations. Like most practices, it is now only a set of signing operations. It becomes part of contemporary life in general, that is, it is framed by signs. It is no longer even the suffering of historical prostitution which used to play the role of the contrary promise of final emancipation . . . None of this remains true. Sign-form seizes labour and rids it of every historical or libidinal significance, and absorbs it in the process of its own reproduction: the operation of the *sign*, behind the empty allusion to what it designates, is to replicate itself. In the past, labour was used to designate the reality of a social production and a social objective of accumulating wealth. Even capital and surplus-value exploited it – precisely where it retained a use-value for the expanded reproduction of capital and its final destruction. It was shot through with finality anyway – if the worker is absorbed in the pure and simple reproduction of his labour power, it is not true that the process of production is experienced as senseless repetition. Labour revolutionises society through its very abjection, as a commodity whose potential always exceeds pure and simple reproduction of value.

Today this is no longer the case since labour is no longer productive but has become reproductive of the *assignation to labour* which is the general habit of a society which no longer knows whether or not it wishes to produce. No more myths of production and no more contents of production: national balance sheets now merely retrace a numerical and statistical growth devoid of meaning, an inflation of the signs of accountancy over which we can no longer even project the phantasy of the collective will. The pathos of growth itself is dead, since no-one believes any longer in the pathos of production, whose final, paranoid and panic-stricken tumescence it was. Today these codes are detumescent. It remains, however, more necessary than ever to reproduce labour as a social ritual as a reflex, as morality, as consensus, as regulation, as the reality principle. The reality principle *of the code*, that is: an immense *ritual of the signs of labour* extends over society in general – since it *reproduces* itself, it matters little whether or not it *produces*. It is much more effective to socialise by means of rituals and signs than by the bound energies of production. You are asked only to become socialised, not to produce or to excel yourself (this classical ethic arouses suspicion instead). You are asked only to consider value, according to the structural definition which here takes on its full social significance, as one term in relation to others, to function as a sign in the general scenario of production, just as labour and production now function only as signs, as terms commutable with non-labour, consumption, communication, etc. – a multiple, incessant, twisting relation across the entire network of other signs. Labour, once voided of its energy and substance (and generally disinvested), is given a new role as the model of social simulation, bringing all the other categories along with it into the aleatory sphere of the code.

An unnervingly strange state of affairs: this sudden plunge into a sort of secondary existence, separated from you by all the opacity of a previous life, where there was a familiarity and an intimacy in the traditional process of labour. Even the concrete reality of exploitation, the violent sociality of labour, is familiar. This has all gone now, and is due not so much to the *operative* abstraction of the *process* of labour, so often described, as to the passage of every *signification* of labour into an *operational* field where it becomes a floating variable, dragging the whole imaginary of a previous life along with it.

Beyond the autonomisation of production as *mode* (beyond the convulsions, contradictions and revolutions inherent in the mode), the *code* of production must re-emerge. This is the dimension things are taking on today, at the end of a 'materialist' history which has succeeded in authenticating it as the real movement of society. (Art, religion and duty have no real history for Marx – only production has a history, or, rather, it is history, it grounds history. An incredible fabrication of labour and production as historical reason and the generic model of fulfilment.)

The end of this religious autonomisation of production allows us to see that all of this could equally have been *produced* (this time in the sense of a stage-production and a scenario) fairly recently, with totally different goals than the internal finalities (that is, the revolution) secreted away within production.

To analyse production as a code cuts across both the material evidence of machines, factories, labour time, the product, salaries and money, and the more formal, but equally 'objective', evidence of surplus-value, the market, capital, to discover the rule of the game which is to destroy the logical network of the agencies of capital, and even the critical network of the Marxian categories which analyse it (which categories are again only an appearance at the second degree of capital, its *critical* appearance), in order to discover the elementary signifiers of production, the social relations it establishes, buried away forever beneath the historical illusion of the producers (and the theoreticians).

The Three Orders of Simulacra

There are three orders of simulacra, running parallel to the successive mutations of the law of value since the Renaissance:

- The *counterfeit* is the dominant schema in the 'classical' period, from the Renaissance to the Industrial Revolution.
- *Production* is the dominant schema in the industrial era.
- Simulation is the dominant schema in the current code-governed phase.

The first-order simulacrum operates on the natural law of value, the second-order simulacrum on the market law of value, and the third-order simulacrum on the structural law of value.

. . .

The Hyperrealism of Simulation

. . .

The very definition of the real is *that of which it is possible to provide an equivalent reproduction*. It is a contemporary of science, which postulates that a process can be reproduced exactly within given conditions, with an industrial rationality which postulates a universal system of equivalences (classical representation is not equivalence but transcription, interpretation and commentary). At the end of this process of reproducibility, the real is not only that which can be reproduced, but *that which is always already reproduced: the* hyperreal.

So are we then at the end of the real and the end of art due to a total mutual reabsorption? No, since at the level of simulacra, hyperrealism is the apex of both art and the real, by means of a mutual exchange of the privileges and prejudices that found them. The hyperreal is beyond representation (cf. Jean-François Lyotard, 'Esquisse d'une économique de l'hyperréalisme', *L'Art vivant*, 36, 1973) only because it is entirely within simulation, in which the barriers of representation rotate crazily, an implosive madness which, far from being ex-centric, keeps its gaze fixed on the centre, on its own abyssal repetition. Analogous to the effect of an internal distance from the dream, allowing us to say that we are dreaming, hyperrealism is only the play of censorship and the perpetuation of the dream, becoming an integral part of a coded reality that it perpetuates and leaves unaltered.

In fact, hyperrealism must be interpreted in inverse manner: *today reality itself is hyperrealist*. The secret of surrealism was that the most everyday reality could become surreal, but only at privileged instants which again arose out of art and the imaginary. Today everyday, political, social, historical, economic, etc., reality has already incorporated the hyperrealist dimension of simulation so that we are now living entirely within the 'aesthetic' hallucination of reality. The old slogan 'reality is stranger than fiction', which still corresponded to the surrealist stage in the aestheticisation of life, has been outrun, since there is no longer any fiction that life can possibly confront, even as its conqueror. Reality has passed completely into the game of reality. Radical disaffection, the cool and cybernetic stage, replaces the hot, phantasmatic phase.

The consummate enjoyment [*jouissance*] of the signs of guilt, despair, violence and death are replacing guilt, anxiety and even death in the total euphoria of simulation. This euphoria aims to abolish cause and effect, origin and end, and replace them with reduplication. Every closed system protects itself in this way from the referential and the anxiety of the referential, as well as from all metalanguage that the system wards off by operating its own metalanguage, that is, by duplicating itself as its own critique. In simulation, the metalinguistic illusion reduplicates and completes the referential illusion (the pathetic hallucination of the sign and the pathetic hallucination of the real).

'It's a circus', 'it's a theatre', 'it's a movie'; all these old adages are ancient naturalist denunciations. This is no longer what is at issue. What is at issue this time is *turning the real into a satellite*, putting an undefinable reality with no common measure into orbit with the phantasma that once illustrated it. This satellisation has subsequently been materialised as the two-room-kitchen-shower which we really have sent into orbit, to the 'spatial power' you could say, with the latest lunar module. The most everyday aspect of the terrestrial environment raised to the rank of a cosmic value, an absolute decor, hypostatised in space. This is the end of metaphysics and the beginning of the era of hyperreality. The spatial transcendence of the banality of the two-room apartment by a cool, machinic figuration in hyperrealism tells us only one thing, however: this module, such as it is, participates in a hyperspace of representation where everyone is already in possession of the technical means for the instant reproduction of his or her own life. Thus the *Tupolev's* pilots who crashed in Bourget were able, by means of their cameras, to see themselves dying first hand. This is nothing other than the short-circuit of the response by the question in the test, a process of instant renewal whereby reality is immediately contaminated by its simulacrum.

A specific class of allegorical and somewhat diabolical objects used to exist, made up of mirrors, images, works of art (concepts?). Although simulacra, they were transparent and manifest (you could distinguish craftsmanship from the counterfeit) with their own characteristic style and *savoir-faire*. Pleasure, then, consisted in locating what was 'natural' within what was artificial and counterfeit. Today, where the real and the imaginary are intermixed in one and the same operational totality, aesthetic fascination reigns supreme: with subliminal perception (a sort of sixth sense) of special effects, editing and script, reality is overexposed to the glare of models. This is no longer a space of production, but a reading strip, a coding and decoding strip, magnetised by signs. Aesthetic reality is no longer achieved through art's premeditation and distancing, but by its elevation to the second degree, to the power of two, by the anticipation and immanence of the code. A kind of unintentional parody hovers over everything, a tactical simulation, a consummate aesthetic enjoyment, is attached to the indefinable play of reading and the rules of the game. Travelling signs, media, fashion and models, the blind but brilliant ambience of simulacra.

Art has for a long time prefigured this turn, by veering towards what today is a turn to everyday life. Very early on the work of art produced a double of itself as the manipulation of the signs of art, bringing about an oversignification of art, or, as Lévi-Strauss said, an 'academicisation of the signifier', irreversibly introducing art to the form of the sign. At this point art entered into infinite *reproduction*, with everything that doubles itself, even the banal reality of the everyday, falling by the same token under the sign of art and becoming aesthetic. The same goes for production, which we might say has today entered into aesthetic reduplication, the phase where, expelling all content and all finality, it becomes somehow abstract and non-figurative. In this way it expresses the pure form of production, taking upon itself, as art does, the value of the finality without end. Art and industry may then exchange their signs: art can become a reproductive machine (Andy Warhol) without ceasing to be art, since the machine is now nothing but a sign. Production can also lose all its social finality as its means of verification, and finally glorify in the prestigious, hyperbolic and aesthetic signs that the great industrial complexes are, 400 m high towers or the numerical mysteries of the Gross National Product.

So art is everywhere, since artifice lies at the heart of reality. So art is dead, since not only is its critical transcendence dead, but reality itself, entirely impregnated by an aesthetic that holds onto its very structurality, has become inseparable from its own image. It no longer even has the time to take on the effect of reality. Reality is no longer stranger than fiction: it captures every dream before it can take on the dream effect. A schizophrenic vertigo of serial signs that have no counterfeit, no possible sublimation, and are immanent to their own repetition – who will say where the reality they simulate now lies? They no longer even repress anything (which, if you like, keeps simulation from entering the sphere of psychosis): even the primary processes have been annihilated. The cool universe of digitality absorbs the universe of metaphor and metonymy. The simulation principle dominates the reality principle as well as the pleasure principle.

Suggested further reading

Baudrillard, J (1988), *Selected Writings* (ed. Poster, M). Oxford: Polity Press
—— (2002) *The Spirit of Terrorism*. London and New York: Verso
Kroker, A, Kroker M and Cook, D (1994 [1984]), *Panic Encyclopaedia. The Definitive Guide to Postmodernism*. London: Macmillan
Norris, C (1992), *Uncritical Theory: Postmodernism, Intellectuals, and the Gulf War*. London: Lawrence and Wishart

Lacan (1901–1981)

At first there is language.

(Lacan, below)

It is a delight to see seduction sweep through psychoanalysis in the works of Lacan.

(Baudrillard, 1988: 153)

Jacques Lacan was a practising psychoanalyst and passionate teacher right up until his death. His influence on psychoanalysis has been huge and controversial; he has been no less important world-wide to academics in the arts and social sciences. Lacan trained as a psychiatrist in Paris in the 1920s, where he mixed in Surrealist circles (his doctoral thesis, on paranoia, provided Salvador Dalí with the theroretical pretext for his so-called 'paranoiac–critical' method of making paintings), and it is possible to see the influence of Surrealism in Lacan's way of thinking and of expounding his thought. Most of his published writings (his famous seminars, given between 1953 and 1977) are transcriptions of his speech; his words can be, notoriously, resistant to readers' wishes for transparency and coherence. Yet some confrontation with his ideas is essential for anyone who is serious in their interest in what is unconscious in the culture and the individual, and whether or not one approves of Lacan's therapeutic procedures (short sessions etc.), his thinking can challenge and encourage thoughtfulness about the practice of psychotherapy, of whatever theoretical orientation.

Lacan's roots are in psychoanalysis, structural linguistics, phenomenology and Hegel. Crucially, for Lacan, if we are subject to the Freudian unconscious we are, in the final analysis, subject to language. For the unconscious, he famously claimed, is structured like a language (Lacan, 1993: 167). It is his radical development of Freud's project – what Lacan called his 'return to Freud' – and particularly the notion of decentring, that qualifies him as a post-modernist. It could, however, also be argued that he was a modernist, in the sense that, for all his phenomenological passion for resisting closure, he ended up by evolving a very elaborate, quasi-mathematical system for explaining what it is to be human in the world; this could seem to have ambitions to be comprehensive and exhaustive.

The emphasis on language is apparent in the extracts we reproduce below, and throughout Lacan's later work.

> If what Freud discovered and rediscovers with a perpetually increasing sense of shock has a meaning, it is that the displacement of the signifier determines the subjects in their acts, in their destiny, in their refusals, their blind spots their end and fate, their innate gifts and social acquisitions . . . without regard for character or sex, and that, willingly or not, everything that might be considered the stuff of psychology, kit and caboodle, will follow the path of the signifier.
>
> (Lacan, in Benvenuto and Kennedy, 1986: 99)

By 'psychology, kit and caboodle' we can also understand him to mean psychology in all its institutional forms – experimental, counselling, clinical, and so on. Lacan most painstakingly followed 'the path of the signifier' in his discussion of Edgar Allan Poe's (1809–1849) story 'The Purloined Letter' – a measure of how far he could distance himself from a technological approach to psychology (although his later work turns increasingly to a kind of algebraic notation). In fact – as the text selected for inclusion below makes clear – Lacan's borrowings from other fields were often characterised by playfulness (he has been heavily rebuked for his borrowings from science by Sokal and Bricmont (1998) – see Chapter 5, below). This is a serious point – it is through the play of the signifier that we are frustrated in our search for meanings but through which, if we can accept this, we can come to play in a more alive and joyful way.

In Poe's story the Queen is caught reading a letter that could compromise her honour. She leaves the letter on the table, under the King's nose, and it thereby escapes his notice. At this moment Minister D enters, sees the letter and immediately grasps the situation. The Minister picks up the letter, and the Queen is powerless, in the King's presence, to stop him; thus the Minister puts the Queen in his power with the (unspoken) threat of exposure. A detective, Dupin, a lover of enigmas (and representative of the analyst), enters Minister D's office, which has been previously searched by the prefect of police at the request of the Queen; the methodical police have failed to find the letter. His eyes protected by green glasses, Dupin, unnoticed by the Minister, spots the letter very visibly hanging on a rack beneath the mantelpiece. Dupin returns the next day on the pretext of getting his snuffbox, and having organised a distraction outside the Minister's window, replaces the letter with another.

What determines the plot of 'The Purloined Letter', for Lacan, is not an interplay of individual psychologies (which is what psychotherapists are generally interested in) but (Felman, 1987) a structure, a repetition and a signifier (the letter) – the story concerns the relation of each player to the signifier, the actual contents of which is never disclosed. All are caught up regardless of individual personality (but not of social position) in something larger – they are, each in a different and complex way, subject to the signifier, trapped by it. Perhaps the question 'how bad a loser are you?' catches something of the threat to humanist and ego-psychological notions (to which Lacan was fiercely opposed) of autonomy and free agency that is implicit in Lacan's use of the story.

The key signifier, for Lacan, the signifier of signifiers, is the phallus (not, note, the penis, but the symbolic law it represents). Here Lacan was in a sense a very orthodox Freudian: the Oedipus complex and its resolution are central to this theorising. It is the *nom du père*, a pun on the *name* of the father (taking the father's name, in patriarchal cultures) and the *No* (*non*) of the father – the threat of castration – that brings about the human subject's very subjecthood, including, crucially, his or her being subject-to the phallus, that is to the signifier, to language. For resolution of the Oedipus complex marks the subject's entry into language, into what Lacan termed the Symbolic register. It marks the subject's move away from the grip of the Imaginary, that is, the fantasy of a mirroring relationship with the mother, or other.

Lacan's emphasis on the role of the phallus in all this provoked much hostility (see for example Irigaray, below). Other feminists, however, found Lacan's way of describing power relations within patriarchy, and his account of the constitution of subjectivity, invaluable (e.g. Grosz, 1990). Mitchell and Rose (1982), for example, while critical of Lacan, are also profoundly influenced by his work, and consider that the relationship of both men and women to the phallus is an important basis on which to rethink the construction of gender. Judith Butler (1990), on the other hand, sees 'phallogocentrism' as containing the means for its own subversion, and argues that the phallic law is inherently vulnerable. It cannot, even so, merely be dismissed (see Grosz, 1990, and Wright, 2000).

In perhaps his most famous paper, 'The Mirror Stage', first given in 1936 and much developed in the following decades (Lacan, 1977), Lacan spelled out his developing notion of the imaginary by means of an image that can be taken as real and/or metaphorical: the baby sees its reflection in a mirror and in this moment of self-recognition (or inevitable mis-recognition) is a moment of alienation; its illusion as to its own wholeness is changed forever. In seeing itself it sees itself as other than itself, and as it is seen by others; this is the birth of what Lacan called the 'split subject' (something far removed from humanist ideas of holism, of the unitary 'self'), and the birth of desire. We are constituted in the eyes and the desire of the other; we desire the (m)other's desire, which can never be 'possessed', it is always horizonal, tantalisingly out of reach, like that which lies at the end of an endless chain of free asssociations. As in the story of the letter, disappointment is guaranteed; ego will always be foiled. Here, furthermore, is where Lacan particularly shows his Hegelian roots (mediated in France through the teachings of Alexandre Kojève, whose lectures Lacan attended): desire is above all the desire for recognition in one's humanness (see Sarup, 1993: 18), and it is perhaps the only recognition we can finally hope for. What delusions are we peddling as therapists if we claim, or encourage our patients and clients to claim, otherwise?

Linked to the Imaginary and the Symbolic is the third of Lacan's registers or orders, the Real – which is all that is 'lacking in the symbolic order, the ineliminable residue of all articulation, the foreclosed element, which may be approached but never grasped' (Sheridan, in Lacan, 1977: x, and see Žižek, below). We will always be getting it wrong. Yet for Lacan the desire to try, hence the importance of language, can never be overestimated, as he suggests in the text we cite:

> One has to realise that we do our dissecting with concepts, not with a knife. Concepts have their specific order in reality. They do not emerge out of human experience – if they did, they would be well made. The first appelations arise out of words themselves. They are instruments for delineating things. Hence every science remains in darkness for a long time, entangled in language . . . The root of the difficulty is that you can only introduce symbols, mathematical or otherwise, by using everyday language, since you have, after all, to explain what you are going to do with them. You are then at a certain level of human exchange, the level of healer in this instance . . . The man speaking to you is a man like any other – he makes use of the wrong language. Oneself is then at issue . . .

Lacan invites us to question the role of the therapist. What are we affirming when we say a trainee is ready to qualify? That the future therapist now has a greater sense that he or she makes use of the wrong language – and that to speak of that sense will also involve using the wrong language? What are we listening for, as therapists, when we listen to language? Is there not always something that eludes us? Lacan also raises the question of when therapy can be said to be over. For Freud it was when the patient was able to live in ordinary unhappiness; for

Lacan it is a case of facing necessary disappointment and incompleteness. Not only, since Freud, is the ego no longer master in its own house (Freud, 1916–17: 285): through Lacan Descartes's 'I think, therefore I am' becomes 'I think where I am not, therefore I am where I do not think', or, 'I think where I cannot say that I am'. This would be so not only for the client, but also for the therapist – with enormous implications for practice, theory and research.

The importance of Lacan is further evident in that all the writers in this chapter, with the possible exceptions of Foucault and Lyotard, have found themselves taking up an explicit position in respect of one or other aspect of his thought.

From Lacan (1988), 'Overture to the Seminar' and 'The Topic of the Imaginary', in *The Seminar of Jacques Lacan, Book 1, Freud's Papers on Technique 1953–1954*, pp. 1–3 and 73–80

OVERTURE TO THE SEMINAR

The master breaks the silence with anything – with a sarcastic remark, with a kick-start.

That is how a buddhist master conducts his search for meaning, according to the technique of *zen*. It behoves the students to find out for themselves the answer to their own questions. The master does not teach *ex cathedra* a ready made science; he supplies an answer when the students are on the verge of finding it.

This kind of teaching is a refusal of any system. It uncovers a thought in motion – nonetheless vulnerable to systematisation, since it necessarily possesses a dogmatic aspect. Freud's thought is the most perennially open to revision. It is a mistake to reduce it to a collection of hackneyed phrases. Each of his ideas possesses a vitality of its own. That is precisely what one calls the dialectic.

Certain of these ideas were, at a given moment, indispensable to Freud, because they supplied an answer to a question that he had formulated previously, in other terms. Hence one only gains a sense of their value by relocating them in their context.

But it is not enough to do some history, the history of thought, and to say that Freud lived in a scientistic century. Rather, with *The Interpretation of Dreams*, something of a different essence, of a concrete psychological density, is reintroduced, namely, meaning.

From the scientistic point of view, Freud appeared at this point to revert to the most archaic thinking – reading something in dreams. He later returns to causal explanations. But when one interprets a dream, one is always up to one's neck in meaning. What is at issue is the subjectivity of the subject, in his desires, in his relation to his environment, to others, to life itself.

Our task, here, is to reintroduce the register of meaning, a register that must itself be reintegrated on its own level.

Brücke, Ludwig, Helmholtz, Du Bois-Reymond had instituted a kind of pledged faith – everything reduces down to physical forces, those of attraction and repulsion. Once one takes these as premises, there's no reason to go beyond them. If Freud did go beyond them, it is because he also took on others. He dared to attach importance to what was happening to him, to the antinomies of his childhood, to his neurotic problems, to his dreams. That is why Freud is for us all a man beset, like anyone else is, by all the contingencies – death, woman, father.

This represents a return to origins, and barely warrants being called science. What holds good in the art of the expert cook, who knows how to joint a bird, to disjoint it with as little resistance as possible, is also true for psychoanalysis. We know that there is a method of conceptualisation proper to each structure. But since this leads to complications, one prefers to cling to a monistic notion of a deduction of the world. That's how one goes astray.

One has to realise that we do our dissecting with concepts, not with a knife. Concepts have their specific order in reality. They do not emerge out of human experience – if they did, they would be well made. The first appelations arise out of words themselves, they are instruments for delineating things. Hence every science remains in darkness for a long time, entangled in language.

At first there is language, already formed, which we use as we would a very poor instrument. From time to time, reversals occur – from phlogiston to oxygen, for instance. Lavoisier introduces the right concept, oxygen, at the same time as his phlogistic. The root of the difficulty is that you can only introduce symbols, mathematical or otherwise, by using everyday language, since you have, after all, to explain what you are going to do with them. You are then at a certain level of human exchange, the level of healer in this instance. So is Freud, despite his denial. But, as Jones has demonstrated, he imposed upon himself right from the beginning the discipline of not dabbling in the speculation to which his nature inclined him. He submitted himself to the discipline of the facts, of the laboratory. He distanced himself from the wrong language.

Let us now turn to the notion of the subject. When one brings it in, one brings in oneself. The man speaking to you is a man like any other – he makes use of the wrong language. Oneself is then at issue.

Thus, Freud knew, from the beginning, that he would only make progress in the analysis of the neuroses if he analysed himself.

The growing importance attributed today to counter-transference means that it is a recognised fact that in analysis the patient is not alone. There are two of us – and not only two.

Phenomenologically, the analytic situation is a structure, that is to say that it is only through that that certain phenomena are isolable, separable. It is another structure, that of subjectivity, which gives human beings the idea that they are comprehensible to themselves.

Hence being neurotic can help one become a good psychoanalyst, and at the beginning, it helped Freud. Like Monsieur Jordain (*sic*) with his prose,[2] we make sense, nonsense, we misunderstand. But the lines of structure still had to be found there. Jung as well, to his own amazement, rediscovers, in the symbols of dreams and religions, certain archetypes, proper to the human race. This is also a structure – but differing from the analytic structure.

Freud introduced the determinism proper to this structure. Hence the ambiguity that is to be found throughout his corpus. For example, is a dream desire or the recognition of desire? Or, again, the ego is on the one hand like an empty egg, differentiated at its surface through contact with the world of perception, but it is also, each time we encounter it, that which says *no* or *me*, *I*, which says *one*, which speaks about others, which expresses itself in different registers.

We are going to employ the techniques of an art of dialogue. Like the good cook, we have to know what joints, what resistances, we will encounter.

The *super-ego* is a law deprived of meaning, but one which nevertheless only sustains itself by language. If I say *you turn to the right*, it's to allow the other to bring his language into line with mine. I think of what goes through his head when I speak to him. This attempt to find an agreement constitutes the communication specific to language. This *you* is so fundamental that it arises before consciousness. Censorship, for example, which is intentional, nevertheless comes into action before consciousness, functioning with vigilance. *You* is not a signal, but a reference to the other – it is order and love.

In the same way, the ego-ideal is an organism of defence established by the ego in order to extend the subject's satisfaction. But it is also the function that depresses most, in the psychiatric meaning of the term.

The *id* is not reducible to a pure and objective given, to the drives of the subject. An analysis never leads to specifying a given quantity of aggressivity or erotism. The point to which analysis leads, the end point of the dialectic of existential recognition, is – *You are this*. In practice this ideal is never reached.

The ideal of analysis is not complete self mastery, the absence of passion. It is to render the subject capable of sustaining the analytic dialogue, to speak neither too early, nor too late. Such is the aim of a training analysis.

The introduction of an order of determinations into human existence, into the domain of meaning, is what we call reason. Freud's discovery is the rediscovery, on fallow ground, of reason.

[2]   'Il y plus de quarante ans que je dis de la prose sans que j'en susse rien' ('I have been speaking prose for more than forty years without knowing it') – Molière, *Le Bourgeois Gentilhomme*, M. Jourdain, Act II, Scene IV.

THE TOPIC OF THE IMAGINARY

. . .

The small talk I will offer you today was announced under the title 'The topic of the imaginary'. Such a subject is quite enough to fill up several years of teaching, but since several questions concerning the place of the imaginary in the symbolic structure crop up while following the thread of our discourse, today's chat may justify its title.

It wasn't without some preconceived plan, the rigour of which will, I hope, become apparent as it is revealed in its entirety, that last time I brought your attention to a case whose particular significance resides in its showing in miniature the reciprocal interplay of those three grand terms we have already had occasion to make much of – the imaginary, the symbolic, and the real.

Without these three systems to guide ourselves by, it would be impossible to understand anything of the Freudian technique and experience. Many difficulties are vindicated and clarified when one brings these distinctions to bear on them. This is indeed the case with the incomprehensions Mlle Gélinier marked upon the other day when dealing with Melanie Klein's text. What matters, when one tries to elaborate upon some experience, isn't so much what one understands, as what one doesn't understand. The value of Mlle Gélinier's report is precisely to have highlighted what, in this text, cannot be understood.

That is why the method of textual commentary proves itself fruitful. Commenting on a text is like doing an analysis. How many times have I said to those under my supervision, when they say to me – *I had the impression he meant this or that* – that one of the things we must guard most against is to understand too much, to understand more than what is in the discourse of the subject. To interpret and to imagine one understands are not at all the same things. It is precisely the opposite. I would go as far as to say that it is on the basis of a kind of refusal of understanding that we push open the door to analytic understanding.

It isn't enough for it to seem to hang together, a text. Obviously, it hangs together within the framework of pat phrases we've grown used to – instinctual maturation, primitive aggressive instinct, oral, anal sadism, etc. And yet, in the register that Melanie Klein brings into play, there appear several contrasts, which I am going to return to in detail.

Everything turns on what Mlle Gélinier found to be peculiar, paradoxical, contradictory in the *ego*'s function – if too developed, it stops all development, but in developing, it reopens the door to reality. How is it that the gate to reality is reopened by a development of the *ego*? What is the specific function of the Kleinian interpretation, which appears to have an intrusive character, a superimposing upon the subject? These are the questions that we will have to touch upon again today.

You should have realised by now that, in the case of this young subject, real, imaginary and symbolic are here tangible, are flush with one another. I have taught you to identify the symbolic with language – now, isn't it in so far as, say, Melanie Klein speaks, that something happens? On the other hand, when Melanie Klein tells us that the objects are constituted by the interplay of projections, introjections, expulsions, reintrojections of bad objects, and that the subject, having projected his sadism, sees it coming back from these objects, and, by this very fact, finds himself jammed up by an anxious fear, don't you have the feeling that we are in the domain of the imaginary?

From then on the whole problem is that of the juncture of the symbolic and of the imaginary in the constitution of the real.

I

To clarify things a little for you, I've concocted a little model for you, a substitute for the mirror-stage.

As I have often underlined, the mirror-stage is not simply a moment in development. It also has an exemplary function, because it reveals some of the subject's relations to his image, in so far as it is the *Urbild* of the ego. Now, this mirror-stage, which no one can deny, has an optical presentation – nor can anyone deny that. Is it a coincidence?

The sciences, and above all those sciences in labour, as ours is, frequently borrow models from other sciences. My dear fellows, you wouldn't believe what you owe to geology. If it weren't for geology, how could one end up thinking that one could move, on the same level, from a recent to a much more ancient layer? It wouldn't be a bad thing, I'll note in passing, if every analyst went out and bought a small book on geology. There was once an analyst geologist, Leuba, who wrote one. I can't recommend you to read it too highly.

Optics could also have its say. At this point I find that I'm not in disagreement with the tradition established by the master – more than one of you must have noticed in the *Traumdeutung*, in the chapter 'The psychology of the dream-process', the famous schema into which Freud inserts the entire proceedings of the unconscious.

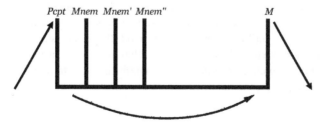

Figure 4 Freud's schema (1900: SE V 538)

Inside, Freud places the different layers which can be distinguished from the level of perception, namely from the instantaneous impression – *Mnem'*, *Mnem'*, etc., both image and memory. These recorded traces are later repressed into the unconscious. It is a very pretty schema, which we will come back to since it will be useful to us. But I'd like to point out that it is accompanied by a commentary which doesn't appear to have ever attracted anyone's attention, even though it was used again in another form in Freud's quasi last work, the *Outline of Psycho-analysis*.

I will read it to you as it is to be found in the *Traumdeutung*. *What is presented to us in these words is the idea of psychical locality* – what is at issue here is precisely the field of psychical reality, that is to say of everything which takes place between perception and the motor consciousness of the ego. *I shall entirely disregard the fact that the mental apparatus with which we are here concerned is also known to us in the form of an anatomical preparation, and I shall carefully avoid the temptation to determine psychical locality in any anatomical fashion. I shall remain upon psychological ground, and I propose simply to follow the suggestion that we should picture the instrument which carries out our mental functions as resembling a compound microscope or a photographic apparatus, or something of the kind. On that basis, psychical locality will correspond to a point inside the apparatus at which one of the preliminary stages of an image comes into being. In the microscope and telescope, as we know, these occur in part at ideal points, regions in which no tangible component of the apparatus is situated. I see no necessity to apologise for the imperfections of this or of any similar imagery. Analogies of this kind are only intended to assist us in our attempt to make the complications of mental functioning intelligible by dissecting the function and assigning its different constituents to different component parts of the apparatus. So far as I know, the experiment has not hitherto been made of using this method of dissection in order to investigate the way in which the mental instrument is put together, and I can see no harm in it. We are justified, in my view, in giving free rein to our speculations so long as we retain the coolness of our judgement and do not mistake the scaffolding for the building. And since at our first approach to something unknown all that we need is the assistance of provisional ideas, I shall give preference in the first instance to hypotheses of the crudest and most concrete description.*[3]

I don't have to tell you that, seeing as advice is given so as not to be followed, since then we haven't missed an opportunity of taking the scaffolding for the building. On the other hand, the authorisation which Freud gives us to make use of supplementary relations so as to bring us closer to an unknown fact incited me into myself manifesting a certain lack of deference in constructing a schema.

---

[3] (1900a) GW II/III 541; stud II 512; SE V 536

Something almost infantile will do for us today, an optical apparatus much simpler than a compound microscope – not that it wouldn't be fun to follow up the comparison in question, but that would take us a bit far out of our way . . .

. . . It is a classical experiment, which used to be performed in the days when physics was fun, in the days when physics was really physics. Likewise, as for us, we find ourselves at a moment in time when psychoanalysis is really psychoanalysis. The closer we get to psychoanalysis being funny the more it is real psychoanalysis. Later on, it will get run in, it will be done by cutting corners and by pulling tricks. No one will understand any longer what's being done, just as there is no longer any need to understand anything about optics to make a microscope. So let us rejoice, we are still doing psychoanalysis.

Put a vast cauldron in place of me – which perhaps could quite happily stand in for me on some days, as a sound-box – a cauldron as close as possible to being a half-sphere, nicely polished on the inside, in short a spherical mirror. If it is brought forward almost as far as the table, you won't see yourselves inside it – hence, even if I were turned into a cauldron, the mirage effect that occurs from time to time between me and my pupils would not come about here. A spherical mirror produces a real image. To each point of a light ray emanating from any point on an object placed at a certain distance, preferably in the plane of the sphere's centre, there corresponds, in the same plane, through the convergence of the rays reflected on the surface of the sphere, another luminous point – which yields a real image of the object.

I am sorry that I haven't been able to bring the cauldron today, nor the experimental apparatuses. You'll have to represent them to yourselves.

Suppose that this is a box, hollow on this side, and that it's placed on a stand, at the centre of the half-sphere. On the box, you will place a vase, a real one. Beneath it, there is a bouquet of flowers. So, what is happening?

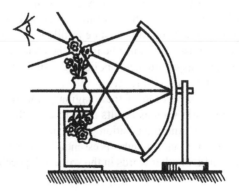

Figure 5 The experiment of the inverted bouquet

The bouquet is reflected in the spherical surface, meeting at the symmetrical point of luminosity. Consequently, a real image is formed. Note that the rays do not quite cross perfectly in my schema, but that is also true in reality, and for all optical instruments – one only ever gets an approximation. Beyond the eye, the rays continue their movement, and diverge once again. But for the eye, they are convergent, and give a real image, since the characteristic of rays which strike the eye in a convergent form is that they give a real image. Convergent in meeting the eye, they diverge in moving away from it. If the rays happen to meet the eye in the opposite sense, then a virtual image is formed. This is what happens when you look at an image in the mirror – you see it where it isn't. Here, on the contrary, you see it where it is – on the one condition that your eye be in the field of the rays which have already crossed each other at the corresponding point.

At that moment, while you do not see the real bouquet, which is hidden, if you are in the right field, you will see a very peculiar imaginary bouquet appear, taking shape exactly in the neck of the vase. Since your eyes have to move linearly in the same plane, you will have an impression of reality, all the while sensing that something is strange, blurred, because the rays don't quite cross over very well. The further away you are, the more parallax comes into play, and the more complete the illusion will be.

This is a fable we will put to a great deal of use. To be sure, this schema has no pretension to touch on anything which has a substantial relation to anything we deal with in analysis, the so-called real or objective relations, or the imaginary relations. But it allows us to illustrate in a particularly simple way what follows on from the strict intrication of the imaginary world and the real world in the psychic economy . . .

2

. . . For there to be an illusion, for there to be a world constituted, in front of the eye looking, in which the imaginary can include the real and, by the same token, fashion it, in which the real can include and, by the same token, locate the imaginary, one condition must be fulfilled – as I have said, the eye must be in a specific position, it must be inside the cone . . .

. . . The eye is here, as so often, symbolic of the subject . . .

. . . So, this eye, what does it mean?

It means that, in the relation of the imaginary and the real, and in the constitution of the world such as results from it, everything depends on the position of the subject. And the position of the subject – you should know, I've been repeating it for long enough – is essentially characterised by its place in the symbolic world, in other words in the world of speech . . .

Suggested further reading

Benvenuto, B and Kennedy, R (1986), *The Works of Jacques Lacan: An Introduction.* London: Free Association Books

Evans, D (1996), *An Introductory Dictionary of Lacanian Psychoanalysis.* London: Routledge

Felman, S (1987), *Jacques Lacan and the Adventure of Insight. Psychoanalysis in Contemporary Culture.* Cambridge, MA: Harvard University Press

Grosz, E (1990), *Jacques Lacan: A Feminist Introduction.* London: Routledge

Derrida (b. 1931)

'MY NAME IS **DERRIDA**, AND I ACCUSE YOU LACAN OF CLAIMING TO BE THE ONE WHO KNOWS – THE **REAL** NARRATOR OF THIS STORY WHO IS NOT SUBJECT TO LANGUAGE. Now let me, Derrida, tell you about what I think about psychotherapy.'

This is the script we would write for Jacques Derrida on his response to Lacan's reading of Poe's story. Derrida will tell us in his own words what he thinks about psychotherapy, in the extract that follows. But first, some introductory comments on this thinker, reactions to whom have varied from accusations of philosophical terrorism (particularly among Anglo-Saxon logical positivists) to veneration almost as a cult figure: merely to invoke his name can be enough to position the speaker at the intellectual cutting edge. For some Derrida is one of the two chief instigators of post-modernism, the other being Foucault (Cahoone, 1996: 336). Many commentators would agree that he has played a dominant role in the late twentieth-century crisis in philosophy, opening up questions as to the whole 'continuing viability of the philosophical tradition deriving from the Greeks' (Matthews, 1996: 165).

Derrida was born in Algeria, went to Paris in the 1950s, and studied phenomenology, in particular the works of Husserl and Heidegger; he was very much influenced by Emmanuel Levinas (see Derrida, 1997a). His enormous influence on the humanities, from linguistics to sociology and feminist studies, started to make itself felt in the 1960s and 1970s, through books such as *Of Grammatology* and *Writing and Difference*, and, in the 1980s, *The Postcard: From Socrates to Freud and Beyond*, among other works.

Like Lacan, he was influenced by Saussure's structural linguistics; he is above all concerned with language. He criticised Lacan, however, for treating the unconscious as if it were the repository of something called 'truth' (the truth of desire, for example) that can be known. For Derrida such concepts as truth, or justice, or nature, or reason, are founded in Western philosophy's very long-standing assumption that there are essences, if only we could find them, which might become the foundations of our beliefs. Derrida, following and reviving the radically reflexive (self-questioning) spirit of Nietzsche, questions the existence of such transcendental meaning ('spirit' would be a good example of a 'transcendental signifier').

Derrida invites the reader to examine the instability of language, and we suggest the implications of this are far-reaching for psychotherapy. He criticises metaphysics, that is, any thought-system that relies on a first principle. A first principle (e.g. 'Truth') is defined by what it excludes (e.g. 'Falsehood'), in a 'binary opposition' to other concepts; one cannot exist without the other, although one may be repressed (Sarup, 1993: 37). The philosophical approach he evolved, more readily called by others than himself 'deconstruction', can be seen to uncover and subvert such oppositions (as Derrida did by looking at the works of the eighteenth-century philosopher Rousseau, the structural anthropologist Lévi-Strauss, and Lacan himself). We would consider very valuable the attempt to read one's patient as a text, and to bring into play a deconstructive stance, as a therapist listening to the patient's utterances and to one's own thoughts – in, for example, opening questions regarding the patient's and one's own supposedly transcendant certainties.

One of the most important concepts developed by Derrida is *différance*, a new word derived from the verb *différer* which means both to differ, and to defer; *différance* encapsulates both meanings, 'difference' and 'deferral' (delay, postponement). It alludes to other features of the instability of language, everything being differentiated and deferred: how words (signifiers) have meaning only in relation to other signifiers, through their differences, and how because these relationships are always in flux ultimate meaning is always deferred: there is no end point. 'Language is thus the play of differences which are generated by signifiers which are themselves the product of those differences' (Sarup, 1993: 44). Such differences we take for granted, and mistake for fixed or given structures. Western culture, Derrida claims, has privileged speech over writing as the guarantor of truthfulness, reinforced by the presence of the speaker (think of 'watch my lips'); he also criticises Husserl for positing the idea that consciousness is like an interior voice to which one listens. Derrida argues that we are subject to the written word (Derrida, 1976). In French there is no phonetic distinction between the endings *-ence* (as in *différence*) and *-ance*. Significantly it is only in writing that the undetected difference shows up, thus the instability and flux of language itself (Sarup, 1993: 44).

For Derrida, as for Nietzsche (Nietzsche, 1977b: 46–7), on whom he draws so fruitfully, metaphor is the very stuff of language. Thus there can be no meaningful difference between literature and more discursive genres, such as philosophy, criticism, or law. All 'work by metaphor, just as poems do, and so are just as fictional' (Sarup, 1993: 47). The passage that follows might thus be read under many 'genre' headings.

Derrida has concerned himself with questions of hospitality and cosmopolitanism (Derrida, 1997b and 2001), engaging particularly in dialogue with intellectuals from the Arab and Muslim worlds; he locates himself and finds himself located as a thinker on a world stage (Roudinesco, 1999). He has also continued his dialogue with, and critique of, psychoanlysis and its practice and institutions. In *États d'âme de la psychanalyse* (States of mind/soul of psychoanalysis;

Derrida, 2000), he examines the crisis of psychoanalysis at the turn of the century, and asks whether psychoanalysis is adequate to the task of addressing new forms of cruelty that are emerging across the social, cultural and political worlds. We might think, for example, of Western European responses to refugees and asylum seekers.

If psychoanalysis cannot manage difference, who can? An earlier moment in Derrida's dialogue with psychoanalysis is reflected in the passage we give below. One reading of the opening remarks, which rely on punning, is that there is a false band (of analysts), and this band has a bond which is also false – it is this false bond which helps them band together (*bander* is also slang – 'to have an erection'). Derrida was very conscious of the history of splits and schisms in the Paris psychoanalytic scene, and the text is a commentary on this. His play on words aims to open up the notion of the *tranche*, which means a slice, as well as being slang for the psychoanalytic session. He is pointing out that if we take a slice from the work of one analytic band and introduce – *tranchefer* it – it to another one, then the second group will confront the first with the madness of their ways.

'Among the thousand and one *faux-bonds* that one might cite as examples, there is the one made by an analyst in relation to his own 'group' by going to a *'tranche'* in another group. And I wager that what I will call the *'confrontation'* effect has an essential relation to all *faux-bonds*, and to the *faux-bond* in the form of a *tranche*, transferring or trancheferring from one group to another' (Derrida, 1987: 504).

From Derrida (1987), 'Du tout', *The Postcard. From Socrates to Freud and Beyond*, pp. 499–515. First published in *Confrontation* I (1978), preceded by this editorial note: 'On 21 November 1977 a session of "Confrontation" with Jacques Derrida was organised around *Glas* (Galilée, 1974), and other texts in thematic relation to the theory, movement and institution of psychoanalysis, notably 'Freud and Scene and Writing' (in *Writing and Difference*); *Le facteur de la verité*; *Fors* (in *Le verbier de l'homme aux loups* by Nicholas Abraham and Maria Torok; English version in *The Georgia Review*); and *Spurs*. In response to René Major's initial questions, Jacques Derrida advanced several introductory propositions. We are reproducing them here in the literality of their recording. Only the title is an exception to this rule.'

DU TOUT

. . . I have not come – if, at least, I have come – with my hands in my pockets in this saloon overflowing with all kinds of bands that are more or less bankable, more or less ready for détente, that are looking out of the corners of their eyes from the bar. Certain of them pretend to be playing poker, peacefully, in a corner. They feign pretending: I am sure that at this very moment all kinds of games are being played *within* each band, and no less ferociously than from one band to another. And since you, René Major, question me about *Glas*, you know that this book, among other things and designedly, is on bands, in bands, the word '*bande*' (noun or verb) and the thing, in every sense, gender and quantity.[4]

Therefore I have come, if, at least, I have come, saying to myself: something will happen tonight only on the condition of your disarmament.

But you might suspect me of exaggerating with this agonistic language: he says that he is disarmed in order to disarm, a well-known device. Certainly. Therefore, I immediately add: I have not come, I did not want to, I still do not want to, I have not come naked.

I have not come naked, not come without anything.

I have come accompanied by a small – how to put it, a small phrase, if it is one, only one, very small.

Further, I am not sure that I assume this small phrase. Nothing yet guarantees that I hold myself accountable for it.

Let us say that I will pronounce this small phrase between quotation marks, as if what is invisible here could take a reading into account. I will pronounce it, let us say, between quotation marks, although I formulated it myself or it formulated itself within me following another small phrase heard at the end of the last session, the only one of the 'Confrontation' sessions that I have attended, outside the one that assembled us more than two years ago around my friends Nicolas Abraham and Maria Torok.

Let us say that I will hold this small phrase between quotation marks despite the fact that I formulated it myself or that it induced itself in me after the last session and the allusive discourse of a given analyst friend, a woman.

This discourse must have immediately found itself plugged into, within me, a system of anticipations, of interests, of hypotheses on the work of an entire logic which since then has formalized itself in the most economical, and also the most elliptical fashion in the following small phrase that, once again, I do not assume, I cite it. *Speech act* theoreticians would say that I mention it rather than *utilize* it, supposing a distinction made in this state is acceptable to analysts' ears. I have made several objections to it in a somewhat polemical text that appeared in the United States under the title *Limited inc.*

---

4 TN. *Bande* as noun has the same senses in French as in English, band as gang and band as strip. On bander as noun and verb, see above, 'To Speculate – On Freud', Part 4 ('Seven: Post-Script'), notes 3 and 6. That *Glas* is on bands and in bands refers to both its formal construction (each page is in two columns) and its content (bands, groups in Hegel and Genet). Derrida is also alluding to the structure of *Confrontation* itself, as a forum that assembled analysts from the four French analytic 'bands' that existed at the time. These were the Association Psychanalytique de Paris (the first French psychoanalytic group), the Association Psychanalytique de France (the first major group to split from the latter, originally including such members as Lacan and Granoff), l'Ecole freudienne (the institute founded by Lacan), and le Quatrième groupe (one of the first 'splits' from the Ecole freudienne). In the year before his death (September 1981) Lacan attempted to dissolve the Ecole freudienne, leading to further changes in the analytic 'bands'.

Here then is this small phrase, it is made to disappoint, I say its lowly, without any punctuation for the moment – its punctuation is in fact mobile, multiple, and essentially labile – I read it then without any punctuation for the moment as if there were a dash of equal length between each word, here it is: *CE-N'EST-PAS-DU-TOUT-UNE-TRANCHE.*[5]

There.

I do not yet know – will I know one day? – if I did well to come here this evening.

I doubtless have come, if I have come, because – it must have been stronger than me.

Not that it simply must have been stronger than me, but because I must have been fascinated, irresistibly grabbed, harpooned by something that gave itself as stronger-than-me.

If it is stronger than me, I have got to go see what it is, which is all that interests me. 'Stronger than me' is a locution that torments me, it imposes itself upon me indiscreetly, at least since the last session when I began to ask myself if I was wise to accept coming here.

In general, until now, until this evening, I have rather easily checked the solicitations or temptations of the 'spectacle', the ingenuousness or political effects of the scenic codes that are available today – the channels, studios, and platforms offered to the intellectuals of our time who believe they are able to make use of them.

This time, apparently, it was stronger than me. But I must say to you now: up to the last moment, just now at the corner café, I asked myself if I would come (this too is happening to me for the first time, think of it what you will), I asked myself if I would not be, as is said, a 'no-show' ['*faux-bond*'].

Some who are here know that in a recently published exchange I took a great interest in the '*faux-bond*', in the word, in all the words engaged in this untranslatable locution, and in the strange 'thing' that a 'faux-bond' is, if at least there is any.[6]

---

[5] TN. This sentence plays on lexical and syntactic undecidability. *Une tranche* is the usual French word for a slice, as in a slice of cake, from the verb *trancher*, to slice. In French psychoanalytic slang, *une tranche* is also the period of time one spends with a given analyst. There is no equivalent English expression. Further, the expression *du tout* can mean either 'of the whole' or 'at all'. Thus, the sentence can mean 'This is not a "slice" [a piece, in the analytic sense or not] of the whole,' or 'This is not at all a "slice" [in any sense]'. The verb *trancher* can also mean to decide on a question or to resolve it in a clear-*cut* way; the English 'trenchant' has a similar sense. Throughout this interview, the senses of *tranche* and 'trench' beckon toward each other, finally coming together in the concluding discussion of schisms and seisms (earthquakes, cracking ground).

[6] TN. As indicated in the text, a *faux-bond* is a 'no-show', but Derrida consistently plays not only on the 'literal' meaning of the expression ('false bound'), but also on the similarity, more striking in English, between 'bond' and 'band'. At *Confrontation*, whatever is not (at all/of the whole) a *tranche* must come from the 'false band'. The recently published exchange Derrida refers to is 'Ja, ou le faux bond' in *Digraphe* 11.

Although I am not, as you all know, and according to the canonic criteria in effect in your four groups of limited responsibility,[7] either analyst or analysand, I am sure that *'faux-bond'* is a word, and a thing, which must interest you.

Among the thousand and one *faux-bonds* that one might cite as examples, there is the one made by an analyst in relation to his own 'group' by going to do a *'tranche'* in another group. And I wager that what I will call the *'confrontation' effect* has an essential relation to all *faux-bonds*, and to the *faux-bond* in the form of a *tranche*, transferring or trancheferring from one group to another.

I am even tempted to believe, in the actual and doubtless limited state of my information, that this problem of the *tranche*, and more precisely of the one that you can go to in another group, this problem which does not with any certainty lead back to the problem of unterminated or interminable analysis, although perhaps touching it to the quick, this problem remains struck by a theoretical and practical, as is said, interdiction. By an interdiction and an entrediction that perhaps organizes the entire suburban network of psychoanalysis in your societies. It is what goes on, but must not be talked of, or can be talked of without being made into a 'critical' problem. And I will soon try to say, if I am left the floor, why the *'confrontation' effect* has an essential relation to a certain lifting – this evening perhaps – only glimpsed, as always, of such an interdiction.

Thus, I almost committed a *faux-bond*. Let us suppose, and this is still only a hypothesis, that I am here and that I have *not* committed a *faux-bond*. Why would I not have done so?

I did not want to abuse it, which perhaps amounts to saying that I did not have the strength, but the strength to do what? In that case, if you had waited for me and if this place had remained empty for an indefinite amount of time, ten minutes one band would say, forty-five to fifty another, then in that case, if you had waited for me, I am sure that something would have occurred.

From myself, from yourselves to myself, there would have been some event, inevitably. And on both sides. I did not have the strength to abuse it, this strange facility. This is why I have said that it will have been stronger than me.

And then I was caught in the trap, in the trap of all traps, the desire still to attend one's own *faux-bond*: to commit a *faux-bond* in relation to oneself and to toll one's own bell (*glas*). It fails every time, and whatever the chance might be.

---

[7] TN. 'Groups of limited responsibility': Derrida is alluding to the common French acronym S.A.R.L., for *société à responsabilité limitée*, meaning a company in which each associate is responsible only to the extent of his investment. This relates to the bond and the band. The question of what bonds an analytic band is put elsewhere by Derrida as, 'is the association ever free?'

Unless, unless the *faux-bond* still has all its chances, this evening. I believe that this hypothesis is still open, I believe it intact.

Suggested further reading

Derrida, J (1998), *The Derrida Reader: Writing Performances* (ed. Wolfeys, J L). Edinburgh: Edinburgh University Press
Forrester, J (1990), *The Seductions of Psychoanalysis. Freud, Lacan and Derrida.* Cambridge: Cambridge University Press
Norris, C (1987), *Derrida.* London: Fontana
Woods, D (ed.) (1992), *Derrida: A Critical Reader.* Oxford: Blackwell

Foucault (1926–1984)

Michel Foucault is possibly best known for his anti-humanist challenge. In announcing the death of the human subject, and the death of the author, and in critiquing the Cartesian model of an isolated, disembodied consciousness, Foucault opened the way to an investigation of the social and discursive practices which lead to the formation of human subjectivity. His thinking on history, on power and knowledge, reason and unreason, the gaze and its relation to coercion and punishment, is of huge potential importance to psychotherapists and counsellors.

One of Foucault's key terms is 'genealogy', which he took from Nietzsche's book *On the Genealogy of Morals*; he meant by it a writing of history that seeks to separate present from past. Instead of looking for continuities (to legitimise and justify the present) he searches out discontinuities and difference – the radical 'foreignness' of the past. He does not try to explain these differences, but allows them to work to undermine present-day assumptions. As a model for the psychotherapist, Foucault's genealogy has much to say for itself.

As a historian Foucault is on the side of Nietzsche rather than Hegel; he is opposed to teleological views, that is, that we are going somewhere historically, in a dialectical 'progress'. In a way that parallels Lyotard's thinking, he rejects grand historical theories and narratives. He is critical of Marxist ideology, preferring to stress local, specific struggles. He is critical too of psychoanalysis, and in particular the notion of repression: power for Foucault is not something that merely weighs on us as a prohibition; it is that which actively produces things: pleasure, knowledge, discourse; it always stands in a productive relation to these things (Sarup, 1993: 79, and see *Discipline and Punish* (1979), and *The History of Sexuality* (1978, 1985, 1986a)). Psychoanalysis allows sexuality to be subsumed within a scientific discourse; sex, in the post-Enlightenment, bourgeois world, lies (in Sarup's paraphrase) at 'the intersection of the discipline of the body and the control of the population'; it is thus a political issue. In the end this scientific, 'technical' or 'instrumental' rationality – the efficient calculation of means and values – leads to disenchantment, and can teach us nothing about how to live our lives (Sarup, 1993: 68–9). It is only by recognising the political nature of these matters – that they are saturated with issues of knowledge and power – that they can be combated.

Foucault's critique of instrumental rationality should not, however, be taken as a naive antagonism to Enlightenment. In his essay 'What is Enlightenment?' Foucault provides a general introduction to his project. He writes of avoiding the 'blackmail' of Enlightenment – that is, feeling one has to take up a position either for or against rationality. The great philosopher of Enlightenment, Immanuel Kant, responding to the question 'what is Enlightenment?' in the 1780s, saw the issue facing philosophy as: what can we know? What limits must knowledge renounce trangressing? Foucault turns the question into a positive. In what is given as universal and necessary, 'what place is occupied by whatever is singular, contingent, and the product of arbitrary constraints?' Here he shows his roots in Nietzsche, and in phenomenology, with its emphasis on the singular and particular, as given to experience, and its abstinence as regards coming up with explanations.

Rather than a search for universal values and structures, Foucault proposes 'a historical investigation into the events that have led us to constitute ourselves and to recognize ourselves as subjects of what we are doing, thinking, saying'. This, therefore, is not transcendental criticism. It is 'genealogical in its design and archaeological in its method'. It is archaeological in that it seeks 'to treat the instances of discourse that articulate what we think, say and do as so many historical events' (i.e. specific, unrepeatable, not universal or pre-ordained), and genealogical in that it will 'separate out, from the contingency that has made us what we are, the possibility of no longer being, doing, or thinking what we are, do, or think'. It is a project which seeks 'to give new impetus . . . to the undefined work of freedom'. (Foucault, 1986b: 45–6)

Foucault's interest in the 'genealogy of knowledge' is thus on one level about how knowledge affects our experience; it is also about that which Reason excludes, and his interest is particularly in the eighteenth century, which is where he sees this exclusion taking place, with the beginnings of professionalisation and the gaze of the 'expert'. For Foucault, as for Nietzsche, there is no pre-existing or inherent order, thus nothing inherent or inevitable in these developments: order is the writing of history itself (Lechte, 1994: 111). Perhaps the best known of his books is one of his earliest, *Madness and Civilization* (Foucault, 1971a [1961]), in which he charted the annexation of madness by medicine, the beginnings of psychiatry, and the coming to being of a new definition of Reason – as 'technical reason' – which definitively excludes Unreason, defining it in the process. The publication of *Madness and Civilization* coincided with the anti-psychiatry movement of the 1960s, and was influential on it. (For an important critique of Foucault's position, see Derrida, 1978b.)

Here is Foucault writing about a parallel series of historical events. This is from the last pages of his *The Birth of the Clinic* (Foucault, 1973) about the beginnings of modern medicine; excluded here are finitude and death themselves:

Western man could constitute himself in his own eyes as an object of science, he grasped himself within his language, and gave himself, in himself and by himself, a discursive existence, only in the opening created by his own elimination: from the experience of Unreason was born psychology, the very possibility of psychology; from the integration of death into medical thought is born a medicine that has given us a science of the individual.

[Medicine therefore has] an importance that is not only methodological, but ontological, in that it concerns man's being as object of positive knowledge . . . The possibility for the individual of being both subject and object of his own knowledge implies an inversion of the structure of finitude . . . Hence the fundamental place of medicine in the over-all architecture of the human sciences. . . . Hence, too, its prestige in the concrete forms of existence: health replaces salvation. . . . This is because medicine offers modern man the obstinate, yet reassuring face of his finitude; in it, death is endlessly repeated, but it also exorcised. . . .

. . . this relation of man to death, which in the first case authorises a scientific discourse in a rational form, and, in the second opens up the source of a language that unfolds endlessly in the void left by the absence of the gods . . .

The formation of clinical medicine [and with it psychotherapy] is merely one of the more visible witnesses to these changes in the fundamental structures of experience. . . . So much . . . [of] contemporary thought, believing it has escaped it since the need of the nineteenth century, has merely rediscovered, little by little, that which made it possible. In the last years of the eighteenth century, European culture outlined a structure that has not yet been unraveled; we are only just beginning to disentangle a few of the threads, which are still so unknown to us that we immediately assume them to be marvellously new or absolutely archaic, whereas for two hundred years (not less, yet not much more), they have constituted the dark, but firm web of our experience.

(Foucault, 1973: 197–9)

How might Foucault's thinking impact on psychotherapy? We might consider the extent to which patients speak of their history in order to relocate themselves, abetted by the therapist as knowledge broker, as the representative of current cultural practices. How then is personal history currently being written, by what vested interests? Implications for training flow from this. If the emphasis is solely on the patient's material, this might leave out the question of where the therapist is responding from.

How does one hear patients from, for example, higher management, or from the old shop floor or production line? How does one hear people's sexual practices; how much are we bound to respond according to the fashion of the time? What is the difference between what can be spoken about to an expensive analyst and to your GP – for example, regarding sexual practices which might be illegal?

Perhaps another discursive practice can break through the patient's speech. Is this to enable a more 'convenient' history to be told, re-managing the patient's knowledge systems, or to make contact with the patient's desire (the 'freedom' to which Foucault alludes)? Is the therapist's role merely to help clients tell their history 'appropriately'?

How far are therapeutic practices, like other discourses, in need of Foucaultian epistemology, that is, of being linked up to the larger 'web of our experience'? For "Thought" . . . is not . . . to be sought only in theoretical formulations such as those of philosophy or science; it can and must be analysed in every manner of speaking, doing, or behaving' (Foucault, 1986b: 334–5). The ideas embodied in a cultural practice are not usually self-evident (see Lechte, 1994: 112); how far are we, even the most (psycho)analytic among us, prepared to be epistemologists of our own practices? The relationship of therapeutic theory to practice is rarely self-evident to the patient, and if we choose to try to make the link is it not always for our own self-interest as therapists?

In his later work Foucault wrote about technologies of the self, finding the mark of a 'technique' in any 'unacknowledged regularity of actions' (Lechte, 1994: 112). How does this function, on the level not only of the individual, but also that of practice, in for example, psychoanalytic thinking about Oedipus? How in danger are we of offering trainings which are forms of indoctrination, training people to follow the knowledge–power nexus while *appearing* to be thoughtful? How might this rub off on the patient's way of telling his or her story, and contribute to the analyst's way of telling his or her story, as a person, a citizen, and so on? In the saying, history-telling tends to change the present to our material advantage.

From Foucault (1971b), 'The Discourse on Language', pp. 7–30

What is so perilous, then, in the fact that people speak, and that their speech proliferates? Where is the danger in that?

Here then is the hypothesis I want to advance, tonight, in order to fix the terrain – or perhaps the very provisional theatre – within which I shall be working. I am supposing that in every society the production of discourse is at once controlled, selected, organised and redistributed according to a certain number of procedures, whose role is to avert its powers and its dangers, to cope with chance events, to evade its ponderous, awesome materiality.

In a society such as our own we all know the rules of *exclusion*. The most obvious and familiar of these concerns what is *prohibited*. We know perfectly well that we are not free to say just anything, that we cannot simply speak of anything, when we like or where we like; not just anyone, finally, may speak of just anything. We have three types of prohibition, covering objects, ritual with its surrounding circumstances, the privileged or exclusive right to speak of a particular subject; these prohibitions inter-relate, reinforce and complement each other, forming a complex web, continually subject to modification. I will note simply that the areas where this web is most tightly woven today, where the danger spots are most numerous, are those dealing with politics and sexuality. It is as though discussion, far from being a transparent, neutral element, allowing us to disarm sexuality and to pacify politics, were one of those privileged areas in which they exercised some of their more awesome powers. In appearance, speech may well be of little account, but the prohibitions surrounding it soon reveal its links with desire and power. This should not be very surprising, for psychoanalysis has already shown us that speech is not merely the medium which manifests – or dissembles – desire; it is also the object of desire. Similarly, historians have constantly impressed upon us that speech is no mere verbalisation of conflicts and systems of domination, but that it is the very object of man's conflicts.

But our society possesses yet another principle of exclusion; not another prohibition, but a division and a rejection. I have in mind the opposition: reason and folly. From the depths of the Middle Ages, a man was mad if his speech could not be said to form part of the common discourse of men. His words were considered null and void, without truth or significance, worthless as evidence, inadmissible in the authentification of acts or contracts, incapable even of bringing about transubstantiation – the transformation of bread into flesh – at Mass. And yet, in contrast to all others, his words were credited with strange powers, of revealing some hidden truth, of predicting the future, of revealing, in all their naiveté, what the wise were unable to perceive. It is curious to note that for centuries, in Europe, the words of a madman were either totally ignored or else were taken as words of truth. They either fell into a void – rejected the moment they were proffered – or else men deciphered in them a naive or cunning reason, rationality more rational than that of a rational man. At all events, whether excluded or secretly invested with reason, the madman's speech did not strictly exist. It was through his words that one recognised the madness of the madman; but they were certainly the medium within which this division became active; they were neither heard nor remembered. No doctor before the end of the eighteenth century had ever thought of listening to the content – how it was said and why – of these words; and yet it was these which signalled the difference between reason and madness. Whatever a madman said, it was taken for mere noise; he was credited with words only in a symbolic sense, in the theatre, in which he stepped forward, unarmed and reconciled, playing his role: that of masked truth.

Of course people are going to say all that is over and done with, or that it is in the process of being finished with, today; that the madman's words are no longer on the other side of this division; that they are no longer null and void, that, on the contrary, they alert us to the need to look for a sense behind them, for the attempt at, or the ruins of some 'œuvre'; we have even come to notice these words of madmen in our own speech, in those tiny pauses when we forget what we are talking about. But all this is no proof that the old vision is not just as active as before; we have only to think of the systems by which we decipher this speech; we have only to think of the network of institutions established to permit doctors and psychoanalysts to listen to the mad and, at the same time, enabling the mad to come and speak, or, in desperation, to withhold their meagre words; we have only to bear all this in mind to suspect that the old division is just as active as ever, even if it is proceeding along different lines and, via new institutions, producing rather different effects. Even when the role of the doctor consists of lending an ear to this finally liberated speech, this procedure still takes place in the context of a hiatus between listener and speaker. For he is listening to speech invested with desire, crediting itself – for its greater exultation or for its greater anguish – with terrible powers. If we truly require silence to cure monsters, then it must be an attentive silence, and it is in this that the division lingers.

It is perhaps a little risky to speak of the opposition between true and false as a third system of exclusion, along with those I have mentioned already. How could one reasonably compare the constraints of truth with those other divisions, arbitrary in origin if not developing out of historical contingency – not merely modifiable but in a state of continual flux, supported by a system of institutions imposing and manipulating them, acting not without constraint, nor without an element, at least, of violence?

Certainly, as a proposition, the division between true and false is neither arbitrary, nor modifiable, nor institutional, nor violent. Putting the question in different terms, however – asking what has been, what still is, throughout our discourse, this will to truth which has survived throughout so many centuries of our history; or if we ask what is, in its very general form, the kind of division governing our will to knowledge – then we may well discern something like a system of exclusion (historical, modifiable, institutionally constraining) in the process of development.

It is, undoubtedly, a historically constituted division. For, even with the sixth-century Greek poets, true discourse – in the meaningful sense-inspiring respect and terror, to which all were obliged to submit, because it held sway over all and was pronounced by men who spoke as of right, according to ritual, meted out justice and attributed to each his rightful share; it prophesied the future, not merely announcing what was going to occur, but contributing to its actual event, carrying men along with it and thus weaving itself into the fabric of fate. And yet, a century later, the highest truth no longer resided in what discourse *was*, nor in what it *did*: it lay in what was *said*. The day dawned when truth moved over from the ritualised act – potent and just – of enunciation to settle on what was enunciated itself: its meaning, its form, its object and its relation to what it referred to. A division emerged between Hesiod and Plato, separating true discourse from false; it was a new division for, henceforth, true discourse was no longer considered precious and desirable, since it had ceased to be discourse linked to the exercise of power. And so the Sophists were routed.

This historical division has doubtless lent its general form to our will to knowledge. Yet it has never ceased shifting: the great mutations of science may well sometimes be seen to flow from some discovery, but they may equally be viewed as the appearance of new forms of the will to truth. In the nineteenth century there was undoubtedly a will to truth having nothing to do, in terms of the forms examined, of the fields to which it addressed itself, nor the techniques upon which it was based, with the will to knowledge which characterised classical culture. Going back a little in time, to the turn of the sixteenth and seventeenth centuries – and particularly in England – a will to knowledge emerged which, anticipating its present content, sketched out a schema of possible, observable, measurable and classifiable objects; a will to knowledge which imposed upon the knowing subject – in some ways taking precedence over all experience – a certain position, a certain viewpoint, and a certain function (look rather than read, verify rather than comment), a will to knowledge which prescribed (and, more generally speaking, all instruments determined) the technological level at which knowledge could be employed in order to be verifiable and useful (navigation, mining, pharmacopoeia). Everything seems to have occurred as though, from the time of the great Platonic division onwards, the will to truth had its own history, which is not at all that of the constraining truths: the history of a range of subjects to be learned, the history of the functions of the knowing subject, the history of material, technical and instrumental investment in knowledge.

But this will to truth, like the other systems of exclusion, relies on institutional support: it is both reinforced and accompanied by whole strata of practices such as pedagogy – naturally – the book-system, publishing, libraries, such as the learned societies in the past, and laboratories today. But it is probably even more profoundly accompanied by the manner in which knowledge is employed in a society, the way in which it is exploited, divided and, in some ways, attributed. It is worth recalling at this point, if only symbolically, the old Greek adage, that arithmetic should be taught in democracies, for it teaches relations of equality, but that geometry alone should be reserved for oligarchies, as it demonstrates the proportions within inequality.

Finally, I believe that this will to knowledge, thus reliant upon institutional support and distribution, tends to exercise a sort of pressure, a power of constraint upon other forms of discourse – I am speaking of our own society. I am thinking of the way Western literature has, for centuries, sought to base itself in nature, in the plausible, upon sincerity and science – in short, upon true discourse. I am thinking, too, of the way economic practices, codified into precepts and recipes – as morality, too – have sought since the eighteenth century, to found themselves, to rationalise and justify their currency, in a theory of wealth and production; I am thinking, again, of the manner in which such prescriptive ensembles as the Penal Code have sought their bases or justifications. For example, the Penal Code started out as a theory of Right; then, from the time of the nineteenth century, people looked for its validation in sociological, psychological, medical and psychiatric knowledge. It is as though the very words of the law had no authority in our society, except insofar as they are derived from true discourse. Of the three great systems of exclusion governing discourse – prohibited words, the division of madness and the will to truth – I have spoken at greatest length concerning the third. With good reason: for centuries, the former have continually tended towards the latter; because this last has, gradually, been attempting to assimilate the others in order both to modify them and to provide them with a firm foundation. Because, if the two former are continually growing more fragile and less certain to the extent that they are now invaded by the will to truth, the latter, in contrast, daily grows in strength, in depth and implacability.

And yet we speak of it least. As though the will to truth and its vicissitudes were masked by truth itself and its necessary unfolding. The reason is perhaps this: if, since the time of the Greeks, true discourse no longer responds to desire or to that which exercises power in the will to truth, in the will to speak out in true discourse, what, then, is at work, if not desire and power? True discourse, liberated by the nature of its form from desire and power, is incapable of recognising the will to truth which pervades it; and the will to truth, having imposed itself upon us for so long, is such that the truth it seeks to reveal cannot fail to mask it.

Thus, only one truth appears before our eyes: wealth, fertility and sweet strength in all its insidious universality. In contrast, we are unaware of the prodigious machinery of the will to truth, with its vocation of exclusion. All those who, at one moment or another in our history, have attempted to remould this will to truth and to turn it against truth at that very point where truth undertakes to justify the taboo, and to define madness; all those, from Nietzsche to Artaud and Tabaille, must now stand as (probably haughty) signposts for all our future work.

There are, of course, many other systems for the control and delimitation of discourse. Those I have spoken of up to now are, to some extent, active on the exterior; they function as systems of exclusion; they concern that part of discourse which deals with power and desire.

I believe we can isolate another group: internal rules, where discourse exercises its own control; rules concerned with the principles of classification, ordering and distribution. It is as though we were now involved in the mastery of another dimension of discourse: that of events and chance.

In the first place, commentary. I suppose, though I am not altogether sure, there is barely a society without its major narratives, told, retold and varied; formulae, texts, ritualised texts to be spoken in well-defined circumstances; things said once, and conserved because people suspect some hidden secret or wealth lies buried within. In short, I suspect one could find a kind of gradation between different types of discourse within most societies: discourse 'uttered' in the course of the day and in casual meetings, and which disappears with the very act which gave rise to it; and those forms of discourse that lie at the origins of a certain number of new verbal acts, which are reiterated, transformed or discussed; in short, discourse which *is spoken* and remains spoken, indefinitely, beyond its formulation, and which remains to be spoken. We know them in our own cultural system: religious or judicial texts, as well as some curious texts, from the point of view of their status, which we term 'literary'; to a certain extent, scientific texts also.

What is clear is that this gap is neither stable, nor constant, nor absolute. There is no question of there being one category, fixed for all time, reserved for fundamental or creative discourse, and another for those which reiterate, expound and comment. Not a few major texts become blurred and disappear, and commentaries sometimes come to occupy the former position. But while the details of application may well change, the function remains the same, and the principle of hierarchy remains at work. The radical denial of this gradation can never be anything but play, utopia or anguish.

Suggested further reading

Derrida, J (1978b [1967]), 'Cogito and the History of Madness', in *Writing and Difference*. Chicago: University of Chicago Press

Forrester, J (1990), 'Michel Foucault and the History of Psychoanalysis', in *The Seductions of Psychoanalysis. Freud, Lacan and Derrida*. Cambridge: Cambridge University Press

Foucault, M (1971), *Madness and Civilization: A History of Insanity in the Age of Reason*. New York: Pantheon

—— (1980), 'Truth and Power', interview with Fontana, A and Pasquino, P, in *Power/Knowledge: Selected Interviews and Other Writings, 1972–77*. New York: Pantheon

—— (1986b), *The Foucault Reader. An Introduction to Foucault's Thought* (ed. Rabinow, P). Harmondsworth: Penguin

Kristeva (b. 1941)

Julia Kristeva was born in Bulgaria and went to Paris as a student in 1965. She became involved in the Marxist group around the radical journal *Tel quel*, and published her doctoral thesis on linguistics. She is professor of linguistics at the University of Paris VII, and a practising psychoanalyst. Her interest in femininity and sexuality particularly revolve around her concern with the inexpressible, the strangeness and otherness of individual and cultural life – with analysing the unanalysable (Lechte, 1994: 141). She is interested in the marginal and repressed aspects of language, and in particular how 'feminine forms of signification which cannot be contained by the rational structure of the symbolic order and which therefore threaten its sovereignty . . . have been relegated to the margins of discourse'. These uncontainable forms of signification she sees as erupting in 'madness, holiness, and poetry' (Sarup, 1993: 123–4). Her interests in the marginal have found expression in her work on the stranger (Kristeva, 1994). This interest comes in part out of the experience of the upheavals and population shifts of post-Second World War Europe: migrant labour (the presence of 'guest workers', the arrival of new ethnic groups with the end of colonialism), and the results, experienced by refugees and asylum seekers, of the collapse of the old Soviet order and of war (in Bosnia and elsewhere). Kristeva herself, as she reminds us, is herself a 'stranger' in France, from behind the Iron Curtain; her stand is one of revolt and opposition, although she questions how far such a stand can be maintained within the 'new world order' (Kristeva, 1998).

Whilst there are major differences between Kristeva and Lacan, Kristeva uses Lacanian theory, with its privileging of the Oedipus complex and the Law of the Father (this has helped make her unpopular among some other feminist thinkers), to form the basis of a theory of signifying practice and the origins of speech and language. This includes a developmental story. Kristeva imagines the pre-Oedipal baby's experience of the mother's/carer's inchoate sounds, heart beats, gurglings, which she sees as the 'raw material' of future ordered and structured language. She calls this raw material the 'semiotic' and pictures the baby occupying a maternal space she terms the 'chora', borrowing the term from Plato's *Timaeus*. It is the enveloping space of the mother's body (something like Winnicott's maternal environment), with its fluid boundaries, that is both the locus for the beginnings of subjectivity and for that which can overwhelm it, for the (Freudian) Death Drive. With potty-training and the adult insistence on cleanliness (*propriété*) and 'regularity', comes the experience of 'abjection' and the entry into Lacan's Symbolic Order, into language. *Propre* in French can mean both 'clean' and 'one's own'; the baby's taking possession of his or her body, with the help of the mother/carer (through the touching and naming of parts) is the moment of entry into language and gendered subjectivity (see Grosz, 1986).

Meanwhile what has had to be 'abjected' subsists; the abject incites both desire and disgust. The abject and abjection can be seen as primers of the culture; they are that which is excluded, and by which culture is defined. They are what lie behind the super-ego injunction 'Keep It Clean'.

> Excrement and its equivalents (decay, infection, disease, corpse, etc.) stand for the danger to identity that comes from without; the ego is threatened by the non-ego, society threatened from its outside, life by death. Menstrual blood, on the contrary, stands for the danger issuing from within the identity (social or sexual); it threatens the relationship between the sexes within a social aggregate and through internalisation, the identity of each sex in the face of sexual difference.
>
> (Kristeva, 1982: 71)

The semiotic for Kristeva can thus be correlated with the polymorphous, pre-Oedipal drives and the erotogenic zones, orifices and organs of Freudian theory. It is, as Sarup has summed it up, 'the "raw material" of signification, the corporeal, libidinal matter that must be harnessed and appropriately channelled for social cohesion and regulation' (Sarup, 1993: 124). There are, however, moments at which this cohesion breaks down or proves unsustainable, and the semiotic overflows its boundaries, and these moments are the moments of the eruption of excess in madness, holiness, poetry, and the art of the avant-garde. 'Although exclusively male in Kristeva's terms, the avant-garde is nevertheless the best representative of the repressed, feminine semiotic order. An important part of Kristeva's argument is that any strengthening of the semiotic, which knows no sexual difference, must lead to a weakening of traditional gender divisions' (Sarup, 1993: 126).

Where is psychotherapy with all this, in its practice, theory and training? Surely through some encouragement of the semiotic we may be able to help our clients, for 'by transgressing the boundaries of the symbolic order the avant-garde creates upheavals and ruptures which may enable what is usually unspoken to be articulated' (Sarup, 1993: 126). Psychoanalysis, psychotherapy and counselling have the potential to free one up to speak more of the abject, and this is why we need them – so we can speak and hear a bit more, and regain some lost contact with the roots of creativity. Yet the excessive avant-garde text, like psychotherapy itself, always 'risks co-option or recuperation in functioning as a "safety-valve" or outlet for what may otherwise have been a more disruptive political practice' (Sarup, 1993: 126). Kristeva herself has been criticised (see for example Owens, 1985: 78 n4) for equating avant-garde practice with the feminine; in this view, her association of women with the pre-symbolic merely works to confirm women's exclusion from representation.

Indeed therapy easily becomes an agent of co-option. Is there any reason to believe that psychotherapy is, often, doing anything other than exercising the Law of the Father, abjecting what it cannot accommodate, or *appropriate*, make clean? Will that which threatens its sovereignty always be relegated to the margins of discourse? Is a good training one which enables participants to carry this out effectively? Ethical codes may be good examples of ways of not thinking about the abject and keeping it in its place. We 'clean up our act' (but things still spill out). One might also think of the gate-keeping, filtering function of the 'scientific committee', of conferences and organisations, and psychoanalysis's particular history of expulsions – usually of the wayward and original thinker – from Jung to Ferenczi to Masud Khan. For the same reasons new ideas can be difficult to introduce within institutions, without them being experienced as a threat. Kristeva's concept of the abject provides a powerful purchase on such experiences.

We would also see links between the operation of the abject and 'technical knowledge', as opposed to, and in place of, thoughtfulness and science more broadly understood: keeping it clean without thinking or experimenting, without getting one's hands dirty, coming to the mess. If you stay with technique you are lifeless, but clean. Perhaps if you start with phenomenology there is less danger of this; the phenomenological is perhaps less of a 'container' of the abject than other kinds of theorising. Think, for example, of the issue of boundaries, which we would argue are often adhered to thoughtlessly, merely as a matter of routine. Such, we suggest, is the anxiety attached to what might flood in if a breach were permitted. How frightening, for example, is the question: should one stick to the boundary and never hit one's patient?

In the extract that follows Kristeva writes about the abject and its relation to the problematics of desire. The abject is something that fascinates desire, but desire is not seduced. The abject cannot be incorporated, or reduced. We cannot think about it, its main characteristic is that it is something that is 'opposed to I'; it leads to a collapse of meaning, as Kristeva seems to be saying can happen in powerful 'super-ego' experiences: 'to each ego its object, to each super-ego its abject'. There is 'a brutish suffering that "I" puts up with. . . . deposits to the father's account. . . . radically separate, loathsome. Not me. Not that. But not nothing'.

From Kristeva (1982), *Powers of Horror. An Essay on Abjection*, pp. 1–2, 5–7, 29–31, 32–4

Approaching Abjection

No Beast is there without glimmer of infinity,
No eye so vile nor abject that brushes not
Against lightning from on high, now tender, now fierce.
Victor Hugo, La Légende des siècles

Neither subject nor object

There looms, within abjection, one of those violent, dark revolts of being, directed against a threat that seems to emanate from an exorbitant outside or inside, ejected beyond the scope of the possible, the tolerable, the thinkable. It lies there, quite close, but it cannot be assimilated. It beseeches, worries, and fascinates desire, which, nevertheless, does not let itself be seduced. Apprehensive, desire turns aside; sickened, it rejects. A certainty protects it from the shameful – a certainty of which it is proud holds on to it. But simultaneously, just the same, that impetus, that spasm, that leap is drawn toward an elsewhere as tempting as it is condemned. Unflaggingly, like an inescapable boomerang, a vortex of summons and repulsion places the one haunted by it literally beside himself.

When I am beset by abjection, the twisted braid of affects and thoughts I call by such a name does not have, properly speaking, a definable *object*. The abject is not an ob-ject facing me, which I name or imagine. Nor is it an ob-jest, an otherness ceaselessly fleeing in a systematic quest of desire. What is abject is not my correlative, which, providing me with someone or something else as support, would allow me to be more or less detached and autonomous. The abject has only one quality of the object – that of being opposed to *I*. If the object, however, through its opposition, settles me within the fragile texture of a desire for meaning, which, as a matter of fact, makes me ceaselessly and infinitely homologous to it, what is *abject*, on the contrary, the jettisoned object, is radically excluded and draws me toward the place where meaning collapses. A certain 'ego' that merged with its master, a superego, has flatly driven it away. It lies outside, beyond the set, and does not seem to agree to the latter's rules of the game. And yet, from its place of banishment, the abject does not cease challenging its master. Without a sign (for him), it beseeches a discharge, a convulsion, a crying out. To each ego its object, to each superego its abject. It is not the white expanse or slack boredom of repression, not the translations and transformations of desire that wrench bodies, nights, and discourse; rather it is a brutish suffering that 'I' puts up with, sublime and devastated, for 'I' deposits it to the father's account [*verse au père – père-version*]: I endure it, for I imagine that such is the desire of the other. A massive and sudden emergence of uncanniness, which, familiar as it might have been in an opaque and forgotten life, now harries me as radically separate, loathsome. Not me. Not that. But not nothing, either. A 'something' that I do not recognize as a thing. A weight of meaninglessness, about which there is nothing insignificant, and which crushes me. On the edge of non-existence and hallucination, of a reality that, if I acknowledge it, annihilates me. There, abject and objection are my safeguards. The primers of my culture.

The improper/unclean

Loathing an item of food, a piece of filth, waste, or dung. The spasms and vomiting that protect me. The repugnance, the retching that thrusts me to the side and turns me away from defilement, sewage, and muck. The shame of compromise, of being in the middle of treachery. The fascinated start that leads me toward and separates me from them . . .

The abjection of self

If it be true that the abject simultaneously beseeches and pulverizes the subject, one can understand that it is experienced at the peak of its strength when that subject, weary of fruitless attempts to identify with something on the outside, finds the impossible within; when it finds that the impossible constitutes its very *being*, that it *is* none other than abject. The abjection of self would be the culminating form of that experience of the subject to which it is revealed that all its objects are based merely on the inaugural *loss* that laid the foundations of its own being. There is nothing like the abjection of self to show that all abjection is in fact recognition of the *want* on which any being, meaning, language, or desire is founded. One always passes too quickly over this word, 'want', and today psychoanalysts are finally taking into account only its more or less fetishized product, the 'object of want'. But if one imagines (and imagine one must, for it is the working of imagination whose foundations are being laid here) the experience of *want* itself as logically preliminary to being and object – to the being of the object – then one understands that abjection, and even more so abjection of self, is its only signified. Its signifier, then, is none but literature. Mystical Christendom turned this abjection of self into the ultimate proof of humility before God, witness Elizabeth of Hungary who 'though a great princess, delighted in nothing so much as in abasing herself'.

The question remains as to the ordeal, a secular one this time, that abjection can constitute for someone who, in what is termed knowledge of castration, turning away from perverse dodges, presents himself with his own body and ego as the most precious non-objects; they are no longer seen in their own right but forfeited, abject. The termination of analysis can lead us there, as we shall see. Such are the pangs and delights of masochism.

Essentially different from 'uncanniness', more violent, too, abjection is elaborated through a failure to recognize its kin; nothing is familiar, not even the shadow of a memory. I imagine a child who has swallowed up his parents too soon, who frightens himself on that account, 'all by himself', and, to save himself, rejects and throws up everything that is given to him – all gifts, all objects. He has, he could have, a sense of the abject. Even before things for him *are* – hence before they are signifiable – he drives them out, dominated by drive as he is, and constitutes his own territory, edged by the abject. A sacred configuration. Fear cements his compound, conjoined to another world, thrown up, driven out, forfeited. What he has swallowed up instead of maternal love is an emptiness, or rather a maternal hatred without a word for the words of the father; that is what he tries to cleanse himself of, tirelessly. What solace does he come upon within such loathing? Perhaps a father, existing but unsettled, loving but unsteady, merely an apparition but an apparition that remains. Without him the holy brat would probably have no sense of the sacred; a blank subject, he would remain, discomfited, at the dump for non-objects that are always forfeited, from which, on the contrary, fortified by abjection, he tries to extricate himself. For he is not mad, he through whom the abject exists. Out of the daze that has petrified him before the untouchable, impossible, absent body of the mother, a daze that has cut off his impulses from their objects, that is, from their representations, out of such daze he causes, along with loathing, one word to crop up – fear. The phobic has no other object than the abject. But that word, 'fear' – a fluid haze, an elusive clamminess – no sooner has it cropped up than it shades off like a mirage and permeates all words of the language with nonexistence, with a hallucinatory, ghostly glimmer. Thus, fear having been bracketed, discourse will seem tenable only if it ceaselessly confront that otherness, a burden both repellent and repelled, a deep well of memory that is unapproachable and intimate: the abject.

Beyond the unconscious

Put another way, it means that there are lives not sustained by *desire*, as desire is always for objects. Such lives are based on *exclusion*. They are clearly distinguishable from those understood as neurotic or psychotic, articulated by *negation* and its modalities, *transgression, denial*, and *repudiation*. Their dynamics challenges the theory of the unconscious, seeing that the latter is dependent upon a dialectic of negativity.

The theory of the unconscious, as is well known, presupposes a repression of contents (affects and presentations) that, thereby, do not have access to consciousness but effect within the subject modifications, either of speech (parapraxes, etc.), or of the body (symptoms), or both (hallucinations, etc.). As correlative to the notion of *repression*, Freud put forward that of *denial* as a means of figuring out neurosis, that of *rejection* (*repudiation*) as a means of situating psychosis. The asymmetry of the two repressions becomes more marked owing to denial's bearing on the object whereas repudiation affects desire itself (Lacan, in perfect keeping with Freud's thought, interprets that as 'repudiation of the Name of the Father').

Yet, facing the ab-ject and more specifically phobia and the splitting of the ego (a point I shall return to), one might ask if those articulations of negativity germane to the unconscious (inherited by Freud from philosophy and psychology) have not become inoperative. The 'unconscious' contents remain here *excluded* but in strange fashion: not radically enough to allow for a secure differentiation between subject and object, and yet clearly enough for a defensive *position* to be established – one that implies a refusal but also a sublimating elaboration. As if the fundamental opposition were between I and Other or, in more archaic fashion, between Inside and Outside. As if such an opposition subsumed the one between Conscious and Unconscious, elaborated on the basis of neuroses.

Owing to the ambiguous opposition I/Other, Inside/Outside – an opposition that is vigorous but pervious, violent but uncertain – there are contents, 'normally' unconscious in neurotics, that become explicit if not conscious in 'borderline' patients' speeches and behavior. Such contents are often openly manifested through symbolic practices, without by the same token being integrated into the judging consciousness of those particular subjects. Since they make the conscious/unconscious distinction irrelevant, borderline subjects and their speech constitute propitious ground for a sublimating discourse ('aesthetic' or 'mystical', etc.), rather than a scientific or rationalist one. . . .

Philosophical sadness and the spoken disaster of the analyst

... It is obvious that the analyst, from the abyss of his silence, brushes against the ghost of the sadness Hegel saw in sexual normalization. Such sadness is the more obvious to him as his ethics is rigorous – founded, as it must be in the West, on the remains of transcendental idealism. But one can also argue that the Freudian stance, which is dualistic and dissolving, unsettles those foundations. In that sense, it causes the sad, analytic silence to hover above a strange, foreign discourse, which, strictly speaking, shatters verbal communication (made up of a knowledge and a truth that are nevertheless heard) by means of a device that mimics terror, enthusiasm, or orgy, and is more closely related to rhythm and song than it is to the World. There is mimesis (some say identification) in the analytic passage through castration. And yet it is necessary that the analyst's interpretative speech (and not only his literary or theoretical bilingualism) be affected by it in order to be analytical. As counterpoise to a purity that found its bearings in disillusioned sadness, it is the 'poetic' unsettlement of analytic utterance that testifies to its closeness to, cohabitation with, and 'knowledge' of abjection.

I am thinking, in short, of the completely mimetic *identification* (transference and countertransference) of the analyst with respect to analysands. That identification allows for securing in their place what, when parcelled out, makes them suffering and barren. It allows one to regress back to the affects that can be heard in the breaks in discourse, to provide rhythm, too, to concatenate (is that what 'to become conscious' means?) the gaps of a speech saddened because it turned its back on its abject meaning. If there is analytic jouissance it is there, in the thoroughly poetic mimesis that runs through the architecture of speech and extends from coenesthetic image to logical and phantasmatic articulations. Without for that matter biologizing language, and while breaking away from identification by means of interpretation, analytic speech is one that becomes 'incarnate' in the full sense of the term. On that condition only, it is 'cathartic' – meaning thereby that it is the equivalent, for the analyst as well as for the analysand, not of purification but of rebirth with and against abjection ...

Something to be Scared of

> A regal soul, inadvertently surrendering to the crab of lust, the octopus of weak mindedness, the shark of individual abjection, the boa of absent morality, and the monstrous snail of idiocracy!
>
> Lautréamont, *Les Chants de Maldoror*

The object as trimming of anguish

When psychoanalysts speak of an object they speak of the object of desire as it is elaborated within the Oedipian triangle. According to that trope, the father is the mainstay of the law and the mother the prototype of the object. Toward the mother there is convergence not only of survival needs but of the first mimetic yearnings. She is the other subject, an object that guarantees my being as subject. The mother is my first object – both desiring and signifiable.

No sooner sketched out, such a thesis is exploded by its contradictions and flimsiness.

Do we not find, *sooner* (chronologically and logically speaking), if not objects at least *pre*-objects, poles of attraction of a demand for air, food, and motion? Do we not also find, in the very process that constitutes the mother as other, a series of semi-objects that stake out the transition from a state of indifferentiation to one of discretion (subject/object) – semi-objects that are called precisely 'transitional' by Winnicott? Finally, do we not find a whole gradation within modalities of separation: a real *deprivation* of the breast, an imaginary *frustration* of the gift as maternal relation, and, to conclude, a symbolic *castration* inscribed in the Oedipus complex; a gradation constituting, in Lacan's brilliant formulation, the object relation insofar as it is always 'a means of masking, of parrying the fundamental fund of anguish' (Seminar of 1956–1957)?

The matter of the object sets in motion, or implicates, the entire Freudian structure. *Narcissism* – beginning with what, or when, does it allow itself to be exceeded by sexual drive, which is drive toward the other? *Repression* – what type of repression yields symbolization, hence a signifiable object, and what other type, on the contrary, blocks the way toward symbolization and topples drive into the lack-of-object of asymbolia or the auto-object of somatization? The connection between the *unconscious and language* – what is the share of language learning or language activity in the constitution of object relation and its transformations?

It is with respect to the phobia of Little Hans that Freud tackles in the clearest fashion the matter of the relation to the object, which is crucial for the constitution of the subject. From the start, fear and object are linked. Can that be by accident? The unending and uncertain identifications of *hysterics* did surely not throw light on Freud's work on this topic. This *obsessional* rumination – which ceaselessly elaborates signs so as better to protect, within the family vault, a sacred object that is missing – was probably of greater avail to him in dealing with the question. But why is it phobia that best allows one to tackle the matter of relation to the object? Why fear *and* object?

Confronted with states of distress that are evoked for us by the child who makes himself heard but is incapable of making himself understood, we, adults, use the word 'fear'. Birth trauma, according to Otto Rank, or the upsetting of the balance of drive integration elaborated by the maternal receptacle (Wilfred R. Bion) in the course of uterine life and by 'good mothering', are theoretical artifacts: they rationalize a 'zero state' of the subject, and also probably a zero state of theory as confronted with what the child has not uttered. *Fear*, therefore, in a first sense, could be the *upsetting* of a bio-drive balance. The constitution of object relation might then be a reiteration of fear, alternating with optimal but precarious states of balance. Fear and object proceed together until the one represses the other. But in which one of us is that fully successful? . . .

Suggested further reading

Grosz, E A (1986), 'Language and the Limits of the Body: Kristeva and Abjection', in Grosz, E A, Threadgold, T, Kelly, D, Cholodenko, A and Colless, E (1986), *Futur*fall. Excursions into Post-Modernity.* Sydney: Power Institute of Fine Arts, University of Sydney
Kristeva, J (ed. Moi, T) (1986), *The Kristeva Reader.* Oxford: Blackwell
Phoca, S and Wright, R (1999), *Introducing Postfeminism.* Duxford: Icon
Smith, A-M (1998), *Julia Kristeva: Speaking the Unspeakable.* London: Pluto Press

Irigaray (b. 1930)

Luce Irigaray was born in Belgium, and trained as a Lacanian psychoanalyst. She continues to practise as an analyst; as a teacher and writer one of her most important contributions has been in opening the way to a critical awareness of the inherent masculine bias in language, for example in the use of the pronoun 'he'. Nothing is gender-neutral; 'neutral' is masculine. For Irigaray, Freudian and Lacanian psychoanalysis has concentrated on men's problems – for example, the Oedipal struggle to leave mother and identify with father – at the expense of mothers and daughters and an understanding of what establishing female identity might mean.

One metaphor she finds for this is the *speculum*. Seeing is privileged in Western discourse, she argues; seeing is the guarantee of Being, what is not seen can easily therefore not exist (out of sight, out of mind). Lacan's mirror is an image of this Western bias towards visible representation, which privileges the male: a flat mirror can only show woman's sexual organs as a hole, a lack. The concave speculum is a different sort of mirror: it allows the inside, the 'cavities' of a woman's body to be seen (Irigaray, 1985a: 89).

For Irigaray psychoanalysis remains, however, an important tool for deconstructing patriarchy, and she makes particular use of the Lacanian notions of 'Real', 'Symbolic' and 'Imaginary'. The Real for Irigaray is the place of mother and death, in patriarchy. The Symbolic is the law founded in the Name of the Father. The Imaginary is the effect of the Symbolic in consciousness and imagination; it is the Imaginary of men. As Lechte comments, anything outside the Symbolic order has to be translated into its terms, unless it is so radically different, like death and the feminine, that no symbolic means are available, and it cannot be communicated. This is especially evident in the field of sexuality, which, as Freud maintained, affects everything. For Irigaray science and language are gendered as male, and this of course affects the institutions of therapy. Any attempt to be 'egalitarian' will always present women as lacking. To speak, women must speak like men. To know their sexuality they must compare it with men's. Women are in society but not of society (Lechte, 1994: 161–2).

Women cannot objectify men in the way men can women. The son's first lesson is to objectify mother, to separate from her; the daughter cannot achieve this separation, and is thus, in Irigaray's clinical experience, more prone to psychosis and melancholia. Delirium might thus be a basis for a feminine language, for the project of working out a symbolic means equivalent to the mother–daughter relationship, to overcome the phenomenon of woman unsymbolised as woman (Lechte, 1994: 163).

Irigaray puts forward a radical repudiation of the Enlightenment ideal of universal reason, or, we might say, the modernist equation between masculinity and rational discourse, of which the female is outside, or a mere residue. Feminine is always deficiency and lack. There is no common genealogy (Kearney and Rainwater, 1996: 411) for sexual identity, except a phallocentric one. Women are thus defective males; male identity is based on fear of the female. It is for this reason that a separatist view of gender is needed.

In her book *Speculum of the Other Woman* (1985a), Irigaray gives a re-reading of the story of the cave from Plato's *Republic*. In Plato, a cave-dweller moves into the light of the outside world having, until this point, lived in the belief that the shadows projected by a fire onto the cave wall are all the reality there is. Plato uses this to illustrate his central theme that the reality we perceive is only a shadow of the world of *Idea* that is reality's template. Irigaray sees the cave as mother (womb) and the outside world as father (*Idea*); thus the prisoner in the cave is moving away from mother and her role in reproduction. She in other words deconstructs it as a founding myth of patriarchy, pointing out how Plato's ideal Republic was far from egalitarian, despite appearances – it was 'monologic' and 'monosexual', and in it women had civic functions only in so far as they came to be like men, and renounced what was specific to them as women (see Sarup, 1993: 120).

Greek myth interests both Irigaray and Cixous (see p. 135 *et seq*, below). The myth of Athena, daughter of Zeus, justifies matricide by saying 'a woman made us do it'; Athena advises Apollo to install patriarchy, by saying Orestes's murder of his mother is legitimate. For Irigaray a 'jamming the theoretical machinery' is necessary, to be undertaken by acts of interpretation and deconstruction. In this and in her anti-Hegelianism (there is no higher synthesis), her thinking synchronises with that of Derrida and Deleuze.

Irigaray recognises that the construction of an identity necessitates the construction of a language of one's own; hence her proclaiming the need for an 'écriture féminine', which she practises herself in her own very different writing styles. This is a way of subverting the male hegemony of the imagination which silences women. The masculine bias of language makes it impossible for women to construct a distinctive identity (Matthews, 1996: 189), and this is something Irigaray feels she has seen most vividly in her female psychotic patients.

If her aim is to construct feminine forms of symbolisation and language coming out of female experience, the practice of psychoanalysis can reinforce patriarchal values, which, if not neutral, are sold as 'transparently natural' (Kearney and Rainwater, 1996: 411). So if one does acknowledge that there are two sexes, what difference does it make to one's practice, as a man or a woman? If we accept Irigaray's argument that phallocentricism is universalised in the history of psychoanalysis, that this is the interpretative lens through which we regard 'healthy development', then we are responsible for perpetuating two of its aspects:

One: not acknowledging the mother, unless it is to incorporate her, as a support for the 'male imaginary' (Sarup, 1993: 118);

Two: perpetuating dominant cultural fantasies. As therapists we are maintaining a culture in which men speak to men, that is 'monologic' and 'monosexual'. How can the 'I' be an 'I' in its own right, and not just in relation to or as a derivative of men?

Since this pervades our culture it pervades *all* therapeutic orientations, not just psychoanalysis. Women's position in the (patriarchal) symbolic order must, furthermore, affect all discourse. How might this also affect men talking to and about men, as well as women talking to and about women, and men talking to and about women, and vice versa?

From Irigaray (1981), 'This Sex Which Is Not One', in Marks and de Courtivron (1981), *New French Feminisms*, pp. 99–105

Female sexuality has always been conceptualized on the basis of masculine parameters. Thus the opposition between 'masculine' clitoral activity and 'feminine' vaginal passivity, an opposition which Freud – and many others – saw as stages, or alternatives, in the development of a sexually 'normal' woman, seems rather too clearly required by the practice of male' sexuality. For the clitoris is conceived as a little penis pleasant to masturbate so long as castration anxiety does not exist (for the boy child), and the vagina is valued for the 'lodging' it offers the male organ when the forbidden hand has to find a replacement for pleasure-giving.

In these terms, woman's erogenous zones never amount to anything but a clitoris-sex that is not comparable to the noble phallic organ, or a hole-envelope that serves to sheathe and massage the penis in intercourse: a non-sex, or a masculine organ turned back upon itself, self-embracing.

About woman and her pleasure, this view of the sexual relation has nothing to say. Her lot is that of 'lack', 'atrophy' (of the sexual organ), and 'penis envy', the penis being the only sexual organ of recognized value. Thus she attempts by every means available to appropriate that organ for herself: through her somewhat servile love of the father–husband capable of giving her one, through her desire for a child–penis, preferably a boy, through access to the cultural values still reserved by right to males alone and therefore always masculine, and so on. Woman lives her own desire only as the expectation that she may at last come to possess an equivalent of the male organ.

Yet all this appears quite foreign to her own pleasure, unless it remains within the dominant phallic economy. Thus, for example, woman's auto-eroticism is very different from man's. In order to touch himself, man needs an instrument: his hand, a woman's body, language . . . And this self-caressing requires at least minimum of activity. As for woman, she touches herself in and of herself without any need for mediation, and before there is any way to distinguish activity from passivity. Woman 'touches herself' all the time, and moreover no one can forbid her to do so, for her genitals are formed of two lips in continuous contact. Thus, within herself, she is already two – but not divisible into one(s) – that caress each other.

This autoeroticism is disrupted by a violent break-in: the brutal separation of the two lips by a violating penis, an intrusion that distracts and deflects the woman from this 'self-caressing' she needs if she is not to incur the disappearance of her own pleasure in sexual relations. If the vagina is to serve also, but not only, to take over for the little boy's hand in order to assure an articulation between autoeroticism and heteroeroticism in intercourse (the encounter with the totally other always signifying death), how, in the classic representation of sexuality, can the perpetuation of autoeroticism for woman be managed? Will woman not be left with the impossible alternative between a defensive virginity, fiercely turned in upon itself, and a body open to penetration that no longer knows, in this 'hole' that constitutes its sex, the pleasure of its own touch? The more or less exclusive – and highly anxious – attention paid to erection in Western sexuality proves to what extent the imaginary that governs it is foreign to the feminine. For the most part, this sexuality offers nothing but imperatives dictated by male rivalry: the 'strongest' being the one who has the best 'hard-on', the longest, the biggest, the stiffest penis, or even the one who, 'pees the farthest' (as in little boys' contests). Or else one finds imperatives dictated by the enactment of sado-masochistic fantasies, these in turn governed by man's relation to his mother: the desire to force entry, to penetrate, to appropriate for himself the mystery of this womb where he has been conceived, the secret of his begetting, of his 'origin'. Desire/need, also to make blood flow again in order to revive a very old relationship – intrauterine, to be sure, but also prehistoric – to the maternal.

Woman, in this sexual imaginary, is only a more or less obliging prop for the enactment of man's fantasies. That she may find pleasure there in that role, by proxy, is possible, even certain. But such pleasure is above all a masochistic prostitution of her body to a desire that is not her own, and it leaves her in a familiar state of dependency upon man. Not knowing what she wants, ready for anything, even asking for more, so long as he will 'take' her as his 'object' when he seeks his own pleasure. Thus she will not say what she herself wants; moreover, she does not know, or no longer knows, what she wants. As Freud admits, the beginnings of the sexual life of a girl child are so 'obscure', so 'faded with time', that one would have to dig down very deep indeed to discover beneath the traces of this civilization, of this history, the vestiges of a more archaic civilization that might give some clue to woman's sexuality. That extremely ancient civilization would undoubtedly have a different alphabet, a different language . . . Woman's desire would not be expected to speak the same language as man's; woman's desire has doubtless been submerged by the logic that has dominated the West since the time of the Greeks.

Within this logic, the predominance of the visual, and of the discrimination and individualization of form, is particularly foreign to female eroticism. Woman takes pleasure more from touching than from looking, and her entry into a dominant scopic economy signifies again, her consignment to passivity: she is to be the beautiful object of contemplation. While her body finds itself thus eroticized, and called to a double movement of exhibition and of chaste retreat in order to stimulate the drives of the 'subject', her sexual organ represents the horror of nothing to see. A defect in this systematics of representation and desire. A 'hole' in its scoptophilic lens. It is already evident in Greek statuary that this nothing-to-see has to be excluded, rejected, from such a scene of representation. Woman's genitals are simply absent, masked, sewn back up inside their 'crack'.

This organ which has nothing to show for itself also lacks a form of its own. And if woman takes pleasure precisely from this incompleteness of form which allows her organ to touch itself over and over again, indefinitely, by itself, that pleasure is denied by a civilization that privileges phallomorphism. The value granted to the only definable form excludes the one that is in play in female autoeroticism. The one of form, of the individual, of the (male) sexual organ, of the proper name, of the proper meaning . . . supplants, while separating and dividing, that contact of at least two (lips) which keeps woman in touch with herself, but without any possibility of distinguishing what is touching from what is touched.

Whence the mystery that woman represents in a culture claiming to count everything, to number everything by units, to inventory everything as individualities. She is neither one nor two. Rigorously speaking, she cannot be identified either as one person, or as two. She resists all adequate definition. Further, she, has no 'proper' name. And her sexual organ, which is not one organ, is counted as none. The negative, the underside, the reverse of the only visible and morphologically designatable organ (even if the passage from erection to detumescence does pose some problems): the penis.

But the 'thickness' of that 'form', the layering of its volume, its expansions and contractions and even the spacing of the moments in which it produces itself as form – all this the feminine keeps secret. Without knowing it. And if woman is asked to sustain, to revive, man's desire, the request neglects to spell out what it implies as to the value of her own desire. A desire of which she is not aware, moreover, at least not explicitly. But one whose force and continuity are capable of nurturing repeatedly and at length all the masquerades of 'femininity' that are expected of her.

It is true that she still has the child, in relation to whom her appetite for touch, for contact, has free rein, unless it is already lost, alienated by the taboo against touching of a highly obsessive civilization. Otherwise her pleasure will find, in the child, compensations for and diversions from the frustrations that she too often encounters in sexual relations *per se*. Thus maternity fills the gaps in a repressed female sexuality. Perhaps man and woman no longer caress each other except through that mediation between them that the child – preferably a boy – represents? Man, identified with his son, rediscovers the pleasure of maternal fondling; woman touches herself again by caressing that part of her body: her baby–penis–clitoris.

What this entails for the amorous trio is well known. But the Oedipal interdiction seems to be a somewhat categorical and factitious law – although it does provide the means for perpetuating the authoritarian discourse of fathers – when it is promulgated in a culture in which sexual relations are impracticable because man's desire and woman's are strangers to each other. And in which the two desires have to try to meet through indirect means, whether the archaic one of a sense-relation to the mother's body, or the present one of active or passive extension of the law of the father. These are regressive emotional behaviors, exchanges of words too detached from the sexual arena not to constitute an exile with respect to it: 'mother' and 'father' dominate the interactions of the couple, but as social roles. The division of labor prevents them from making love. They produce or reproduce. Without quite knowing how to use their leisure. Such little as they have, such little indeed as they wish to have. For what are they to do with leisure? What substitute for amorous resource are they to invent? Still . . .

Perhaps it is time to return to that repressed entity, the female imaginary. So woman does not have a sex organ? She has at least two of them, but they are not identifiable as ones. Indeed, she has many more. Her sexuality, always at least double, goes even further: it is plural. Is this the way culture is seeking to characterize itself now? Is this the way texts write themselves/ are written now? Without quite knowing what censorship they are evading? Indeed, woman's pleasure does not have to choose between clitoral activity and vaginal passivity, for example. The pleasure of the vaginal caress does not have to be substituted for that of the clitoral caress. They each contribute, irreplaceably, to woman's pleasure. Among other caresses . . . Fondling the breasts, touching the vulva, spreading the lips, stroking the posterior wall of the vagina, brushing against the mouth of the uterus, and so on. To evoke only a few of the most specifically female pleasures. Pleasures which are somewhat misunderstood in sexual difference as it is imagined – or not imagined, the other sex being only the indispensable complement to the only sex.

But woman has sex organs more or less everywhere. She finds pleasure almost anywhere. Even if we refrain from invoking the hystericization of her entire body, the geography of her pleasure is far more diversified, more multiple in its differences, more complex, more subtle, than is commonly imagined – in an imaginary rather too narrowly focused on sameness.

'She' is indefinitely other in herself. This is doubtless why she is said to be whimsical, incomprehensible, agitated, capricious . . . not to mention her language, in which 'she' sets off in all directions leaving 'him' unable to discern the coherence of any meaning. Hers are contradictory words, somewhat mad from the standpoint of reason, inaudible for whoever listens to them with ready-made grids, with a fully elaborated code in hand. For in what she says, too, at least when she dares, woman is constantly touching herself. She steps ever so slightly aside from herself with a murmur, an exclamation, a whisper, a sentence left unfinished . . . When she returns, it is to set off again from elsewhere. From another point of pleasure, or of pain. One would have to listen with another ear, as if hearing an 'other meaning' always in the process of weaving itself, of embracing itself with words, but also of getting rid of words in order not to become fixed, congealed in them. For if 'she' says something, it is not, it is already no longer, identical with what she means. What she says is never identical with anything, moreover; rather, it is contiguous. It touches (upon). And when it strays too far from that proximity, she breaks off and starts over at 'zero': her body-sex.

It is useless, then, to trap women in the exact definition of what they mean, to make them repeat (themselves) so that it will be clear; they are already elsewhere in that discursive machinery where you expected to surprise them. They have returned within themselves. Which must not be understood in the same way as within yourself. They do not have the interiority that you have, the one you perhaps suppose they have. Within themselves means within the intimacy of that silent, multiple, diffuse touch. And if you ask them insistently what they are thinking about, they can only reply: Nothing. Everything. . . .

However, in order for woman to reach the place where she takes pleasure as woman, a long detour by way of the analysis of the various systems of oppression brought to bear upon her is assuredly necessary. And claiming to fall back on the single solution of pleasure risks making her miss the process of going back through a social practice that her enjoyment requires. . . .

How can [woman] this object of transaction [among men] claim a right to pleasure without removing her/itself from established commerce? With respect to other merchandise in the marketplace, how could this commodity maintain a relationship other than one of aggressive jealousy? How could material substance enjoy her/itself without provoking the consumer's anxiety over the disappearance of his nurturing ground? How could that exchange – which can in no way be defined in terms 'proper' to woman's desire – appear as anything but a pure mirage, mere foolishness, all too readily obscured by a more sensible discourse and by a system of apparently more tangible values?

Suggested further reading

Irigaray, L (ed. Whitford, M) (1992), *The Irigaray Reader*. Oxford: Blackwell
—— (1994) *Thinking the Difference*. London: Routledge

Cixous (b. 1937)

Hélène Cixous was closely identified with the group 'Psychanalyse et Politique' ('Psych et Po') in the 1970s, which challenged the structures of patriarchal oppression in psychoanalytic theory. 'Psych et Po' was suspicious that groups describing themselves as feminist were merely reformists seeking to take part in the dominant structures of masculine power. In the later 1970s and the 1980s, particularly through her writing for the theatre, she turned her attention towards liberation as well as gender politics, writing about post-colonial struggles (such as in India and Cambodia). She is against all dualistic thinking, since it is oppositions like Man/Woman, Activity/Passivity, Culture/Nature that continue to keep these structures in place (see the extract below). These oppositions are moreover always hierarchical – there is always a battle, and '"victory" always comes down to the same thing: things get hierarchical'. One category assumes dominance over the other, to the extent that the latter is silenced or made invisible.

Cixous proposes instead multiplicity and openness of meaning; her thought has strong links to Derrida's, to deconstruction and the concept of *différance* (difference and deferral). She is also a profound reader of Nietzsche, an admirer of the (for Cixous, atypically masculine) excesses of his style and thought, and his insistence on the bodily roots of human culture. Her avoidance of oppositions is directed towards a recognition, like Nietzsche's, that the production of meaning is always provisional and in flux, never completed. She is in favour of a celebration of the subjective and corporeal, and of diversity, on both a macro- and a micro-political scale, over cultural homogeneity and uniformity.

She writes in the essay 'Sorties', below (the title could mean 'exits', 'outings', 'departures', 'overflows', 'outbursts', 'launchings'), about women speaking, and emphasises how women's public speech, in contrast to men's, has its roots in song, and is an event of the body, not 'objective' or 'universalised' but an intervention in the present: 'she involves her story in history'. Cixous's image of the 'self-absorbed masculine . . . pocketing itself again' and the woman who 'launches forth . . . (and) seeks to love' might recall Bloom and Molly in Joyce's *Ulysses*, Joyce being another writer Cixous admires and has written about. Hoffmann, Kleist, Poe, all figures from nineteenth-century Romanticism, are others. She also admires Shakespeare, Genet and Bataille; the Brazilian writer Clarice Lispector (see for example Lispector, 1992), introduced her to a liberating excessiveness, an elusive- and allusive-ness, and she felt she had discovered a kindred spirit, a writer of fictions like herself who, in Sarup's phrase, aims 'to reject the constraining masks of social identity in favour of a Heideggerian notion of the multiple and temporal experience of Being' (Sarup, 1993: 114)

Cixous's main strategy is to open up a place for feminine writing. Feminine writing, for Cixous, cannot be defined other than by its closeness to voice. Speech for Cixous is close to song and thus to the archaic, to the unconscious and mythical. Cixous asserts 'the associative logic of music over the linear logic of philosophical and literary discourse; thus speaking is a powerfully transgressive act for women, and writing is a privileged space for transformation' (Sarup, 1993: 112). Speaking, she says, is a way of by-passing the patriarchal order. She opposes, not surprisingly, the Cartesian view that mind and body are separate, siding, rather, with Freud in that respect ('the ego is a bodily ego'). Writing is inevitably something that is made and understood in relation to bodies, and women's relationships to their bodies are deeply culturally inscribed. Writing thus conceptualised leads to an engagement with the unconscious, myth, and dream, and can profoundly shake our illusions of autonomy and conscious control.

Cixous writes of woman's 'gift' as an alternative economy, alternative to the masculine 'exchange' economy which implies the certainty of immediate return. Some of this thinking she draws from the work of Georges Bataille (1897–1962), who was moved less by production and consumption than by art and games. The sun gives without receiving (Bataille, 1991); but for Cixous women are not like the sun (although men might wish they were). Cixous writes that really there is no free gift, but there is a difference in the why and the how of the gift. This other relation to giving consists in 'the values that the gesture of giving affirms, causes to circulate; in the type of profit the giver draws from the gift, and the use to which he or she puts it' (Cixous, 1986: 87). A *sortie* is also an item of expenditure, an *outgoing*; Cixous's ideas on the gift have echoes of the Levinasian choice 'for generosity and communication' (Wild, in Levinas, 1969: 14–15).

Cixous also rejects Freud's and Lacan's views on sexual difference, in order 'to maintain plurality' (Sarup, 1993: 111). Freud too, of course, maintained that we are plural in sexuality, 'polymorphously perverse' (Freud, 1905), and in this respect he could be adduced in support of Cixous's project to expose myths underlying patriarchy, myths which work to lend it an aura of 'naturalness'. Cixous is, for example, like Irigaray, interested in Greek myths that diminish the seriousness of matricide.

If Irigaray is turning the tables, rewriting Freud's phallocentric stories to privilege the vagina, in a reversal, and Kristeva can sometimes seem to catch herself doing this and seek another resolution, by means of the semiotic, Cixous attempts to look at sexual difference by sustaining a notion of bisexuality. This is consistent with her opposition to all forms of dualistic thinking based on oppositions and hierarchies. In order to pursue this she needs to look at how women are located in culture, and at how things are set up, in the dominant order, so that where women are placed is not questioned. Woman is like Sleeping Beauty, the dormant negative subject, until kissed by the man. She is always therefore subordinate to his desire; only his wanting to kiss her will bring her to life. Cixous refers to Hegel's Master and Slave parable, and says women are more caught up in it than men. A subject requires the recognition of an other to differentiate from him- or herself. The problem is that this recognition is experienced as a threat, so it is followed almost immediately by a repression, so that the subject can return 'to the security and certainty of self-knowledge' (Sarup, 1993: 110). Within a patriarchal set-up sexual difference is always caught up in a structure of power where otherness is only tolerated when it is repressed. Hence there is always an inequality of power.

This is the culture in which psychoanalytic writing and practice are located, and within which psychoanalysis and psychotherapy need to be reflective. We would argue that this culture traps men as well as women: if to kiss Sleeping Beauty and to bring her to life is men's desire, men's desire is to have someone who desires men's desire in that way.

Is there sufficient recognition, in psychotherapy, of the conflict inherent in binary oppositions, which Cixous writes about? Is it not inevitable that our relationships with our patients, and their apparently 'natural' relations outside therapy, are based on the dominance of one and repression of the other, with the element of our being locked together in violent conflict repressed? Do psychotherapy trainings teach us convincingly to speak in a way in which the violence we have done to our patients is repressed? Do we then learn suitably to camouflage this violence we have done to our patients over the years, in the name of helping them with their violence? Are we teaching patients not to speak about the violence we are doing to them – and might it be that when they *can* do this, they are ready to leave? Having achieved this, perhaps both therapist and patient may be more able to engage critically with current cultural practices.

It might be argued that humanist therapists are very well placed to take on Cixous's thinking. Humanists tend to be sceptical of dualistic ideas, particularly 'head versus heart', and to be concerned about over-intellectualisation and the dominance of unfeeling, masculinised discourse. However, they often seem simply to swap the terms of the polarity, privileging heart over head. Humanists also typically attempt to establish a relation of equality between therapist and client. Yet this can be done in such a way that violence itself is repressed; saying we are equal can be to enact a denial and set up a form of repression, and of oppression (a repression of the language of oppression).

Cixous raises questions about what we are attuned to in patriarchy. The tune opens up the unconscious, thus the opportunity to speak as a woman. There is no doubt a danger that psychoanalysis will re-convert this into its own discursive language, ensuring the continuation of male culture. If psychoanalysis is subversive, is it subversive to women finding their voice?

In the following extract Cixous starts with the question 'Where is she?', and follows this by writing about the polarities signalled above, organised in hierarchies which privilege the masculine. But she presents this in a non-discursive, poetic way. She links this way of writing with the economy of femininity and, with that, the possibility of love. For a feminist practice of writing cannot be '*theorised*, enclosed, coded, which does not mean it does not exist. But it will always exceed the discourse governing the phallocentric system' . . .

Cixous, 'Sorties', in Cixous and Clément (1986), *The Newly Born Woman*, pp. 66–79

Where is she?
Activity/Passivity
Sun/Moon
Culture/Nature
Day/Night

Father/Mother
Head/Heart

Intelligible/Palpable
Logos/Pathos
Form, convex, step, advance, semen, progress.
Matter, concave, ground – where steps are taken, holding- and dumping-ground.
Man

Woman
　　Always the same metaphor: we follow it, it carries us, beneath all its figures, wherever discourse is organized. If we read or speak, the same thread or double braid is leading us throughout literature, philosophy, criticism, centuries of representation and reflection.
　　Thought has always worked through opposition,
　　Speaking/Writing Parole/Ecriture
　　High/Low
Through dual, hierarchical oppositions. Superior/Inferior. Myths, legends, books. Philosophical systems. Everywhere (where) ordering intervenes, where a law organizes what is thinkable by oppositions (dual, irreconcilable; or sublatable, dialectical). And all these pairs of oppositions are couples. Does that mean something? Is the fact that Logocentrism subjects thought – all concepts, codes and values – to a binary system, related to 'the' couple, man/woman?

Nature/History
Nature/Art
Nature/Mind
Passion/Action

　　Theory of culture, theory of society, symbolic systems in general – art, religion, family, language – it is all developed while bringing the same schemes to light. And the movement whereby each opposition is set up to make sense is the movement through which the couple is destroyed. A universal battlefield. Each time, a war is let loose. Death is always at work.

Father/son Relations of authority, privilege, force.

The Word/Writing Relations: opposition, conflict, sublation, return.

Master/slave Violence. Repression.

We see that 'victory' always comes down to the same thing: things get hierarchical. Organization by hierarchy makes all conceptual organization subject to man. Male privilege, shown in the opposition between activity and passivity, which he uses to sustain himself. Traditionally, the question of sexual difference is treated by coupling it with the opposition: activity/ passivity.

There are repercussions. Consulting the history of philosophy – since philosophical discourse both orders and reproduces all thought – one notices that it is marked by an absolute *constant* which orders values and which is precisely this opposition, activity/passivity. [. . .]

Writing Femininity Transformation

And there is a link between the economy of femininity – the open, extravagant subjectivity, that relationship to the other in which the gift doesn't calculate its influence – and the possibility of love; and a link today between this 'libido of the other' and writing.

At the present time, *defining* a feminine practice of writing is impossible with an impossibility that will continue; for this practice will never be able to be *theorized*, enclosed, coded, which does not mean it does not exist. But it will always exceed the discourse governing the phallocentric system; it takes place and will take place somewhere other than in the territories subordinated to philosophical-theoretical domination. It will not let itself think except through subjects that break automatic functions, border runners never subjugated by any authority. But one can begin to speak. Begin to point out some effects, some elements of unconscious drives, some relations of the feminine Imaginary to the Real, to writing.

What I have to say about it is also only a beginning, because right from the start these features affect me powerfully.

First I sense femininity in writing by: a privilege of voice: writing and voice are entwined and interwoven and writing's continuity/voice's rhythm take each other's breath away through interchanging, make the text gasp or form it out of suspenses and silences, make it lose its voice or rend it with cries.

In a way, feminine writing never stops reverberating from the wrench that the acquisition of speech, speaking out loud, is for her – 'acquisition' that is experienced more as tearing away, dizzying flight and flinging oneself, diving. Listen to woman speak in a gathering (if she is not painfully out of breath): she doesn't 'speak', she throws her trembling body into the air, she lets herself go, she flies, she goes completely into her voice, she vitally defends the 'logic' of her discourse with her body; her flesh speaks true. She exposes herself. Really she makes what she thinks materialize carnally, she conveys meaning with her body. *She inscribes* what she is saying because she does not deny unconscious drives the unmanageable part they play in speech.

Her discourse, even when 'theoretical' or political, is never simple or linear or 'objectivized', universalized; she involves her story in history.

Every woman has known the torture of beginning to speak aloud, heart beating as if to break, occasionally falling into loss of language, ground and language slipping out from under her, because for woman speaking – even just opening her mouth – in public is something rash, a transgression.

A double anguish, for even if she transgresses, her word almost always falls on the deaf, masculine ear, which can only hear language that speaks in the masculine.

We are not culturally accustomed to speaking, throwing signs out toward a scene, employing the suitable rhetoric. Also, it is not where we find our pleasure: indeed, (one pays a certain price for the use of a discourse. The logic of communication requires an economy both of signs – of signifiers – and of subjectivity. The orator is asked to unwind a thin thread, dry and taut. We like uneasiness, questioning. There is waste in what we say. We need that waste. To write is always to make allowances for superabundance and uselessness while slashing the exchange value that keeps the spoken word on its track. That is why writing is good, letting the tongue try itself out – as one attempts a caress, taking the time a phrase or a thought needs to make oneself loved, to make oneself reverberate.

It is in writing, from woman and toward woman, and in accepting the challenge of the discourse controlled by the phallus, that woman will affirm woman somewhere other than in silence, the place reserved for her in and through the Symbolic. May she get out of booby-trapped silence! And not have the margin or the harem foisted on her as her domain!

In feminine speech, as in writing, there never stops reverberating something that, having once passed through us, having imperceptibly and deeply touched us, still has the power to affect us – song, the first music of the voice of love, which every woman keeps alive.

The Voice sings from a time before law, before the Symbolic took one's breath away and reappropriated it into language under its authority of separation. The deepest, the oldest, the loveliest Visitation. Within each woman the first, nameless love is singing.

In woman there is always, more or less, something of 'the mother' repairing and feeding, resisting separation, a force that does not let itself be cut off but that runs codes ragged. The relationship to childhood (the child she was, she is, she acts and makes and starts anew, and unties at the place where, as a same she even others herself), is no more cut off than is the relationship to the 'mother', *as it consists of* delights and violences. Text, my body: traversed by lilting flows; listen to me, it is not a captivating, clinging 'mother'; it is the equivoice that, touching you, affects you, pushes you away from your breast to come to language, that summons *your* strength; it is the rhyth-me that laughs you; the one intimately addressed who makes all metaphors, all body(?) – bodies(?) – possible and desirable, who is no more describable than god, soul, or the Other; the part of you that puts space between yourself and pushes you to inscribe your woman's style in language. Voice: milk that could go on forever. Found again. The lost mother/bitter-lost. Eternity: is voice mixed with milk.

Not the origin: she doesn't go back there. A boy's journey is the return to the native land, the *Heimweh* Freud speaks of, the nostalgia that makes man a being who tends to come back to the point of departure to appropriate it for himself and to die there. A girl's journey is farther – to the unknown, to invent.

How come this privileged relationship with voice? Because no woman piles up as many defences against instinctual drives as a man does. You don't prop things up, you don't brick things up the way he does, you don't with-draw from pleasure so 'prudently'. Even if phallic mystification has contaminated good relations in general, woman is never far from the 'mother' (I do not mean the role but the 'mother' as no-name and as source of goods). There is always at least a little good mother milk left in her. She writes with white ink.

Voice! That, too, is launching forth and effusion without return. Exclamation, cry, breathlessness, yell, cough, vomit, music. Voice leaves. Voice loses. She leaves. She loses. And that is how she writes, as one throws a voice – forward, into the void. She goes away, she goes forward, doesn't turn back to look at her tracks. Pays no attention to herself. Running break-neck. Contrary to the self-absorbed, masculine narcissism, making sure of its image, of being seen, of seeing itself, of assembling its glories, of pocketing itself again. The reductive look, the always divided look returning, the mirror economy; he needs to love himself. But she launches forth: she seeks to love. Moreover, this is what Valéry sensed, marking his Young Fate in search of herself with ambiguity, masculine in her jealousy of herself: 'seeing herself see herself', the motto of all phallocentric speculation/specularization, the motto of every Teste; and feminine in the frantic descent deeper deeper to where a voice that doesn't know itself is lost in the sea's churning.

Suggested further reading

Cixous, H (1976), 'The Laugh of the Medusa', *Signs*, 1: 875–99
—— (1994), (ed. Sellers, S) *The Hélène Cixous Reader*. London: Routledge
Shiach, N (1991), *Hélène Cixous: A Politics of Writing*. London: Routledge

Deleuze (1925–1995) and Guattari (1930-1992)

> The question we must ask is whether the things produced by desire – a dream, an act of love, a realised Utopia – will ever achieve the same value on the social plane as the things produced commercially, such as cars or cooking fat?
>
> (Guattari, 1984: 255)

Gilles Deleuze and Félix Guattari's main challenge consists in their notion of the 'anti-Oedipus', and the book of that name first published in 1972. In it they argued their radical opposition to the Freudian and Lacanian emphasis on the Oedipus complex and the signifier (Lacan), which in their view restricted 'the plural libido of madness' within a narrow family model. The book became the best-selling manifesto for an anti-psychiatry 'à la française' (Roudinesco and Plon, 1997: 412). Deleuze and Guattari inveighed against the whole Freudian family romance, and set out a new conceptualisation of the polyvalence of human desire: a 'material psychiatry' based on the liberation of the flow of desire, which they termed 'schizo-analysis'. Their thinking has echoes of Marcuse's influential, libertarian post-Marxism of the 1950s (Marcuse, 1955).

The philosopher Deleuze and the psychoanalyst Guattari were both steeped in the Lacanian tradition – Guattari had been analysed by Lacan – and both were committed leftists, Guattari being particularly involved as a militant anti-colonialist during the Algerian war of independence, and later in the ecological movement. Deleuze's writing moved from the history of philosophy to a very individual style of literary criticism; he has been described as an outsider on the French philosophical scene, although like Derrida and Foucault he has been enthusiastically taken up in English- speaking academia (Lechte, 1994: 101). Both authors drew on the libertarian spirit that had filled Lacan's teaching, but they were critical of the dogmatism that they saw taking it over as the 1970s advanced.

Their critique of psychoanalysis in general was that it had become a form of social control: it repressed desire through the imposition of Lack, Culture and Law on the unconscious (Sarup, 1993: 94). This view is directly anti-Lacanian; they were against what they saw as the psychoanalytic priesthood, which offered only a mythical Oedipal explanation of desire. Desire is determined for Lacan by lack, guilt and fear of castration; for Deleuze and Guattari, on the contrary, desire is produced directly from the unconscious, which is thus inherently revolutionary in character; it is active revolutionary desire which 'is always mingled with an opposing, reactive desire for repression', and invites repression because of its revolutionary potential. Furthermore, desire cannot be confined to the family unit; it is 'a productive feature of political economy'. Taking up the 1960s slogan 'the personal is political', they saw libido and the social as inseparable and intersecting. Following Wilhelm Reich (1897–1957; see *The Mass Psychology of Fascism*, 1933, discussed in Rycroft, 1971), they believed the unconscious is a disruptive, political force.

They affirm fluidity and spontaneity, against patriarchal authority and its familial definitions of desire; turning Lacan on his head, they affirm the Imaginary against the Symbolic, which they characterise as tyrannical and dictatorial. There is in the Imaginary and the revolutionary unconscious no distinction between word and deed. Hence Lacan's Real is not at all beyond reach: it is what desire realises. Deleuze and Guattari come up with a formulation that combines Marxist and Freudian/Lacanian thought with an ironic nod in the direction of Descartes: we are 'desiring machines'. What 'desiring machines' produce is an effect: *délire*, delirium. Capitalism requires 'desiring machines who acquiesce to their own slavery' (Kearney and Rainwater, 1996: 403).

The terms 'schizophrenia' and 'paranoia' are the two polar types of desire which Deleuze and Guattari associate respectively with the revolutionary and the fascist. The schizophrenic becomes the model revolutionary because he or she has not been fully Oedipalised (this chimes with Laing and anti-psychiatry in the UK). Sarup paraphrases: 'it is not enough to fight fascism on the streets; we must also fight it in our own heads, setting our revolutionary schizophrenia against our own fascist paranoia' (Sarup, 1993: 93). In Deleuze and Guattari's 'schizoanalysis' children, the primitive and the mad thus occupy a privileged place, in that they are in touch with the power of the pre-Symbolic. Paranoic investment on the other hand has its own rewards under capitalism, through the seduction of power, status and money (which leads to the repression of non-conforming desire).

Real, productive *délire* is thus schizophrenia, based on flight, whereas reactionary desire is based on the authoritarian structure of the hierarchical state, which is echoed in the reductive theory of the Oedipus complex. Productive desire is akin to the Nietzschian will to power (Sarup, 1993: 97), and Deleuze and Guattari can be seen as ultra-Nietzschians, raising Nietzschian yes-saying 'to the *n*th degree' (Lechte, 1994: 104). They espouse the principle of horizontality inspired by Nietzsche: desire is not defined vertically and Oedipally, in terms of a hierarchy and a lack (negatively), but horizontally, in relation to the society (positively).

Deleuze and Guattari see Freudian/Lacanian psychoanalysis as an 'interpreting machine', with interpretation as impoverishment. Followers of Marx and Freud, they claim, often interpret others' lives impoverishingly by always returning to a master-code. Deleuze and Guattari are not attacking interpretation *per se*, so long as it is 'immanent' rather than 'transcendent'. In other words there must be respect for the other's internal norms, values and complexities, rather than deferral to an external code or value system as the final arbiter. Thus we would argue, following their thinking, that counselling and psychotherapeutic theories may be of interest in terms of their *implications* for the client/patient. If they are to be studied with a view to *application*, then this will lead to transcending the individual, that is, deadening individuality in the name of helping. All this could be said to be an argument for post-phenomenology: do all you can not to reduce complexity.

Deleuze and Guattari raise further fundamental questions. To what extent is our role to encourage our patients in their ability to seduce and be seduced by power, status and money, and to repress non-conforming desire? This is not just a question of opening up their potential for revolutionary desire – what of the therapist's own? To what extent should we blank-screen our own desire? Even if we do, how far might we recognise our desire for power, status and money, in our desire to be therapists? Desire is both in our patients and in ourselves. Where does this leave the notion of having 'no desire' (Bion, 1967): does not 'no desire' equal a desire for capitalism to go on working? There is an argument (see Irigaray, above) that to say one is neutral in terms of sexuality is to condone the patriarchal; similarly to claim to be value-free is to make a political choice for capitalism.

An example: What does one say to a patient whose desire is to go on being manipulated or exploited by their parents or partner – should we say 'carry on'? In not doing this, the therapist is making a political choice. As therapists we are all the time translating or mediating between the patient and the culture we are in.

At the same time Deleuze and Guattari can remind us that therapy is also marginal and subversive – that it can be something to do with revolutionary desire. Or can this, too, be professionalised? In therapy, perhaps, we can at least help our patients be less afraid of becoming mad. In the passage that follows, Deleuze and Guattari critique a definition of schizophrenia as a problem related to ego and body-image. Such thoughts are rehearsed elsewhere in their work too, particularly in *A Thousand Plateaux* (Deleuze and Guattari, 1987), where the idea of the 'body without organs', a phrase borrowed from Antonin Artaud, is developed. This is not the organic, Oedipal or hysterical body, with its tell-tale organs, but a body like the social or political body, always in the process of formation and deformation, like desire itself (Lechte, 1994: 104). It exists in a mobile, expansive and horizontal relationship to the collectivity ('rhizomatic', to use another of the authors' terms), rather than in a vertical and hierarchical one to the father and the law.

From Deleuze and Guattari (1984), *Anti-Oedipus: Capitalism and Schizophrenia*, pp. 22–28 and 34–35

A Materialist Psychiatry

. . . A truly materialist psychiatry can be defined . . . by the twofold task it sets itself: introducing desire into the mechanism, and introducing production into desire.

There is not very great difference between false materialism and typical forms of idealism. The theory of schizophrenia is formulated in terms of three concepts that constitute its trinary schema: dissociation (Kraepelin), autism (Bleuler), and space–time or being-in-the-world (Binswanger). The first of these is an explanatory concept that supposedly locates the specific dysfunction or primary deficiency. The second is an ideational concept indicating the specific nature of the effect of the disorder: the delirium itself or the complete withdrawal from the outside world, 'the detachment from reality, accompanied by a relative or an absolute predominance of [the schizophrenic's] inner life'.

The third concept is a descriptive one, discovering or rediscovering the delirious person in his own specific world. What is common to these three concepts is the fact that they all relate the problem of schizophrenia to the ego through the intermediary of the 'body image' – the final avatar of the soul, a vague conjoining of the requirements of spiritualism and positivism.

The ego, however, is like daddy–mommy: the schizo has long since ceased to believe in it. He is somewhere else, beyond or behind or below these problems, rather than immersed in them. And wherever he is, there are problems, insurmountable sufferings, unbearable needs. But why try to bring him back to what he has escaped from, why set him back down amid problems that are no longer problems to him, why mock his truth by believing that we have paid it its due by merely figuratively taking our hats off to it? There are those who will maintain that the schizo is incapable of uttering the word *I*, and that we must restore his ability to pronounce this hallowed word. All of which the schizo sums up by saying: they're fucking me over again. 'I won't say *I* any more, I'll never utter the word again; it's just too damn stupid. Every time I hear it, I'll use the third person instead, if I happen to remember to. If it amuses them. And it won't make one bit of a difference.' And if he does chance to utter the word *I* again, that won't make any difference either. He is too far removed from these problems, too far past them.

Even Freud never went beyond this narrow and limited conception of the ego. And what prevented him from doing so was his own tripartite formula – the Oedipal, neurotic one: daddy–mommy–me. We may well ponder the possibility that the analytic imperialism of the Oedipus complex led Freud to rediscover, and to lend all the weight of his authority to, the unfortunate misapplication of the concept of autism to schizophrenia. For we must not delude ourselves: Freud doesn't like schizophrenics. He doesn't like their resistance to being oedipalized, and tends to treat them more or less as animals. They mistake words for things, he says. They are apathetic, narcissistic, cut off from reality, incapable of achieving transference; they resemble philosophers – 'an undesirable resemblance'.

The question as to how to deal analytically with the relationship between drives (*pulsions*) and symptoms, between the symbol and what is symbolized, has arisen again and again. Is this relationship to be considered *causal*? Or is it a relationship of *comprehension*? A mode of *expression*? The question, however, has been posed too theoretically. The fact is, from the moment that we are placed within the framework of Oedipus – from the moment that we are measured in terms of Oedipus – the cards are stacked against us, and the only real relationship, that of production, has been done away with. The great discovery of psychoanalysis was that of the production of desire, of the productions of the unconscious. But once Oedipus entered the picture, this discovery was soon buried beneath a new brand of idealism: a classical theater was substituted for the unconscious as a factory; representation was substituted for the units of production of the unconscious; and an unconscious that was capable of nothing but expressing itself – in myth, tragedy, dreams – was substituted for the productive unconscious.

Every time that the problem of schizophrenia is explained in terms of the ego, all we can do is 'sample' a supposed essence or a presumed specific nature of the schizo, regardless of whether we do so with love and pity or disgustedly spit out the mouthful we have tasted. We have 'sampled' him once as a dissociated ego, another time as an ego cut off from the world, and yet again – most temptingly – as an ego that had not ceased to be, who was there in the most specific way, but in his very own world, though he might reveal himself to a clever psychiatrist, a sympathetic superobserver – in short, a phenomenologist. Let us remember once again one of Marx's caveats: we cannot tell from the mere taste of wheat who grew it; the product gives us no hint as to the system and the relations of the production. The product appears to be all the more specific, incredibly specific and readily describable, the more closely the theoretician relates it to *ideal forms of causation, comprehension, or expression*, rather than to *the real process of production on which it depends*. The schizophrenic appears all the more specific and recognizable as a distinct personality if the process is halted, or if it is made an end and a goal in itself, or if it is allowed to go on and on endlessly in a void . . . But the moment that one describes, on the contrary, the material process of production, the specificity of the product tends to evaporate, while at the same time the possibility of another outcome, another end result of the process appears. Before being a mental state of the schizophrenic who has made himself into an artificial person through autism, schizophrenia is the process of the production of desire and desiring-machines. How does one get from one to the other, and is this transition inevitable? This remains the crucial question. Karl Jaspers has given us precious insights, on this point as on so many others, because his 'idealism' was remarkably atypical. Contrasting the concept of process with those of reaction formation or development of the personality, he views process as a rupture or intrusion, having nothing to do with an imaginary relationship with the ego; rather, it is a relationship with the 'demoniacal' in nature. The one thing Jaspers failed to do was to view process as material economic reality, as the process of production wherein Nature = Industry, Nature = History.

To a certain degree, the traditional logic of desire is all wrong from the very outset: from the very first step that the Platonic logic of desire forces us to take, making us choose between *production* and *acquisition*. From the moment that we place desire on the side of acquisition, we make desire an idealistic (dialectical, nihilistic) conception, which causes us to look upon it as primarily a lack: a lack of an object, a lack of the real object . . .

In point of fact, if desire is the lack of the real object, its very nature as a real entity depends upon an 'essence of lack' that produces the fantasized object. Desire thus conceived of as production, though merely the production of fantasies, has been explained perfectly by psychoanalysis. On the very lowest level of interpretation, this means that the real object that desire lacks is related to an extrinsic natural or social production, whereas desire intrinsically produces an imaginary object that functions as a double of reality, as though there were a 'dreamed-of object behind every real object', or a mental production behind all real productions. This conception does not necessarily compel psychoanalysis to engage in a study of gadgets and markets, in the form of an utterly dreary and dull psychoanalysis of the object: psychoanalytic studies of packages of noodles, cars, or 'thingumajigs'. But even when the fantasy is interpreted in depth, not simply as an object, but as a specific machine that brings desire itself front and center, this machine is merely theatrical, and the complementarity of what it sets apart still remains: it is now need that is defined in terms of a relative lack and determined by its own object, whereas desire is regarded as what produces the fantasy and produces itself by detaching itself from the object, though at the same time it intensifies the lack by making it absolute: an 'incurable insufficiency of being', an 'inability-to-be that is life itself'. Hence the presentation of desire as something *supported* by needs, while these needs, and their relationship to the object as something that is lacking or missing, continue to be the basis of the productivity of desire (theory of an underlying support). In a word, when the theoretician reduces desiring-production to a production of fantasy, he is content to exploit to the fullest the idealist principle that defines desire as a lack, rather than a process of production, of 'industrial' production . . .

If desire produces, its product is real. If desire is productive, it can be productive only in the real world and can produce only reality. Desire is the set of *passive syntheses* that engineer partial objects, flows, and bodies, and that function as units of production. The real is the end product, the result of the passive syntheses of desire as autoproduction of the unconscious. Desire does not lack anything; it does not lack its object. It is, rather, the *subject* that is missing in desire, or desire that lacks a fixed subject; there is no fixed subject unless there is repression. Desire and its object are one and the same thing: the machine, as a machine of a machine. Desire is a machine, and the object of desire is another machine connected to it. Hence the product is something removed or deducted from the process of producing: between the act of producing and the product, something becomes detached, thus giving the vagabond, nomad subject a residuum. The objective being of desire is the Real in and of itself. There is no particular form of existence that can be labeled 'psychic reality'. As Marx notes, what exists in fact is not lack, but passion, as a 'natural and sensuous object'. Desire is not bolstered by needs, but rather the contrary; needs are derived from desire: they are counterproducts within the real that desire produces. Lack is a countereffect of desire; it is deposited, distributed, vacuolized within a real that is natural and social. Desire always remains in close touch with the conditions of objective existence; it embraces them and follows them, shifts when they shift, and does not outlive them. For that reason it so often becomes the desire to die, whereas need is a measure of the withdrawal of a subject that has lost its desire at the same time that it loses the passive syntheses of these conditions. This is precisely the significance of need as a search in a void: hunting about, trying to capture or become a parasite of passive syntheses in whatever vague world they may happen to exist. It is no use saying: We are not green plants; we have long since been unable to synthesize chlorophyll, so it's necessary to eat. . . . Desire then becomes this abject fear of lacking something. But it should be noted that this is not a phrase uttered by the poor or the dispossessed. On the contrary, such people know that they are close to grass, almost akin to it, and that desire 'needs' very few things – *not those leftovers that chance to come their way, but the very things that are continually taken from them* – and that what is missing is not things a subject feels the lack of somewhere deep down inside himself, but rather the objectivity of man, the objective being of man, for whom to desire is to produce, to produce within the realm of real.

The real is not impossible; on the contrary, within the real everything is possible, everything becomes possible. Desire does not express a molar lack within the subject; rather, the molar organization deprives desire of its objective being. Revolutionaries, artists, and seers are content to be objective, merely objective: they know that desire clasps life in its powerfully productive embrace, and reproduces it in a way that is all the more intense because it has few needs. And never mind those who believe that this is very easy to say, or that it is the sort of idea to be found in books . . . We know very well where lack – and its subjective correlative – come from. Lack is created, planned, and organized in and through social production. It is counterproduced as a result of the pressure of antiproduction; the latter falls back on (*se rabat sur*) the forces of production and appropriates them. It is never primary; production is never organized on the basis of pre-existing need or lack (*manque*). It is lack that infiltrates itself, creates empty spaces or vacuoles, and propagates itself in accordance with the organization of an already existing organization of production. The deliberate creation of lack as a function of market economy is the art of a dominant class. This involves deliberately organizing wants and needs amid an abundance of production, making all of desire teeter and fall victim to the great fear of not having one's needs satisfied; and making the object dependent upon a real production that is supposedly exterior to desire (the demands of rationality), while at the same time the production of desire is categorized as fantasy and nothing but fantasy . . .

What we are really trying to say is that capitalism, through its process of production, produces an awesome schizophrenic accumulation of energy or charge, against which it brings all its vast powers of repression to bear, but which nonetheless continues to act as capitalism's limit. For capitalism constantly counteracts, constantly inhibits this inherent tendency while at the same time allowing it free rein; it continually seeks to avoid reaching its limit while simultaneously tending toward that limit. Capitalism institutes or restores all sorts of residual and artificial, imaginary, or symbolic territorialities, thereby attempting, as best it can, to recode, to rechannel persons who have been defined in terms of abstract quantities. Everything returns or recurs: States, nations, families. That is what makes the ideology of capitalism 'a motley painting of everything that has ever been believed'. The real is not impossible; it is simply more and more artificial. Marx termed the twofold movement of the tendency to a falling rate of profit, and the increase in the absolute quantity of surplus value, the law of the counteracted tendency. As a corollary of this law, there is the twofold movement of decoding or deterritorializing flows on the one hand, and their violent and artificial reterritorialization on the other. The more the capitalist machine deterritorializes, decoding and axiomatizing flows in order to extract surplus value from them, the more its ancillary apparatuses, such as government bureaucracies and the forces of law and order, do their utmost to reterritorialize, absorbing in the process a larger and larger share of surplus value.

There is no doubt that at this point in history the neurotic, the pervert, and the psychotic cannot be adequately defined in terms of drives, for drives are simply the desiring-machines themselves. They must be defined in terms of modern territorialities. The neurotic is trapped within the residual or artificial territorialities of our society, and reduces all of them to Oedipus as the ultimate territoriality – as reconstructed in the analyst's office and projected upon the full body of the psychoanalyst (yes, my boss is my father, and so is the Chief of State, and so are you, Doctor). The pervert is someone who takes the artifice seriously and plays the game to the hilt: if you want them, you can have them – territorialities infinitely more artificial than the ones that society offers us, totally artificial new families, secret lunar societies. As for the schizo, continually wandering about, migrating here, there, and everywhere as best he can, he plunges further and further into the realm of deterritorialization, reaching the further limits of the decomposition of the socius on the surface of his own body without organs. It may well be that these peregrinations are the schizo's own particular way of rediscovering the earth. The schizophrenic deliberately seeks out the very limit of capitalism: he is its inherent tendency brought to fulfillment, its surplus product, its proletariat, and its exterminating angel. He scrambles all the codes and is the transmitter of the decoded flows of desire. The real continues to flow. In the schizo, the two aspects of *process* are conjoined: the metaphysical process that puts us in contact with the 'demoniacal' element in nature or within the heart of the earth, and the historical process of social production that restores the autonomy of desiring-machines in relation to the deterritorialized social machine. Schizophrenia is desiring-production as the limit of social production. Desiring-production, and its difference in regime as compared to social production, are thus end points, not points of departure. Between the two there is nothing but an ongoing process of becoming that is the becoming of reality. And if materialist psychiatry may be defined as the psychiatry that introduces the concept of production into consideration of the problem of desire, it cannot avoid posing in eschatological terms the problem of the ultimate relationship between the analytic machine, the revolutionary machine, and desiring-machines.

Suggested further reading

Deleuze, G and Guattari, F (1987), *A Thousand Plateaux*, Minneapolis: University of Minnesota Press

Levinas (1905–1995)

> The face is exposed, menaced, as if inviting us to an act of violence. At the same time, the face is what forbids us to kill.
>
> (Levinas, 1985: 86)

For Emmanuel Levinas, every face says 'do not do violence to me, and do not let me die alone'. If, as psychotherapists, we are responsible for our clients' responsibility, for the face of the other, then we will do less violence to others. Importantly, such responsibility does not come out of a consideration of what is good for oneself. It is about what it might really mean to put the other first in a therapeutic situation, as in life.

Levinas was born in Lithuania in 1905 of Jewish parents. He was in the Ukraine during the Russian Revolution, and as a young man he went to France, where he was to spend most of the rest of his life, surviving a prisoner-of-war camp in the Second World War. In 1928–9 he visited Freiburg, where he attended Husserl's lectures. This was his decisive encounter with phenomenology and through this, with Heidegger. Levinas is now seen as largely responsible for taking phenomenology to France. He greatly influenced Sartre, Merleau-Ponty, Lyotard and Derrida, although it was not until he was 55 that he gained serious academic respectability, when he became a full professor. His international reputation was established with the publication of *Totality and Infinity* in 1961. He was also responsible for the academic revival of Talmudic studies in France.

'[T]he face is not "seen" . . . it is uncontainable, it leads you beyond. It is in this that the signification of the face makes it escape from being, as a correlate of a knowing' (Levinas, 1985: 86–7). For Levinas, 'to be, or not to be' is the wrong question. Concern with 'being' leads to a focus on self-knowledge and knowing: the idea that through knowing myself I can come to know the Universe. This is the Western notion of making consciousness transparent: the contents of consciousness becomes identified with knowledge, and from this follows the idea that all can ultimately be known. Whilst the acquisition of such 'knowledge' may well be appropriately catered for through the computer interface, through the face-to-face a middle ground can be sought, as the face-to-face moves us to an infinity, to a recognition of the infinite unknowability of the other, which is beyond the tyranny of egocentricity. The latter leads through appropriation to a violence that leaves as our only choice totalitarianism or anarchy, to totalising moves: egocentricity must claim a central position from which to *know*, a central position that can only be maintained by its claim to be the sole vantage point from which to know.

> Absolute knowledge, such as it has been sought, promised or recommended by philosophy, is a thought of the Equal. Being is embraced in the truth. Even if the truth is considered as never definitive, there is a promise of a more complete and adequate truth. Without doubt, the finite being that we are cannot in the final account complete the task of knowledge; but in the limit where this task is accomplished, it consists in making the other become the Same. On the other hand, the idea of the Infinite implies a thought of the Unequal.
>
> (Levinas, 1985: 91)

The post-Socratic emphasis on *being* is the foundation of Western ideas about knowledge and intelligibility: by studying the products of our own consciousness we believe we come to know. In the process, however, the other is relegated to the status of a bit player, a mere version of, and less than, me. Yet the hope of the Western project is that one day we will know it all. I will become the possessor of knowledge and be in a known transparent world where nothing is hidden from me, for everything will be intelligible. It is this delusion of ideal intelligibility that leads us to violence: what moves me is to make the world transparent to me, and the face of the other is not there to stop me.

It is only through heteronomy, as described below, that a post-modern therapy can take place. For it is only through the face of the other that one can learn of the infinite.

The primacy given to the ontological – with devastating consequences – has formed the unquestioned basis of most counselling and psychotherapy, with its emphasis on autonomy, ego-centricity, or notions of a bounded unitary self, etc. (Loewenthal, 1996). Levinas challenges the ontological, by suggesting that ethical questions must always come before those of being; this is part of his critique of Heidegger, as he expounds it in the extract we give below. This challenge, it seems to us that Levinas is saying, comes out of phenomenological rather than moral necessity: phenomenologically, the face of the other is prior to ourselves.

Levinas points out that 'Every philosophy seeks truth. Sciences too can be defined by this search. . . . ' (Levinas, in Peperzak, 1993: 88), and psychotherapy is no exception in claiming that it also seeks the truth. Yet Western culture contains two major philosophical traditions, the Greek and the Hebraic, each with its own underlying assumptions about the ways truth, in terms of relationships, can be thought about and experienced. Furthermore, it is the Greek notion of autonomy that has more often than not assumed cultural dominance over the notion of heteronomy.

Levinas raises questions about notions of 'absolute' and scientific truth. 'Truth implies experience . . . for experience deserves its name only if it transports us beyond what constitutes our nature' (Levinas, in Pepezak, 1993: 88). It leads towards a 'beyond'. He is saying that truth is not something outside experience, and yet, although this may seem contradictory, it is beyond our nature. But this does not mean that one's experiences are the yardstick for truth. We cannot claim to have the truth because it is our experience ('I've experienced it so you can't take it away from me'). Experience is that which gets us in touch with that which is other than what we are. It is not 'what we are', and it takes us beyond what we have been. So what we feel 'at home' with may stop us genuinely experiencing. We can conceive of and experience our environment as something complicit with us and submissive to our preconceptions, but genuine experience in the Levinasian sense is a reaching towards a beyond, beyond what familiarly surrounds us. Can it therefore only be in relationship where the other is put first, in dwelling with the absolutely other, that truth is to be found? We will not arrive at truth if we see the beyond as something to be colonised and incorporated. It will always be beyond: absolutely other.

This has enormous implications for ethics, ethical practice and so-called ethical committees. We cannot appropriate truth to our experience – it is outside of us (there are parallels here with Wittgenstein: knowledge is not arrived at through contemplation of our 'inner worlds'). We have always to be prepared to go beyond our 'gut reactions'. Only then do we have a chance, momentarily, to reach a truth with another.

When speaking of ethics we do not have in mind codes of conduct. These can be seen as unethical since, however well intended in their systematisation, they are putting the code rather than the other first. Levinasian ethics is not, therefore, about my right to exist, it is not even just about the other's right to exist: it is about my responsibility for the other's responsibility to others.

Levinas thus helps us raise crucial questions about ethics and vested interest – for example within our counselling/psychotherapy training organizations. Our 'truth', our theoretical orientation or club membership, can never be a home we can be at home in (in contrast to Heidegger's 'dwelling'). If we feel at home we may be perpetrating violence.

Truth for Levinas is leaving 'being at home' (and leaving 'being' at home). One cannot be at home with the truth. Something 'feels' 'right'. Is it always wrong if it feels right (and vice versa)? There's great complexity here.

Philosophy for Levinas would be about putting the other first, so if we are 'at home' it is always about me first, my place in the sun. Then philosophy needs to legitimise the corruption – to make us feel at home. This is easier to see if we think of someone we don't like. We should invite onto our ethics committees people from outside of the family.

Levinas has called truth the 'daughter' of experience (Levinas, in Peperzak, 1993: 88). Perhaps this is best thought about against the background of Freud's question 'What does woman want?' Levinas is talking about the unknown, which he equates with the infinite (rather than the ideal – the idealised and oppressed woman of patriarchy). The Other is always mediated by culture.

In contrast to heteronomy, Levinas describes the Greek notion of autonomy in terms of 'the free adherence to a proposition', and of 'the feat of remaining the same despite the unknown lands into which thought seems to lead'.

> Perceived in this way, philosophy would be engaged in reducing to the Same all that is opposed to it as *other*. It would be moving toward *auto-nomy*, a stage in which nothing irreducible would limit thought any longer, in which, consequently, thought, non-limited, would be free.
>
> Freedom, autonomy, *the reduction of the Other to the Same*, lead to this formula: the conquest of being by man over the course of history. This reduction does not represent some abstract schema; it is man's Ego.
>
> (Levinas, in Peperzak, 1993: 88)

This is Descartes ('I am a machine that thinks'), versus Lacan (being subject to). In autonomy one is subject to nothing, it is as if we *were* the subject. Autonomy sells. The notion of 'disappointment guaranteed' is more difficult.

Notions of autonomy tend to go unquestioned in our culture. The Hebraic notion of heteronomy gets left out, in a received historical view that civilisation in the West went from Egypt to Athens and Rome. We are not saying that the idea of autonomy should be abandoned, but that heteronomy must come first, autonomy second. Most of counselling and psychotherapy has wrongly chosen autonomy over heteronomy, encompassing every Other in the Same. Thus the client/patient is in danger of becoming a bit player on the therapist's stage, with the further danger that as a result of therapy everyone else becomes a bit player on the client/patient's stage.

But what, it might be asked, obliges me to put the other first? You are onto-logically free not to, Levinas would answer – free to refuse the other. But this can never invalidate the other's prior claim upon you. On the other hand we can, as John Wild wrote in his Introduction to Levinas's *Totality and Infinity*, make a free 'choice for generosity and communication' (Wild, in Levinas, 1969: 14–15).

Let us examine some implications for current schools of therapy. Let us imagine a patient: a mother searching for the forgiveness of her estranged daughter. Would the person-centred counsellor encourage the mother to go in the direction that she appears to want to go in? Or would the counsellor feel uneasy about this? Would the behaviourist devise a programme to help the mother assert herself and get what she wants? Would a psychoanalyst develop the mother's ego strength so she is more able to carry out her chosen task? All these approaches, which we have grossly caricatured and oversimplified, can be seen as unethical (and delusional) in that they attempt to promote an autonomy which is at the expense of the other. The mother would be putting her daughter first, if she gave a primacy to her responsibility for her daughter's responsibility; instead she is putting herself first in seeking her daughter's forgiveness.

An extended version of the discussion above is Loewenthal and Snell (2001). There is a useful collection of essays regarding Levinas and psychotherapy in

Bernasconi and Wood (1988), and Gordon (1999) discusses the implications of Levinas for ethical practice. Some further references appear in Gondek (1995–6: 138 n5). Gans (1997) provides a helpful reading of the implications of Levinas for counselling and psychotherapy: psychotherapy as an ethical practice.

Derrida (1995) argues that Levinas has been caught in a Christian conspiracy that developed the notion of ethics because Christians could not take life's rawness, and Grosz (1996) has argued that Levinas has ignored gender. For others, what Levinas has to say about ethical practice may appear like a form of humanism. If so, it is a post-modern humanism since, unlike Hamlet, ethical practitioners try not to be at the centre of the world, but always to be subject to ethics.

From Levinas, in Peperzak (1993), *To the Other. An Introduction to the Philosophy of Emmanuel Levinas*, pp. 88–113

Philosophy and the Idea of the Infinite

1. Autonomy and Heteronomy

Every philosophy seeks truth. Sciences, too, can be defined by this search, for from the philosophic *eros*, alive or dormant in them, they derive their noble passion. If this definition seems too general and rather empty, it will, however, permit us to distinguish two directions the philosophical spirit takes, and this will clarify its physiognomy. These directions interact in the idea of truth.

1. Truth implies experience. In the truth, a thinker maintains a relationship with a reality distinct from him, other than him – 'absolutely other' . . . For experience deserves its name only if it transports us beyond what constitutes our nature. Genuine experience must even lead us beyond the Nature that surrounds us, which is not jealous of the marvellous secrets it harbors, and, in complicity with men, submits to their reason and inventions; in it men also feel themselves to be at home. Truth would thus designate the outcome of a movement that leaves a world that is intimate and familiar, even if we have not yet explored it completely, and goes toward another region, toward a *beyond*, as Plato puts it. Truth would imply more than exteriority: transcendence. Philosophy would be concerned with the absolutely other; it would be heteronomy itself. Let us go yet further. Distance alone does not suffice to distinguish transcendence from exteriority. Truth, the daughter of experience, has very lofty pretensions; it opens upon the very dimension of the ideal. In this way, philosophy means metaphysics, and metaphysics inquires about the divine.

2. But truth also means the free adherence to a proposition, the outcome of a free research. The freedom of the investigator, the thinker on whom no

constraint weighs, is expressed in truth. What else is this freedom but the thinking being's refusal to be alienated in the adherence, the preserving of his nature, his identity, the feat of remaining the same despite the unknown lands into which thought seems to lead? Perceived in this way, philosophy would be engaged in reducing to the Same all that is opposed to it as *other*. It would be moving toward *auto-nomy*, a stage in which nothing irreducible would limit thought any longer, in which, consequently, thought, non-limited, would be free. Philosophy would thus be tantamount to the conquest of being by man over the course of history.

Freedom, autonomy, the *reduction of the Other to the Same*, lead to this formula: the conquest of being by man over the course of history. This reduction does not represent some abstract schema; it is man's Ego. The existence of an Ego takes place as an identification of the diverse. So many events happen to it, so many years age it, and yet the Ego remains the Same! The Ego, the Self, the ipseity (as it is called in our time), does not remain invariable in the midst of change like a rock assailed by the waves (which is anything but invariable); the Ego remains the Same by making of disparate and diverse events a history – its history. And this is the original event of the identification of the Same, prior to the identity of a rock, and a condition of that identity.

Autonomy or heteronomy? The choice of Western philosophy has most often been on the side of freedom and the Same . . . Thus Western thought very often seemed to exclude the transcendent, encompass every Other in the Same, and proclaim the philosophical birthright of autonomy.

2. Narcissism, or the Primacy of the Same

Autonomy, the philosophy which aims to ensure the freedom, or the identity of beings, presupposes that freedom itself is sure of its right, is justified without recourse to anything further, is complacent in itself, like Narcissus. When, in the philosophical life that realizes this freedom, there arises a term foreign to the philosophical life, other – the land that supports us and disappoints our efforts, the sky that elevates us and ignores us, the forces of nature that aid us and kill us, things that encumber us or serve us, men who love us and enslave us – it becomes an obstacle; it has to be surmounted and integrated into this life. But truth is just this victory and this integration. In evidence the violence of the encounter with the non-I is deadened. The commerce with exterior truth as enacted in true cognition is thus not opposed to freedom but coincides with it. The search for truth becomes the very respiration of a free being, exposed to exterior realities that shelter, but also threaten, its freedom. Thanks to truth, these realities, whose plaything I am in danger of becoming, are understood by me.

The 'I think', thought in the first person, the soul conversing with itself or, qua reminiscence, rediscovering the teachings it receives, thus promote freedom. Freedom will triumph when the soul's monologue will have reached universality, will have encompassed the totality of being, encompassing even the animal individual which lodged this thought. Every experience of the world, of the elements and objects, lends itself to this dialectic of the soul conversing with itself, enters into it, belongs to it. The things will be ideas, and will be conquered, dominated, possessed in the course of an economic and political history in which this thought will be unfolded. It is doubtless for this reason that Descartes will say that the soul might be the origin of the ideas that relate to exterior things, and thus *account* for the real.

The essence of truth will then not be in the heteronomous relationship with an unknown God, but in the already-known which has to be uncovered or freely invented in oneself, and in which everything unknown is comprised. It is fundamentally opposed to a God that reveals. Philosophy is atheism, or rather unreligion, negation of a God that reveals himself and puts truths into us. This is Socrates' teaching when he leaves to the master only the exercise of maieutics:[8] every lesson introduced into the soul was already in it. The I's identification, its marvellous autarchy, is the natural crucible of this transmutation of the Other into the Same. Every philosophy is – to use Husserl's neologism – an egology. And when Descartes comes to discern an acquiescence of the will in even the most rational truth, he not only explains the possibility of error but sets up reason as an ego and truth as dependent on a movement that is free, and thus sovereign and justified.

This identification requires mediation. Whence a second characteristic of the philosophy of the same: its recourse to Neuters. To understand the non-I, access must be found through an entity, an abstract essence which is and is not. In it is dissolved the other's *alterity*. The foreign being, instead of maintaining itself in the impregnable fortress of its singularity, instead of facing, becomes a theme and an object. It fits under a concept already or dissolves into relations. It falls into the network of a priori ideas, which I bring to bear so as to capture it. To know is to surprise in the individual confronted, in this wounding stone, this upward plunging pine, this roaring lion, that by which it is not this very individual, this foreigner, that by which it is already betrayed and by which it gives the free will, vibrant in all certainty, hold over it, is grasped and conceived, enters into a concept. Cognition consists in grasping the individual, which alone exists, not in its singularity which does not count, but in its generality, of which alone there is science.

And here every power begins. The surrender of exterior things to human freedom through their generality does not only mean, in all innocence, their comprehension, but also their being taken in hand, their domestication, their possession. Only in possession does the I complete the identification of the diverse. To possess is, to be sure, to maintain the reality of this other one

---

[8]   Editors' note: maieutics is the Socratic art of midwifery, helping in the birth of thoughts.

possessed, but to do so while suspending its independence. In a civilization which the philosophy of the Same reflects, freedom is realized as a wealth. Reason, which reduces the other, is appropriation and power . . .

. . . let us . . . observe that this supremacy of the Same over the Other seems to be integrally maintained in the philosophy of Heidegger, the most renowned of our time. When Heidegger traces the way of access to each real singularity through Being, which is not a particular being nor a genus in which all the particulars would enter, but is rather the very act of being which the verb to be, and not the substantive, expresses (and which, with M. De Waelhens, we write with a capital 'B'), he leads us to the singularity across a Neuter which illuminates and commands thought and renders intelligible. When he sees man possessed by freedom rather than possessing freedom, he puts over man a Neuter which illuminates freedom without putting it in question. And thus he is not destroying but summing up a whole current of Western philosophy.

The *Dasein* Heidegger puts in place of the soul, consciousness, or the Ego retains the structure of the Same. Independence – autarchy – came to the Platonic soul (and to all its counterfeit versions) from its homeland, the world of Ideas; according to the *Phaedo*, the soul is related to that world and consequently cannot encounter anything really foreign in it. Reason, the power to maintain oneself identical above the variations of becoming, formed the soul of this soul. Heidegger contests this dominant position for man, but leaves *Dasein* in the Same, qua mortal. The possibility of being annihilated is in fact constitutive of *Dasein*, and thus maintains its ipseity. This nothingness is a death, is my death, my possibility (or impossibility), my power. No one can substitute himself for me to die. The supreme moment of resoluteness is solitary and personal.

To be sure, for Heidegger man's freedom depends on the light of Being, and thus does not seem to be a principle. But that was also the case in classical idealism, where free will was considered the lowest form of freedom, and true freedom obeyed universal reason. The Heideggerian freedom is obedient, but obedience makes it arise and does not put it into question, does not reveal its injustice. Being, equivalent to the independence and extraneousness of realities, is equivalent to phosphorescence, light. It converts into intelligibility. The 'mystery' essential to this 'dark light' is a modality of this conversion. Independence ends in radiation. *Being and Time*, Heidegger's first and principal work, perhaps always maintained but one thesis: Being is inseparable from the comprehension of Being; Being already invokes subjectivity. But Being *is not* a being. It is a Neuter which orders thought and beings, but which hardens the will instead of making it ashamed. The consciousness of his finitude does not come to man from the idea of infinity, that is, is not revealed as an imperfection, does not refer to the Good, does not know itself to be wicked. Heideggerian philosophy precisely marks the apogee of a thought in which the finite does not refer to the infinite (prolonging certain tendencies of Kantian philosophy: the separation between the understanding and reason, diverse themes of transcendental dialectics), in which every deficiency is but weakness and every fault committed against oneself – the outcome of a long tradition of pride, heroism, domination, and cruelty.

Heideggerian ontology subordinates the relation with the other to the relation with the Neuter, Being, and it thus continues to exalt the will to power, whose legitimacy the Other (*Autrui*) alone can unsettle, troubling good conscience. When Heidegger calls attention to the forgetting of Being, veiled by the diverse realities it illuminates, a forgetting for which the philosophy developed from Socrates on would be guilty, when he deplores the orientation of the intellect toward technology, he maintains a regime of power more inhuman than mechanism and which perhaps does not have the same source as it. (It is not sure that National Socialism arises from the mechanist reification of men, and that it does not rest on peasant enrootedness and a feudal adoration of subjugated men for the masters and lords who command them). This is an existence which takes itself to be natural, for whom its place in the sun, its ground, its *site*, orient all signification – a pagan *existing*. Being directs it building and cultivating, in the midst of a familiar landscape, on a maternal earth. Anonymous, neuter, it directs it, ethically indifferent, as a heroic freedom, foreign to all guilt with regard to the Other.

Indeed this earth-maternity determines the whole Western civilization of property, exploitation, political tyranny, and war. Heidegger does not discuss the pre-technological power of possession effected in the enrootedness of perception (which no one has described so brilliantly as he), in which the most abstract geometrical space is in the last analysis embedded, but which cannot find any place in the whole infinity of mathematical extension. The Heideggerian analyses of the world which in *Being and Time* were based on gear or fabricated things are in his later philosophy borne by the vision of the lofty landscapes of nature, an impersonal fecundity, matrix of particular beings, inexhaustible matter of things.

Heidegger not only sums up a whole evolution of Western philosophy. He exalts it by showing in the most dramatic way its anti-religious essence become a religion in reverse. The lucid sobriety of those who call themselves friends of truth and enemies of opinion would thus have a mysterious prolongation! In Heidegger atheism is a paganism, the pre-Socratic text anti-Scriptures. Heidegger shows in what intoxication the lucid sobriety of philosophers is steeped.

To conclude, the well-known theses of Heideggerian philosophy – the pre-eminence of Being over beings, of ontology over metaphysics – end up affirming a tradition in which the Same dominates the Other, in which freedom, even the freedom that is identical with reason, precedes justice. Does not justice consist in putting the obligation with regard to the Other before obligations to oneself, in putting the Other before the Same?

3. The Idea of the Infinite

By reversing the terms we believe we are following a tradition at least as ancient, that which does not read right in might and does not reduce *every other* to the Same. Against the Heideggerians and neo-Hegelians for whom philosophy begins with atheism, we have to say that the tradition of the Other is not necessarily religious, that it is philosophical. Plato stands in this tradition when he situates the Good above Being, and, in the *Phaedrus*, defines true discourse as a discourse with gods. But what we find most distinctive is the Cartesian analysis of the idea of the infinite, although we shall retain only the *formal design* of the structure it outlines.

In Descartes the I that thinks maintains a relationship with the Infinite. This relationship is not that which connects a container to a content, since the I cannot contain the Infinite, nor that which binds a content to a container, since the I is separated from the Infinite. The relationship which is thus described negatively is the idea of the Infinite in us . . .

4. The Idea of the Infinite and the Face of the Other (Autrui)

Experience, the idea of the infinite, occurs in the relationship with the Other (*Autrui*). The idea of the infinite is the social relationship . . .

5. The Idea of the Infinite is Desire

The ethical relationship is not grafted on to an antecedent relationship of cognition, it is a foundation and not a superstructure. To distinguish it from cognition is not to reduce it to a subjective sentiment. The idea of the infinite, in which being overflows the idea, in which the Other overflows the Same, breaks with the inward play of the soul and alone deserves the name experience, a relationship with the exterior. It is then more *cognitive* than cognition itself, and all objectivity must participate in it . . .

. . . [T]he infinite is not the object of a contemplation, that is, is not proportionate to the thought that thinks it. The idea of the infinite is a thought which at every moment *thinks more than it thinks*. A thought that thinks more than it thinks is Desire. Desire 'measures' the infinity of the infinite . . .

Suggested further reading

Bernasconi, R and Wood, D (eds) 1988, *The Provocation of Levinas. Rethinking the Other*. London: Routledge

Gans, S. (1997) 'Lacan and Levinas: Towards an Ethical Psychoanalysis', *Journal of the British Society for Phenomenology*, Vol. 28, No. 1, January

Gondek, H (1995–6) 'Cogito and Separation. Lacan/Levinas', *Journal of European Psychoanalysis*, No. 2, Fall – pp. 133–68

Gordon. P (1999), *Face to Face: Therapy as Ethics*. London: Constable

Levinas, E (1969 [1961]), *Totality and Infinity. An Essay on Exteriority* (trans. Lingis, A). Pittsburgh: Duquesne University Press
—— (1981) 'Ethics of the Infinite', in Kearney, R (1995), *States of Mind. Dialogues with Contemporary Thinkers on the European Mind.* Manchester: Manchester University Press
—— (1985) *Ethics and Infinity. Conversations with Philippe Nemo* (trans. Cohen, R). Pittsburgh: Duquesne University Press
—— (1989) 'Ethics as First Philosophy', in Levinas, E (ed. Hand, S) *The Levinas Reader.* Oxford: Blackwell
Loewenthal, D, and Snell, R (2001), 'Psychotherapy as the Practice of Ethics', in Palmer-Barnes, F and Murdin, L (eds), *Values and Ethics in the Practice of Psychotherapy.* Buckingham: Open University Press

Žižek (b. 1949)

Slavoj Žižek was born in Ljubljana, Slovenia, in former Yugoslavia, and he is still based there. His background is in philosophy, sociology and psychoanalysis. The focus of his interest moved from German thinking – Heidegger, and the Frankfurt School – to French. His major contribution lies in his use of Lacanian theory for the analysis of philosophy, ideology and culture – particularly visual art and cinema, and especially the films of Alfred Hitchcock. He has described himself as 'a psychoanalytically oriented (Lacanian) philosopher' (Žižek, 1999: 110), and claims to keep Lacan open in the same way as Lacan claimed to keep Freud open. In the 1990s his interests and those of the Slovene Lacanian school (a society for theoretical rather than clinical psychoanalysis, whose practical interests are leftist-political) shifted towards the English-speaking world.

Žižek's use of Lacan is based on the notion of the Real, in terms of the failure of language: the Real always resists incorporation, however much the Symbolic attempts it (Wright, in Žižek, 1999: 3): for example, in trying to bring the multi-directedness of bodily drives into language. The Real can never be experienced, but only known through its manifestations in the everyday. We may know there is something else moving us, which we may find ourselves representing in strange or surprising ways, but there is always a residue that is unrepresentable. ('Because something is happening here. But you don't know what it is. Do you, Mister Jones', in the words of Bob Dylan's 'Ballad of a Thin Man'.) In so far as we are constituted by language we face a void – that of which language cannot speak. We try to fill the gap with what Žižek has termed 'the sublime object of ideology', that which we imagine the other to possess, what Lacan called *petit objet a*: that which will fill the gap and complete us.

What are the implications for psychotherapy? Žižek can help point up the fallacy of therapies that pretend we can know what is going on, in an attempt to master the Real. We tend to think it is because we do not really *want* to know the 'contents' of the unconscious (for example, getting the measure of how much I *really* desired to have sex with my mother); Žižek would say here is something else that we cannot know. We can never be anything other than alienated. We are for example alienated in our adherence to Oedipal theory – necessarily and futilely. When we are in touch with the Real, we search for explanations; the source of the uneasy glance between therapist– patient, self–other, is the Real. Both therapist and patient are, in Lacanian terms, alienated in the signifier; therapy can more clearly show the failure of language, and thus in therapy one can be closer to the Real. We complain of being 'stuck' with a patient; this is when we are doing therapy. The Real manifests itself perhaps when we feel most driven towards explanation – when things become unbearable or too close.

When we get too close to the Real we go to therapy, and there is always the danger of therapy becoming a normalising process. A sense of the Real is an awareness that we are not able to think about something: not the actual, say, sexual abuse, but the possibility of something being there that cannot be spoken. This, Žižek insists, is what drives us. How do we help people with this 'too-much'? How can we help our clients/patients so that the Real does not overwhelm them, but so that they can play and be open to the unknown? By overkill, of interpretation or reconstruction? This would be to close down, to treat the Real as if it does not exist. Perhaps all we can do is help people be more poetic, to paint multiple pictures where the signifiers are never stable; thus one's interpretations can never be stable. Otherwise psychotherapy and psychoanalysis end in theoretical turgidity, like a horrendous super-ego. Freed up to be more open to the Real, the person may feel more exposed (like philosophers who go mad). When the Real becomes too much, there is breakdown. Fear of this can keep us from playing. Do free associations stop with the Real?

Žižek makes a particular distinction between modernism and post-modernism. He disagrees with the philosopher Jürgen Habermas's distinction. For Habermas modernism is characterised by reliance on reason rather than on traditional authority, and post-modernism means a deconstructing, or unmasking, of the hidden power agenda of this reason. Habermas thus sees deconstruction as post-modern, an attack on reason. For Habermas, there is the possibility of 'sincere, truth-governed speech' (Cahoone, 1996: 589), so that discourse is not merely a matter of power and self-interest (a more post-Marxist view). Rationality for Habermas has a communicative essence: 'rationality is inherently linguistic and discursive hence social' (Cahoone, 1996: 589). Žižek gives this a 'new twist'. In a way Habermas is a post-modernist without knowing it, he says. The way Habermas constructs an opposition modernism–post-modernism – seeing post-modernism as the deconstruction of universals – presupposes a universal, and a procedure. This is modernist. So the line of demarcation between modern and post-modern must lie elsewhere. Habermas is post-modern, however, in that he claims freedom is possible only on the basis of a fundamental alienation (in comparison with the first-generation Frankfurt School, who believed alienation could be overcome). Modernism tended to locate freedom in a utopian idea of unity and harmony; Habermas rejects this modernist notion of freedom, finding it instead in what modernists called alienation, in the existence of differing and competing worlds.

In another way, Žižek says, Habermas is still a modernist. Žižek sees deconstruction, unmasking, as a quintessentially modernist enterprise: Freud, Marx and Nietzsche used a logic of unmasking. As a procedure of unmasking, deconstruction relies on language and the movement of unchanged signifiers – thus it is structuralist and modernist. Deconstructionists are only really structuralists: the idea of 'post-', Žižek says, is in fact an Anglo-Saxon academic perception of French philosophy, of the work of Derrida, Foucault, or Deleuze. This is why Lacan assumes such importance in Žižek's work: only the post-structuralist Lacan marks the post-modern break, because he draws attention to what lies outside the signifier, after language has failed – to the Real (Žižek, 1999: 37 etc.).

Žižek illustrates this distinction in the extract that follows by looking at two films, Antonioni's *Blow-Up* and Hitchcock's *Lifeboat*. *Blow-up* is about the search for a missing body which may not exist. A non-existent ball in a tennis match enables someone to join the game: fantasy can conceal what does not exist. In Hitchcock's film, set in the Second World War, a German sailor is caught by British sailors – the horror on his face is shown. What is obscene for Žižek is shown by post-modernism, and concealed by modernism. The obscene object is the incestuous maternal object. It is not an absence but a disgusting presence. (Might it not be argued, however, that this kind of thinking, at least the reference to the 'incestuous maternal object', is itself a bit reductive, a potential closing down?)

Žižek also discusses Kafka's *The Trial*. Modernist misreadings suggest the novel is about an absent God or an inner emptiness. In fact there is a disgusting presence that is too close. The judges in the courtroom look through pornographic books. Later a man and woman are having sex in the back of the room. The Law that allows this, and which the victim is unable to escape, is a 'punitive super-ego that is driven by an obscene and anarchic *jouissance*'. There is the Symbolic Law, and the Real; they are in the same space, with only a thin boundary between them. The Law is invested with boundless enjoyment; rather than being an ideal of justice it is engulfed by uncontrollable drives. 'The Freudian super-ego has closer links with the id than the ego does' (Wright, in Žižek, 1999: 38). In other words, we might say that when one is into 'shoulds', one easily gets hot under the collar. The super-ego, for Žižek, is haunted by infinite guilt, although it appears to itself all-knowing. Law is necessary but not true; if you can't invest the Law as necessary, you get flooded with *jouissance*. Super-ego colonises the Law with enjoyment. The psychotic is persecuted by the Symbolic, while the neurotic can hold onto a supposition of the other's consistency.

In Žižek's reading of Lacan, Freudian language is extended to notions of Law and *jouissance*, and not just restricted to super-ego and id, and this may help us as therapists to think and respond differently. Rather than, for example, encouraging us to ease the severity of a punitive super-ego, perhaps Žižek helps keep open questions about speaking, the use of language, and its consistency, in therapeutic practice. If there is a constant risk of *jouissance* flooding the Law, what is our place in social control? A client/patient says they get pleasure from something, for example from hitting their child. Can the therapist hear this? Is psychotherapy a secondary enforcement of the Law? Is the therapist's investment in the Law necessarily such that she or he must seek out expressions of remorse in the patient? This would be for the therapist, not the patient, although it may be done in the name of the patient. It might be an attempt to stop the therapist going mad.

Modernism wants to close the circle, so there is no gap. Žižek takes a Lacanian way of keeping it open, and perhaps our job as therapists is to re-open the gap for our patients, to enable both *jouissance* and the Law, to stay with the lack of consistency between the Law and the Real, with permanent unresolvedness, and not get stuck in attempted resolutions.

From Žižek (1991), 'The Obscene Object of Post-Modernity', *Looking Awry: An Introduction to Jacques Lacan through Popular Culture*, pp. 141–50

The Postmodernist Break: Modernism versus Postmodernism

When the topic of "postmodernism" is discussed in "deconstructivist" circles, it is obligatory – a sign of good manners, so to speak – to begin with a negative reference to Habermas, with a kind of distancing from him. In complying with this custom, we would like to add a new twist: to propose that Habermas is himself postmodernist, although in a peculiar way, without knowing it. To sustain this thesis, we will question the very way Habermas constructs the opposition between modernism (defined by its claim to a universality of reason, its refusal of the authority of tradition, its acceptance of rational argument as the only way to defend conviction, its ideal of a communal life guided by mutual understanding and recognition and by the absence of constraint) and postmodernism (defined as the "deconstruction" of this claim to universality, from Nietzsche to "poststructuralism"); the endeavour to prove that this claim to universality is necessarily, constitutively "false", that it masks a particular network of power relations; that universal reason is as such, in its very form, "repressive" and "totalitarian"; that its truth claim is nothing but an effect of a series of rhetorical figures. This opposition is simply false: for what Habermas describes as "postmodernism" is the immanent obverse of the modernist project itself; what he describes as the tension between modernism and postmodernism is the immanent tension that has defined modernism from its very beginning. Was not the aestheticist, anti-universalist ethics of the individual's shaping his life as a work of art always part of the modernist project? Is the genealogic unmasking of universal categories and values, the calling into question of the universality of reason not a modernist procedure *par excellence*? Is not the very essence of theoretical modernism, the revelation of the "effective contents" behind the "false consciousness" (of ideology, of morality, of the ego), exemplified by the great triad of Marx–Nietzsche–Freud? Is not the ironic, self-destructive gesture by means of which reason recognizes in itself the force of repression and domination against which it fights – the gesture at work from Nietzsche to Adorno and Horkheimer's *Dialectic of Enlightenment* – is not this gesture the supreme act of modernism? As soon as fissures appear in the unquestionable authority of tradition, the tension between universal reason and the particular contents escaping its grasp is inevitable and irreducible.

The line of demarcation between modernism and postmodernism must, then, lie elsewhere. Ironically, it is Habermas himself who, on account of certain crucial features of his theory, belongs to postmodernism: the break between the first and the second generation of the Frankfurt school, that is, between Adorno, Horkheimer, and Marcuse on the one side and Habermas on the other, corresponds precisely to the break between modernism and postmodernism. In Adorno and Horkheimer's *Dialectic of Enlightenment*, in Marcuse's *One-Dimensional Man*, in their unmasking of the repressive potential of "instrumental reason", aiming at a radical revolution in the historical totality of the contemporary world and at the utopian abolition of the difference between "alienated" life spheres, between art and "reality", the modernist project reaches its zenith of self-critical fulfilment. Habermas is, on the other hand, postmodern precisely because he recognizes a positive condition of freedom and emancipation in what appeared to modernism as the very form of alienation: the autonomy of the aesthetic sphere, the functional division of different social domains, etc. This renunciation of the modernist utopia, this acceptance of the fact that freedom is possible only on the basis of a certain fundamental "alienation", attests to the fact that we are in a postmodernist universe.

This confusion concerning the break between modernism and postmodernism comes to a critical point in Habermas's diagnosis of poststructuralist deconstructionism as the dominant form of contemporary philosophical postmodernism. The use of the prefix "post-" in both cases should not lead us astray (especially if we take into account the crucial but usually overlooked fact that the very term "poststructuralism", although designating a strain of French theory, is an Anglo-Saxon and German invention. The term refers to the way the Anglo-Saxon world perceived and located the theories of Derrida, Foucault, Deleuze, etc. – in France itself, nobody uses the term "poststructuralism".) Deconstructionism is a modernist procedure *par excellence*; it presents perhaps the most radical version of the logic of "unmasking" whereby the very unity of the experience of meaning is conceived as the effect of signifying mechanisms, an effect that can take place only insofar as it ignores the textual movement that produced it. It is only with Lacan that the "postmodernist" break occurs, insofar as he thematizes a certain real, traumatic kernel whose status remains deeply ambiguous: the real resists symbolization, but it is at the same time its own retroactive product. In this sense we could even say that deconstructionists are basically still "structuralists" and that the only "poststructuralist" is Lacan, who affirms enjoyment as "the real Thing", the central impossibility around which every signifying network is structured.

Hitchcock as Postmodernist

In what, then, does the postmodernist break consist? Let's begin with Antonioni's *Blow-Up*, perhaps the last great modernist film. As the hero develops photographs shot in a park, his attention is attracted to a stain that appears on the edge of one of the photographs. When he enlarges the detail, he discovers the contours of a body there. Though it is the middle of the night, he rushes to the park and indeed finds the body. But on returning to the scene of the crime the next day, he finds that the body has disappeared without leaving a trace. The first thing to note here is that the body is, according to the code of the detective novel, the object of desire *par excellence*, the cause that starts the interpretive desire of the detective (and the reader): How did it happen? Who did it? The key to the film is only given to us, however, in the final scene. The hero, resigned to the cul-de-sac in which his investigation has ended, takes a walk near a tennis court where a group of people – without a tennis ball – mime a game of tennis. In the frame of this supposed game, the imagined ball is hit out of bounds and lands near the hero. He hesitates a moment and then accepts the game: bending over, he makes a gesture of picking up the ball and throwing it back into the court. This scene has, of course, a metaphorical function in relation to the rest of the film. It indicates the hero's consenting to the fact that "the game works without an object": even as the mimed tennis game can be played without a ball, so his own adventure proceeds without a body.

"Postmodernism" is the exact reverse of this process. It consists not in demonstrating that the game works without an object, that the play is set in motion by a central absence, but rather in displaying the object directly, allowing it to make visible its own indifferent and arbitrary character. The same object can function successively as a disgusting reject and as a sublime, charismatic apparition: the difference, strictly structural, does not pertain to the "effective properties" of the object, but only to its place in the symbolic order.

One can grasp this difference between modernism and postmodernism by analyzing the effect of horror in Hitchcock's films. At first, it seems that Hitchcock simply respects the classical rule (already known by Aeschylus in *The Oresteia*) according to which one must place the terrifying object or event outside the scene and show only its reflections and its effects on the stage. If one does not see the object directly, one fills out its absence with fantasy projections (one sees it as more horrible than it actually is). The elementary procedure for evoking horror would be, then, to limit oneself to reflections of the terrifying object in its witnesses or victims.

As is well known, this is the crucial axis of the revolution in horror movies accomplished in the 1940s by the legendary producer Val Lewton (*Cat People, The Seventh Victim*, etc.). Instead of directly showing the terrifying monster (vampire, murderous beast), its presence is indicated only by means of off-screen sounds, by shadows, and so on, and thus rendered all the more horrible. The properly Hitchcockian approach, however, is to *reverse* this process. Let's take a small detail from *Lifeboat*, from the scene where the group of allied castaways welcome on board their boat a German sailor from the destroyed submarine: their surprise when they find out that the person saved is an enemy. The traditional way of filming this scene would be to let us hear the screams for help, to show the hands of an unknown person gripping the side of the boat, and then *not* to show the German sailor, but to move the camera to the shipwrecked survivors: it would then be the perplexed expression on their faces that would indicate to us that they had pulled something unexpected out of the water. What? When the suspense was finally built up, the camera would finally reveal the German sailor. But Hitchcock's procedure is *the exact contrary* of this: what he does not show, precisely, is the shipwrecked survivors. He shows the German sailor climbing on board and saying, with a friendly smile, "Danke schön!" Then he *does not* show the surprised faces of the survivors; the camera remains on the German. If his apparition provoked a terrifying effect, one can only detect it by *his* reaction to the survivor's reaction: his smile dies out, his look becomes perplexed . . . One shows an ordinary object or an activity, but suddenly, through the reactions of the milieu to this object, *reflecting themselves in the object itself,* one realizes that one is confronting the source of an inexplicable terror. The terror is intensified by the fact that this object is, in its appearance, completely ordinary: what one took only a moment ago for a totally common thing is revealed as evil incarnate.

Such a postmodernist procedure seems to us much more subversive than the usual modernist one, because the latter, by not showing the Thing, leaves open the possibility of grasping the central emptiness under the perspective of an "absent God". The lesson of modernism is that the structure, the inter-subjective machine, works as well if the Thing is lacking, if the machine revolves around an emptiness; the postmodernist reversal shows *the Thing itself as the incarnated, materialized emptiness.* This is accomplished by showing the terrifying object directly and then by revealing its frightening effect to be simply the effect of its place in the structure. The terrifying object is an everyday object that has started to function, by chance, as that which fills in the hole in the Other (the symbolic order) . . .

. . . The most familiar things take on a dimension of the uncanny when one finds them in another place, a place that "is not right". And the thrill effect results precisely from the familiar, domestic character of what one finds in this Thing's forbidden place – here we have the perfect illustration of the fundamental ambiguity of the Freudian notion of *das Unheimliche.*

The opposition between modernism and postmodernism is thus far from being reducible to a simple diachrony; we are even tempted to say that postmodernism in a way *precedes* modernism. Like Kafka – who logically, not only temporally, precedes Joyce – the postmodernist *inconsistency* of the

Other is retroactively perceived by the modernist gaze as its *incompleteness*. If Joyce is the modernist *par excellence*, the writer of the symptom ("the symptom Joyce", as Lacan puts it), of the interpretive delirium taken to the infinite, of the *time* (to interpret) where each stable moment reveals itself to be nothing but a "condensation" of a plural signifying process, Kafka is in a certain way already postmodernist, the antipode of Joyce, the writer of fantasy, of the *space* of a nauseous inert presence. If Joyce's text provokes interpretation, Kafka's blocks it.

It is precisely this dimension of a non-dialecticizable, inert presence that is mis-recognized by a modernist reading of Kafka, with its accent on the inaccessible, absent, transcendent agency (the Castle, the Court), holding the place of the lack, of the absence as such. From this modernist perspective, the secret of Kafka would be that in the heart of the bureaucratic machinery, there is only an emptiness, nothing: bureaucracy would be a mad machine that "works by itself", as in *Blow-Up* where the game is played without a body–object. One can read this conjunction in two opposed ways, which nevertheless share the same theoretical frame: theological and immanentist. One reading takes the elusive, inaccessible, transcendent character of the center (of the Castle, of the Court) as a mark of an "absent God" (the universe of Kafka as an anguished universe, abandoned by God); the other reading takes the emptiness of this transcendence as an "illusion of perspective", as a reverse form of the apparition of the immanence of desire (the inaccessible transcendence, the central lack, is then only the negative form of the apparition of the surplus of desire, of its productive movement, over the world of objects *qua* representations).

These two readings, although opposed, miss the same point: the way this absence, this empty place, is always already filled out by an inert, obscene, revolting *presence*. The Court in *The Trial* is not simply absent, it is indeed present under the figures of the obscene judges who, during night inter-rogations, glance through pornographic books; the Castle is indeed present under the figure of subservient, lascivious, and corrupt civil servants. Which is why the formula of the "absent God" in Kafka does not work at all: for Kafka's problem is, on the contrary, that in this universe God is *too present*, in the guise of various obscene, nauseous phenomena. Kafka's universe is a world in which God – who up to now had held himself at an assured distance – has gotten too close to us. Kafka's universe is a "universe of anxiety", why not? – on condition, however, that one takes into account the Lacanian definition of anxiety (what provokes anxiety is not the loss of the incestuous object but, on the contrary, its very *proximity*). We are too close to *das Ding*, that is the theological lesson of postmodernism. Kafka's mad, obscene God, this "Supreme Being of Evil", is exactly the same as God *qua* Supreme Good – the difference lies only in the fact that we have got too close to Him.

. . .

The Obscene Law

In Kafka's universe, the Court is – above all – lawless, in a formal sense: it is as if the chain of "normal" connections between causes and effects were suspended, put in parenthesis. Every attempt to establish the Court's mode of functioning by logical reasoning is doomed in advance to fail. All the oppositions noted by K. (between the anger of the judges and the laughter of the public on the benches; between the merry right side and the severe left side of the public) prove false as soon as he tries to base his tactics on them . . .

The fatal error of K. was to address the Court, the Other of the Law, as a homogeneous entity, attainable by means of consistent argument, whereas the Court can only return him an obscene smile, mixed with signs of perplexity . . .

Suggested further reading

Žižek, S (1999), *The Žižek Reader* (ed. Wright E and Wright, E). Oxford: Blackwell, pp. 39–51
—— (2001), *On Belief*. London: Routledge
—— (2002), *Welcome to the Desert of the Real! Five Essays on September 11th and Related Dates*. London and New York: Verso

Wittgenstein (1889–1951)

> A philosophical problem has the form: 'I don't know my way about'.
>
> (Wittgenstein, 2001: 49e)

> Philosophy is a battle against the bewitchment of our intelligence by means of language.
>
> (Wittgenstein, 2001: 47e)

Having found ourselves referring to him at different places throughout the book, we debated whether Wittgenstein should have a section to himself. In a sense, he haunts the preceding pages, even when we have not alluded to him directly; we include him at the end of the post-modern section because of his special concern with language, and his insistence on the complexity and multiplicity of its uses.

Ludwig Wittgenstein was born in Vienna, the son of an industrialist. He studied philosophy in Cambridge in 1911–13, and fought in the Austrian army in the First World War. During his captivity as an Italian prisoner-of-war, he wrote his *Tractatus Logico-Philosophicus*, published in English translation with an introduction by Bertrand Russell in 1922. He gave up his family fortune, and, for a time in the early 1920s, his career as a philosopher, to teach in rural elementary schools in Austria; he also considered becoming a monk. He returned in 1929 to Cambridge, where he taught philosophy until 1947; he was made professor in 1939. He became a British subject in 1938. The main work of his later period is *Philosophical Investigations*, the first versions of which appeared in 1945 and 1949 (the edition we cite below is the second English edition of 1958).

The meaning of language, for Wittgenstein, lies in its use; it is a 'form of life' (Wittgenstein, 2001: 88e). Wittgenstein teaches that only by attending carefully to language, to the elusive power of which we are prisoners (Heaton, 2000: 5), can we hope to distinguish lies from truth, to free ourselves from deception and delusion. If he is modern in implying that freedom from illusion and deception is ever possible – 'the clarity we are aiming at is indeed *complete* clarity' (Wittgenstein, 2001: 51e) – he is post-modern in his estimation of the difficulties: language creates and masks our cover-stories, but our only means of trying to uncover cover-stories is by using words, which bring other errors and weave new cover-stories in their turn. The notion of language games, later developed by Lyotard, comes from Wittgenstein. Like Levinas, he stresses the importance of the struggle to be clear, in the hope that there can be moments of truth and meeting. In his use of a dry wit, and of paradox – to shake us up, to loosen up our habitual and entrapping metaphors – his writing can echo Lacan's. He gives primacy to ordinariness, and in that sense he is similar to Heidegger: he does not elevate scientific or technical language, as if this could help us with our problems of living and how to think about our lives. On the contrary, Wittgenstein and Heidegger would seem to agree, such language merely distracts us.

Wittgenstein embraces confusion, and his particular way of engaging with it is not to start with grand theory. He resists closure at every turn: for Wittgenstein, in the words of a commentator, 'there were no philosophical results, in the form of answers to questions, but only the growth and dissolution of philosophical puzzlement' (Harvey, 1967: 893). He said he was concerned with 'the concepts of meaning, of understanding . . . states of consciousness' (Wittgenstein, 2001: vii). He opens up much that is fundamental for therapeutic practice: the invitation to the patient to make their own sense through speaking with us, the search for the liberating word which does not set out from the ground of an established theory. He offers an invitation to therapists and patients to be ignorant, to be in our practice as people. This is different from trying to build up a knowledge base and establish a science, which is what much psychoanalysis does: it invites one 'to enter a world of secure moorings' (Heaton, 2000: 11). As therapists influenced by Wittgenstein, we are not entering a secure world. But neither would we be very secure if we stayed in the world of our knowledgeable certainties. For 'when we follow the rules, things do not turn out as we had assumed . . . we are therefore as it were entangled in our own rules . . . This entanglement in our rules is what we want to understand (i.e. get a clear view of)' (Wittgenstein, 2001: 50e).

In reading Wittgenstein one can have the experience of not being able to anticipate where he will go next, where his thought will take him. There is never a sense of falling into a schema. This process of reading catches for us something important about the practice of psychotherapy – to be able to see one's client/patient as one might approach a text by Wittgenstein; to attend to the silences and disruptions. Wittgenstein wrote, 'my thoughts were soon crippled if I tried to force them on in any single direction against their natural inclination' (Wittgenstein, 2001: vii): a lesson for therapists in the practice of encouraging free association. One senses his philosophising was a form of therapy for himself, a clarifying of errors that led him astray.

His sister had been in analysis with Freud, his Viennese compatriot, and he maintained a respect for what he called Freud's 'extraordinary scientific achievement', while describing psychoanalysis itself as a 'foul practice', dangerous for those who do not think clearly – '*So hold onto your brains!*' (Wittgenstein, in Bouveresse, 1995: xix). He questioned the need for the notion of an unconscious. Our errors come from language, and there is no need to postulate further. 'Since everything lies open to view there is nothing to explain' (Wittgenstein, 2001: 50e). If this way of looking at things lacks the explanatory power of the Freudian unconscious, it has the virtue of keeping us close to experience, while theories of great explanatory power always tend to remove us further from it.

'Let the use of words teach you their meanings', Wittgenstein advised (Wittgenstein, 2001: 20, cited in Heaton, 2000: 17). As Heaton writes, it is sense and nonsense that are important, rather than the truth of a theory (Heaton, 2000: 16); Wittgenstein encourages us to have the courage of our foolishness. 'Don't for heaven's sake, be afraid of talking nonsense! Only don't fail to pay attention to your nonsense . . . Always come down from the barren heights of cleverness into the green valleys of folly' (Wittgenstein, 1998: 64, 86). This is fundamentally different from the starting place of most trainings – for how do you use theory to make sense of what makes sense or nonsense? Theory, after all, can imprison us, and a reading of Wittgenstein can underline for us that a slow cure is all important. 'A *picture* held us captive. And we could not get outside it, for it lay in our language and language seemed to repeat it to us inexorably' (Wittgenstein, 2001: 48e); it is only by means of a patient untangling of the words we use that a dissolution of the transference can take place – including transference to theory itself, and that includes the theory of transference. Perhaps the end of analysis is signalled in Wittgenstein's observation that 'The real discovery is the one that makes me capable of stopping doing philosophy when I want to' (Wittgenstein, 2001: 51e). Therapy and free association are like Wittgenstein's writing: not a linear process, more a kind of a walking around until some clarity or relief emerges.

In looking at ethics, Wittgenstein reminds us how we are involved with judgements of value, and of how confusion can arise between absolute and relative judgements of value, and statements of fact. If I have behaved preposterously towards you, and I show no regret, and you say to me 'you *ought* to want to behave better', this would be an example of an absolute judgement of value. If you tell me I play tennis badly, in the face of my response that I know, but do not want to play any better, this would be a relative judgement; it is also a mere statement of facts (that I play tennis badly). It can be phrased in such a way that it loses all resemblance to a judgement of value. The reverse is also true. 'Instead of saying "This is the right way to Grantchester", I could equally well have said, "This is the right way you have to go if you want to get to Grantchester in the shortest time" . . . ' (Wittgenstein, 1965, in Cahoone, 1996: 193). But it is not true of absolute values: 'no statement of fact can ever be, or imply, a judgement of absolute value'. Be wary of 'facts', Wittgenstein warns us. There is no sense, he concludes, in talking about the 'right road', the one everyone would logically have to take – any more than there is an 'absolute good', 'the one which everybody, independent of his tastes and inclinations, would necessarily bring about or feel guilty for not bringing about. And I want to say that such a state of affairs is a chimera. No state of affairs has, in itself, the coercive power of an absolute judge' (Wittgenstein, 1965, cited in Cahoone, 1996: 194–5). The responsibility is on us.

As a therapist I may feel, therefore, that I need to be especially interested in experience, meaning and intention, as focal points for my attention in my practice. But I use these notions in a loose and confused way. In *Philosophical Investigations* Wittgenstein raises questions about the relationship of language to experience which psychotherapy has perhaps still to explore with real rigour. How do I describe my experience? How do I use words to stand for my sensations? (Wittgenstein, 2001: 91e). Someone else might understand, so my language cannot just be a private one; I do not peer into some supposed 'inner world' and report on what I see in it. Speech is different from that. Yet no one can know my experience or think my thoughts for me, any more than they can wear my hat for me (Wittgenstein, 1998: 2e).

'Are the words for sensations tied up with my natural expressions of my sensation?' '[T]he verbal expression of pain replaces crying and does not describe it' (Wittgenstein, 2001: 89e): speech is not just reportage but also action. 'It is what human beings say that is true and false, and they agree in the language they use. This is not agreement in opinions, but in form of life' (Wittgenstein, 2001: 88e). There must be agreement not just in terms of definition, but in terms of judgement – of a kind of common-sense consensus.

While it might make sense to say of another, 'I doubt whether he is in pain', it makes no sense to say of myself 'I doubt whether I am in pain' (Wittgenstein, 2001: 89e). To make such a statement, while it might appear to be an expression of philosophical doubt, would be to be trapped in a language-game. Language can take us away from common sense and the ordinary; Wittgenstein might be describing a state which psychoanalysts would call hysterical (and Marxists a state of extreme alienation).

In providing examples of language-games – this, it could be said, became the whole of his philosophical activity – Wittgenstein engages in a constant opening up of distinctions. 'The language-game 'I mean (or meant) *this*' is different from 'I thought of . . . as I said it'. The latter is akin to 'It reminded me of . . . ' 'Mere explanation of a word does not refer to an occurrence at the moment of speaking' – words are detached from what happens in the speaking of them; to say I mean or meant something is not the same as saying I thought something. Speaking happens in time – but we are not speaking about an experience in that time. When we talk about meaning we are not talking about experience nor our intentions. The words have no 'experience-content'. '"Talking" (whether out loud or silently) and "thinking" are not concepts of the same kind; even though they are in closest connection' (Wittgenstein, 2001: 217e).

How then do I find the right word? (Wittgenstein, 2001: 218e). Wait, Wittgenstein at first seems to be saying, until a word occurs to you. In the following passage, he finds words to convey the mystery of speech, of finding oneself in words (with echoes of Lacan's *parole pleine*, full speech), and of how this is an experience of embodiment (with echoes of Levinas's meditations on the face):

> At last a word comes: *"That's it!"* *Sometimes* I can say why. This is simply what searching, this is what finding, is like here.
>
> But doesn't the word that occurs to you somehow 'come' in a special way? Just attend and you'll see! – Careful attention is no use to me. All it could discover would be what is *now* going on in *me*. And how can I, precisely now, listen for it at all? I ought to have to wait until a word occurs to me anew. This, however, is the queer thing: it seems as though I did not have to wait on the occasion, but could give myself an exhibition of it, even when it is not actually taking place. How? – I *act* it – But *what* can I learn in this way? What do I reproduce? – Characteristic accompaniments. Primarily: gestures, faces, tones of voice.
>
> (Wittgenstein, 2001: 218e–219e)

As a mental training for therapists, a daily reading of *Philosophical Investigations* might be as salutary as the crossword recommended to his students by Lacan.

In the extract we give below, Wittgenstein seems to take us back to phenomenology, although he did not see himself as particularly coming from this Continental tradition. He proposes doing away with explanation and letting description take its place. It is worth the reader asking what happens to him or her in the process of reading. One has an experience: in showing us how we can 'bump our heads' against errors of thought, Wittgenstein takes us through something, compels us to live it. What he aims for, as a psychoanalysis or a course of psychotherapy might aim, is what he calls 'perspicuity': 'to get a clear view of the state . . . that troubles us'. This, we would argue, *is* the therapy, rather than a search for explanations which can produce the further confusions which arise 'when language is like an engine idling'.

From Wittgenstein (2001 [1958]), *Philosophical Investigations*. pp. 47e–52e

109. It was true to say that our considerations could not be scientific ones. It was not of any possible interest to us to find out empirically 'that, contrary to our preconceived ideas, it is possible to think such-and-such' – whatever

that may mean. (The conception of thought as a gaseous medium.) And we may not advance any kind of theory. There must not be anything hypothetical in our considerations. We must do away with all *explanation*, and description alone must take its place. And this description gets its light, that is to say its purpose, from the philosophical problems. These are, of course, not empirical problems; they are solved, rather, by looking into the workings of our language, and that in such a way as to make us recognize those workings: *in despite of* an urge to misunderstand them. The problems are solved, not by giving new information, but by arranging what we have always known. Philosophy is a battle against the bewitchment of our intelligence by means of language.

110. "Language (or thought) is something unique" – this proves to be a superstition (*not* a mistake!), itself produced by grammatical illusions.
And now the impressiveness retreats to these illusions, to the problems.

111. The problems arising through a misinterpretation of our forms of language have the character of *depth*. They are deep disquietudes; their roots are as deep in us as the forms of our language and their significance is as great as the importance of our language. – Let us ask ourselves: why do we feel a grammatical joke to be *deep*? (And that is what the depth of philosophy is.)

112. A simile that has been absorbed into the forms of our language produces a false appearance, and this disquiets us. "But *this* isn't how it is!" – we say. "Yet *this* is how it has to *be*!"

113. "But *this* is how it is –" I say to myself over and over again. I feel as though, if only I could fix my gaze absolutely sharply on this fact, get it in focus, I must grasp the essence of the matter.

114. (*Tractatus Logico-Philosophicus*, 4.5): "The general form of propositions is: This is how things are." – That is the kind of proposition that one repeats to oneself countless times. One thinks that one is tracing the outline of the thing's nature over and over again, and one is merely tracing round the frame through which we look at it.

115. A *picture* held us captive. And we could not get outside it, for it lay in our language and language seemed to repeat it to us inexorably.

116. When philosophers use a word – "knowledge", "being", "object", "I", "proposition", "name" – and try to grasp the *essence* of the thing, one must always ask oneself: is the word ever actually used in this way in the

language-game which is its original home? – What *we* do is to bring words back from their metaphysical to their everyday use.

117. You say to me: "You understand this expression, don't you? Well then – I am using it in the sense you are familiar with." – As if the sense were an atmosphere accompanying the word, which it carried with it into every kind of application.

If, for example, someone says that the sentence "This is here" (saying which he points to an object in front of him) makes sense to him, then he should ask himself in what special circumstances this sentence is actually used. There it does make sense.

118. Where does our investigation get its importance from, since it seems only to destroy everything interesting, that is, all that is great and important? (As it were all the buildings, leaving behind only bits of stone and rubble.) What we are destroying is nothing but houses of cards and we are clearing up the ground of language on which they stand.

119. The results of philosophy are the uncovering of one or another piece of plain nonsense and of bumps that the understanding has got by running its head up against the limits of language. These bumps make us see the value of the discovery.

120. When I talk about language (words, sentences, etc.) I must speak the language of every day. Is this language somehow too coarse and material for what we want to say? *Then how is another one to be constructed?* – And how strange that we should be able to do anything at all with the one we have! In giving explanations I already have to use language full-blown (not some sort of preparatory, provisional one); this by itself shews that I can adduce only exterior facts about language.

Yes, but then how can these explanations satisfy us? – Well, your very questions were framed in this language; they had to be expressed in this language, if there was anything to ask!

And your scruples are misunderstandings. Your questions refer to words; so I have to talk about words.

You say: the point isn't the word, but its meaning, and you think of the meaning as a thing of the same kind as the word, though also different from the word. Here the word, there the meaning. The money, and the cow that you can buy with it. (But contrast: money, and its use.)

121. One might think: if philosophy speaks of the use of the word "philosophy" there must be a second-order philosophy. But it is not so: it is, rather, like the case of orthography, which deals with the word "orthography" among others without then being second-order.

122. A main source of our failure to understand is that we do not *command a clear view* of the use of our words. – Our grammar is lacking in this sort of perspicuity. A perspicuous representation produces just that understanding which consists in 'seeing connexions'. Hence the importance of finding and inventing *intermediate cases*.

The concept of a perspicuous representation is of fundamental significance for us. It earmarks the form of account we give, the way we look at things. (Is this a 'Weltanschauung'?)

123. A philosophical problem has the form: "I don't know my way about".

124. Philosophy may in no way interfere with the actual use of language; it can in the end only describe it.

For it cannot give it any foundation either.

It leaves everything as it is.

It also leaves mathematics as it is, and no mathematical discovery can advance it. A "leading problem of mathematical logic" is for us a problem of mathematics like any other.

125. It is the business of philosophy, not to resolve a contradiction by means of a mathematical or logico-mathematical discovery, but to make it possible for us to get a clear view of the state of mathematics that troubles us: the state of affairs *before* the contradiction is resolved.

(And this does not mean that one is sidestepping a difficulty.)

The fundamental fact here is that we lay down rules, a technique, for a game, and that then when we follow the rules, things do not turn out as we had assumed. That we are therefore as it were entangled in our own rules.

This entanglement in our rules is what we want to understand (i.e. get a clear view of).

It throws light on our concept of *meaning* something. For in those cases things turn out otherwise than we had meant, foreseen. That is just what we say when, for example, a contradiction appears: "I didn't mean it like that."

The civil status of a contradiction, or its status in civil life: there is the philosophical problem.

126. Philosophy simply puts everything before us, and neither explains nor deduces anything. – Since everything lies open to view there is nothing to explain. For what is hidden, for example, is of no interest to us.

One might also give the name "philosophy" to what is possible before all new discoveries and inventions.

127. The work of the philosopher consists in assembling reminders for a particular purpose.

128. If one tried to advance *theses* in philosophy, it would never he possible to debate them, because everyone would agree to them.

129. The aspects of things that are most important for us are hidden because of their simplicity and familiarity. (One is unable to notice something – because it is always before one's eyes.) The real foundations of his enquiry do not strike a man at all. Unless *that* fact has at some time struck him. – And this means: we fail to be struck by what, once seen, is most striking and most powerful.

130. Our clear and simple language-games are not preparatory studies for a future regularization of language – as it were first approximations, ignoring friction and air-resistance. The language-games are rather set up as *objects of comparison* which are meant to throw light on the facts of our language by way not only of similarities, but also of dissimilarities.

131. For we can avoid ineptness or emptiness in our assertions only by presenting the model as what it is, as an object of comparisons, so to speak, a measuring-rod; not as a preconceived idea to which reality *must* correspond. (The dogmatism into which we fall so easily in doing philosophy.)

132. We want to establish an order in our knowledge of the use of language: an order with a particular end in view; one out of many possible orders; not *the* order. To this end we shall constantly be giving prominence to distinctions which our ordinary forms of language easily make us overlook. This may make it look as if we saw it as our task to reform language.
Such a reform for particular practical purposes, an improvement in our terminology designed to prevent misunderstandings in practice, is perfectly possible. But these are not the cases we have to do with. The confusions which occupy us arise when language is like an engine idling, not when it is doing work.

133. It is not our aim to refine or complete the system of rules for the use of our words in unheard-of ways.
For the clarity that we are aiming at is indeed *complete* clarity. But this simply means that the philosophical problems should *completely* disappear.
The real discovery is the one that makes me capable of stopping doing philosophy when I want to. – The one that gives philosophy peace, so that it is no longer tormented by questions which bring *itself* in question. – Instead, we now demonstrate a method, by examples; and the series of examples can be broken off. – Problems are solved (difficulties eliminated), not a *single* problem.
There is not *a* philosophical method, though there are indeed methods, like different therapies.

134. Let us examine the proposition: "This is how things are." – How can I say that this is the general form of propositions? – It is first and foremost *itself* a proposition, an English sentence, for it has a subject and a predicate. But how is this sentence applied – that is, in our everyday language? For I got it from there and nowhere else.

We may say, e.g.: "He explained his position to me, said that this was how things were, and that therefore he needed an advance". So far, then, one can say that that sentence stands for any statement. It is employed as a propositional *schema*, but *only* because it has the construction of an English sentence. It would be possible to say instead "such and such is the case", "this is the situation", and so on. It would also be possible here simply to use a letter, a variable, as in symbolic logic. But no one is going to call the letter "p" the general form of propositions. To repeat: "This is how things are" had that position only because it is itself what one calls an English sentence. But though it is a proposition, still it gets employed as a propositional variable. To say that this proposition agrees (or does not agree) with reality would be obvious nonsense. Thus it illustrates the fact that *one* feature of our concept of a proposition is, *sounding like a proposition*.

Suggested further reading

Bouveresse, J (1995), *Wittgenstein Reads Freud. The Myth of the Unconscious*. Princeton, NJ: Princeton University Press

Heaton, J (2000), *Wittgenstein and Psychoanalysis*. Duxford: Icon Books

Wittgenstein, L (1965), 'Lecture on Ethics', *The Philosophical Review*, Vol. 74, No. 1 (January), pp. 3–12, in Cahoone (ed.) (1996), *From Modernism to Postmodernism. An Anthology*. Oxford: Blackwell

—— (1998), *Culture and Value* (revised 2nd edition, ed. von Wright, G R). Oxford: Blackwell

—— (2001 [1958]), *Philosophical Investigations*. Oxford: Blackwell

Chapter 5

Some critiques of post-modernism

We have looked at some criticisms of the selected thinkers as they have arisen in our discussions; in this final chapter we explore some further criticisms of post-modernism, and question what will be next.

At a European psychotherapy conference held in Paris at the end of the 1990s there was little mention of the World Cup football which was taking place in France at the same time. Whilst some may worry about the suitability of therapists who are not engaged in this way in popular culture, what was more alarming was the dearth of papers relating to cultural developments in European, and particularly French, thinking in the last thirty to forty years.

Rather than dwelling on post-war, and post-modern European thinking, the conference showed considerable interest in American reductionism and Eastern mysticism (for a stinging critique of Western Buddhism see Žižek 2001: 12–15). Why is this? We can speculate that post-war European thought presents much more of an intellectual challenge than that offered by many American and Eastern approaches. Furthermore, as we have suggested in this book, post-modernism challenges the egocentric/Frank Sinatra 'I Did It My Way' schools of counselling and psychotherapy. In contrast to other disciplines – from literary criticism to architecture and geography – counselling, psychotherapy and psychoanalysis constitute one of the few areas left which are still resistant to such developments in European thinking. For example, few students of counselling and psychotherapy in the UK are seriously encouraged to engage with Lacan, and when he is mentioned at all it can still be in such cursory terms as these:

> Lacan . . . was violently anti-authoritarian and declaimed against the International Psycho-Analytic Association, yet when he was in authority over his own society he was enormously authoritarian seemingly without knowing it . . . when the blind spot is as gross as in the example just quoted it is difficult to have any confidence that such a person could be a good mediator of the psychoanalytic process.
>
> (Symington, 1986: 331)

This is the only reference to Lacan in an otherwise useful and respected introduction to psychoanalysis. We are not suggesting that Lacan and Lacanianism are beyond criticism (as with other approaches there is, of course, the danger that they can be used as forms of violent technique, applied without thought); Lacan is, however, a key example of someone who – by taking developments in linguistics seriously – provides huge potential for us to be more thoughtful about our practice.

Besides this kind of attack from within psychotherapy/psychoanalysis, there have been criticisms of post-modern, Continental, thinking from a number of other, diverse positions. These positions might often be in heated opposition to one another. We would point to three: a liberal, humanist position (for example, Centore, 1991, and see Habermas, below); a Marxist position (for example, Callinicos, 1990, and Eagleton, below); and a 'revisionist' scientific position. For example, Myerson (2001) argues that far from grand narratives being defunct, as Lyotard claimed, there is now a new grand narrative, the threat of ecological disaster, and this provides science with a new legitimacy, since only science is adequate to address this threat. While there is some substance to this argument, Myerson seems insufficiently critical of the role of scientific, instrumental rationality in bringing the threat into being in the first place. Wariness regarding a too narrowly 'scientific' approach to a solution might be in order.

In sympathy with Myerson's stance would probably, however, be Sokal and Bricmont (1998), who fiercely question the use made of mathematics and physics by some French intellectuals, including Lacan, Kristeva and Derrida. Their book *Intellectual Impostures* followed a successful hoax (the publication of a phoney article, parodying post-modern procedures, in a radical science journal), and takes the philosophers to task for misusing mathematics and science to bolster the respectability of various of their arguments. In our first extract, below, Sokal and Bricmont outline the aim of their book.

In response to their criticisms, we consider that while issues of fact in terms of epistemic relativism must be explored carefully, as must the place, use and misuse of science, this should not be taken as a way of dismissing arguments which need to be struggled with if we wish to examine the places clients and their therapists can take up in our current world. It is easy for writers and reporters to provide readers with what they want, as the *Guardian* newspaper in the UK partially recognised – in a double-edged way – in its review of Sokal and Bricmont's book: 'Sometimes newspapers tell us exactly what we want to hear. Last year, the *Guardian* reported from Paris that "modern French philosophy is a load of old tosh"' (Christy, 1998). There are attacks from both within and outside the profession of psychotherapy on this Continental thinking. Because this thinking questions the very bases of vested interest, in which we are of course implicated, it is perhaps inevitable that those interests should be eager to find ammunition with which to counter-attack – sometimes through ambivalent or ironic protestations of support. As Foucault has argued, regimes of power have managed to change questions of truth and falsehood into questions of what is scientific and what is unscientific (Foucault, 1980). Sokal and Bricmont may be right in demonstrating, for example, Lacan's use of the language of science to lend vicarious prestige to his project; but does this therefore leave it bereft of value? It is perhaps their assumption that it does that led Derrida to respond to the original hoax with a laconic 'le pauvre Sokal' (Sturrock, 1998).

We provide criticism of post-modernism from another direction, in extracts from the American philosopher Richard Rorty (1991), and from Jürgen Habermas (1987). Rorty is a challenging and cogent philosophical spokesperson for the liberal, humanist tradition (he draws from the late nineteenth-century American Pragmatists, James, Dewey, *et al.*). For Rorty, philosophy has lost its function in the West in so far as it can no longer claim to be foundational of knowledge, as in its previous tradition. Post-modernists might celebrate this: for Rorty this post-modern anti-foundationalism leads to a separation of philosophy and politics. Philosophy is left with little to do; it can only contribute to a conversation about culture, and needs to refind or remake its roots, pragmatically, in terms of a cultural 'solidarity'. Like most post-modernists, Rorty does not see the search for objective 'truth' as philosophy's task; he feels, however, that philosophy must reach towards ways of formulating 'the good'.

Does Rorty nostalgically want philosophy to return to a time when knowledge and the good were linked, and could this really be possible? Post-modernists would question whether our interest in knowledge is really bound up with a search for the good. Post-modern thinkers, with the exception of Levinas, rarely talk of the good. They would tend to think of knowledge as having to do with power, appropriation and totalisation, rather than acceptance. We would argue the case that professionalisation of knowledge in counselling, psychotherapy, psychology, and related professions, can lead to less truth and justice, not more.

Habermas's thinking comes out of the background of the Frankfurt School, with its emphasis on materialist approaches to history. For Habermas, 'We cannot dismiss a priori the suspicion that postmodern thought merely claims a transcendent status . . . We cannot exclude from the outset the possibility that neoconservatism and aesthetically inspired anarchism, in the name of a farewell to modernity, are merely trying to revolt against it once again. It could be that they are merely cloaking their complicity with the venerable tradition of counter-Enlightenment in the garb of post-Enlightenment' (Habermas, 1987: 4–5).

As Cahoone writes, rationality for Habermas is inherently linguistic, and social (Cahoone, 1996: 589). The extract below provides a brief overview of Habermas's three major areas of concern with regard to post-modernism. First, he says, post-modern discourses which radically critique reason give no account of their own position; the post-modern critique of reason is fundamentally flawed because it shows 'reckless disregard for its own foundations'. Second, post-modern critiques are inherently contradictory, 'guided by normative intuitions that go beyond what they can accommodate in terms of the indirectly affirmed "other of reason"'; how can rational language affirm an 'other of reason', except in bad faith? Third, post-modern discourses are a 'totalizing repudiation of modern forms of life', at best indifferent to 'effects that ensure freedom and those that remove it'.

Habermas grounds his thinking in a notion of the self; he likes the reassurance of a self at the centre, stating that he is concerned that post-modernism throws out 'precisely what a modernity reassuring itself once meant by the concepts of self-consciousness, self-determination, and self-realisation' (Habermas, 1987: 337 etc). He raises serious questions about post-modernism's potential inconsistencies and intellectual dishonesties. Yet he seems to yearn for a time when it was possible to see the individual at the centre of her or his world, subject perhaps only to 'truth' and 'freedom', or to a political or social programme with a 'rational' basis, that is, one that could, in theory, be formally defined and agreed upon.

Perhaps Habermas is not interested in signs because they might lead down a chain of signifiers over which he would have no control. For Habermas, it is rationality that will get us there – rather than justice to another in the moment. We do not feel that Lyotard's criticism of his position has been overturned: for Lyotard the consensus in which Habermas seeks to locate legitimacy 'does violence to the heterogeneity of language games' (Lyotard, 1984: xxv). A Habermasian, late-modern way of thinking has, however, won in important respects in the world of psychotherapy. At the start of the twenty-first century psychotherapy would seem increasingly to have gone down the path of empiricism, as can be seen, for example, in cognitive-behavioural thinking, which tacitly privileges that which is measurable and outcome-based. This is different from asking: 'What is the world of our patients and clients?'

Before we consider the final extract, we must signal the work of the American Marxist scholar Fredric Jameson, which has been very influential, since the early 1980s, in focusing debate on the nature and value of post-modernism, especially for thinkers on the left. Jameson's evolving project has been to develop a theoretical understanding of the post-modern as a function of social, political, economic and cultural relations within late capitalism. Jameson tends to use a language which can be powerfully evocative, or, depending on the reader, obscurely 'post-modern', and this is suggestive of the extent to which his project involves his immersion in post-modern culture. Drawing on Lyotard and Baudrillard, Deleuze and Lacan, he has seen the post-modern as characterised by new experiences of time and space: the speeding up of time, as fashion succeeds fashion, and, spatially, the localisation of the global – ethnic identities, for example, becoming life-style choices, in the consumerist West. Jameson's seminal essay of 1984, 'Postmodernism, or, the Cultural Logic of Late Capitalism' (in Jameson, 1996), could be read as a sort of polemic in favour of post-modernism. The essay also, however, spoke to a wide audience on the left, which was concerned to reclaim socialist values perceived to be lost or dissipated within the extreme forms of relativism and the intensive commodification characteristic of the post-modern era. For Jameson has sought 'to reconfirm the privileged status of Marxism as a mode of analysis of capitalism proper' (Jameson in Lyotard, 1984: xiii). Jameson's work can be taken to affirm that even within global capitalism there is an area of universal value, a non-commodified, non-capitalised space, available as a basis for the rehabilitation of internationalist, transformational ideals. Anderson (1998) is a useful introduction to Jameson's thinking.

A broadly similar position is taken up by Terry Eagleton – a British professor of English on the political left – who also derives his critical approach from a notion of universal human value. In contrast to Habermas, Eagleton (Eagleton, 1996) sees post-modernism as being about 'the final penetration of the rationalizing impulse of modernity into the inner sanctum of the subject'. Like Habermas, he asks whether post-modernism is radical or conservative. From a Marxist point of view, he sees post-modernism as part of the problem, not the solution. Structuralism brought technological determinism into the mind itself, 'treating individuals as the mere empty locus of impersonal codes', and this mimicked the way advanced capitalist society, as 'both libertarian and authoritarian', treats people but pretends it does not. The market is a 'decentered network of desire', and 'the political ambivalences of postmodernism match this contradiction exactly'. 'Politically oppositional but economically complicit', it helps to hold the potential anarchy of the market in place. Eagleton raises the question for our book: does post-modernism shore capitalism up in the name of questioning it? Its cultural relativism and suspicion of, or distaste, for ideas of solidarity, tell against it as something of any use in the fight against technical, totalising thinking. If this is the case, then in a way our thinkers have failed and modernity triumphs.

In some respects we go along with Eagleton's view. At the same time, we have argued that we also need to be open, alert and attentive to the state of the culture now, to be on the edge of something, as it manifests itself in the language of our clients/patients and the unconscious that seeps through, erupts out of, or is otherwise embodied in this language. If we are to be attentive to our clients then this requires attention to the ways our discourse with them is constructed. We need to be attentive to the way that language currently shapes us. There are always limits to our thinking; at worst, to look at the culture we were in (or wish we had been) is to be in the wrong place, to remain nostalgically fixated on older struggles and polarisations – although, as phenomenologists, we might hope to be cognisant of the ways such struggles and polarisations subsist in 'sedimented' form in the present.

We must also acknowledge that a certain post-modern movement may have passed, for us to be able to write about it at all. The new edge is (always already) elsewhere. By a horrible irony, we found ourselves drafting this concluding section on 11 September 2001 – in a common room down the corridor from our office at the University of Surrey a TV was relaying live pictures of the burning towers. Whatever is next, we hope that in producing this book we are playing a part in fostering a recognition that what we all hold in common is that we are 'subject to(o)'. This, we hope, can also help give us courage and humility in fighting against the hardness and inhumanity of a world view founded in purely 'technical' reason. It is a view which can lead, for example, to the claim that the possessor of the smartest and most powerful weaponry has, by virtue of this very power, the moral obligation to police and subjugate regimes of which he does not morally approve. Technical reason, as Foucault and others have tirelessly demonstrated, can become technical justification for quite other agendas.

We have argued in this book that with the increasing professionalisation of therapy, post-modern thinking provides an important way of exploring questions of value, for example such questions as: on what basis are 'standards' set in therapy? To what extent does the other (whether 'subject', 'client', 'patient', 'object', 'student', 'consumer', 'user' or 'person') merely become part of a supporting cast in a drama set up to preserve the therapist's privilege, and to protect the therapist's approach? When are perversions intolerable? When in imposing standards are we treating others as puppets? Related issues have included: what are the implications for the training and evaluation of counsellors and psychotherapists?

If we accept as part of post-modernism that the postal principle is broken, that the message sent is not the one received, then surely therapists have no choice but to be interested in language and the stories we tell. Once this is taken on, it would certainly seem naïve to suppose – and thinkers on the left ought not to be naïve – that solidarity and consensus are ever easily given, or achieved through the application of 'reason'. The post-modern challenges the singularity of the modern narrative. As clients and patients we can operate like movie directors, editing, having biases, or toeing the party line. Post-modernism reminds us that there are histories, not just history; it can help us, when we need reminding, to see that the therapist's job is far from facilitating the client to tell a story, as if it were *the* story.

In this book we endorse the post-modern attempt to 'demolish ideological positions built on the idea of an epistemic subject being the centre of the world instead of being part of the text of the world'. We share Løvlie's view: 'In the name of the death of the subject [the post-modern] blend of contextualism and irony actually recaptures the modern individual in his or her position as . . . critical subject' (Løvlie, 1992: 132–3). The development of psychotherapy since the 1960s has taken place within an era of individualism, where questions of value centre on the person. We have moved from God to Science to the Person – so is the person the new God, and which person is it, the therapist or the client? When corporations and nations act within this individualistic ethic, it can lead to scenarios such as the USA's refusal to sign up to the Kyoto and other international agreements. As psychotherapists do we think that this is a good model for relationships? How healthy is it for our work, our clients/patients, and indeed our world, if we ignore the critique of autonomy which, for us, is one of the major and defining contributions of Continental post-modern philosophy?

From Sokal and Bricmont (1998), *Intellectual Impostures*, pp. 3–6

The goal of this book is to make a limited but original contribution to the critique of the admittedly nebulous *Zeitgeist* that we have called 'postmodernism'. We make no claim to analyse postmodernist thought in general; rather, our aim is to draw attention to a relatively little-known aspect, namely the repeated abuse of concepts and terminology coming from mathematics and physics. We shall also analyse certain confusions of thought that are frequent in postmodernist writings and that bear on either the content or the philosophy of the natural sciences.

The word 'abuse' here denotes one or more of the following characteristics:

1 Holding forth at length on scientific theories about which one has, at best, an exceedingly hazy idea. The most common tactic is to use scientific (or pseudo-scientific) terminology without bothering much about what the words actually mean.

2 Importing concepts from the natural sciences into the humanities or social sciences without giving the slightest conceptual or empirical justification. If a biologist wanted to apply, in her research, elementary notions of mathematical topology, set theory or differential geometry, she would be asked to give some explanation. A vague analogy would not be taken very seriously by her colleagues. Here, by contrast, we learn from Lacan that the structure of the neurotic subject is exactly the torus (it is no less than reality itself . . .), from Kristeva that poetic language can be theorized in terms of the cardinality of the continuum . . . , and from Baudrillard that modern war takes place in a non-Euclidean space . . . – all without explanation.

3 Displaying a superficial erudition by shamelessly throwing around technical terms in a context where they are completely irrelevant. The goal is, no doubt, to impress and, above all, to intimidate the non-scientist reader. Even some academic and media commentators fall into the trap. Roland Barthes is impressed by the precision of Julia Kristeva's work . . . and *Le Monde* admires the erudition of Paul Virilio . . .

4 Manipulating phrases and sentences that are, in fact, meaningless. Some of these authors exhibit a veritable intoxication with words, combined with a superb indifference to their meaning.

These authors speak with a self-assurance that far outstrips their scientific competence. Lacan boasts of using 'the most recent development in topology' . . . and Latour asks whether he has taught anything to Einstein. . . . They imagine, perhaps, that they can exploit the prestige of the natural sciences in order to give their own discourse a veneer of rigour. And they seem confident that no one will notice their misuse of scientific concepts. No one is going to cry out that the king is naked.

Our goal is precisely to say that the king is naked (and the queen too). But let us be clear. We are not attacking philosophy, the humanities or the social sciences in general; on the contrary, we feel that these fields are of the utmost importance and we want to warn those who work in them (especially students) against some manifest cases of charlatanism. In particular, we want to 'deconstruct' the reputation that certain texts have of being difficult because the ideas in them are so profound. In many cases we shall demonstrate that if the texts seem incomprehensible, it is for the excellent reason that they mean precisely nothing.

There are many different degrees of abuse. At one end, one finds extrapolations of scientific concepts, beyond their domain of validity, that are erroneous but for subtle reasons. At the other end, one finds numerous texts that are full of scientific words but entirely devoid of meaning. And there is, of course, a continuum of discourses that can be situated somewhere between these two extremes. Although we shall concentrate in this book on the most manifest abuses, we shall also briefly address some less obvious confusions concerning chaos theory . . .

Let us stress that there is nothing shameful in being ignorant of calculus or quantum mechanics. What we are criticizing is the pretension of some celebrated intellectuals to offer profound thoughts on complicated subjects that they understand, at best, at the level of popularizations.

At this point, the reader may naturally wonder: Do these abuses arise from conscious fraud, self-deception, or perhaps a combination of the two? We are unable to offer any categorical answer to this question, due to the lack of (publicly available) evidence. But, more importantly, we must confess that we do not find this question of great interest. Our aim here is to stimulate a critical attitude, not merely towards certain individuals, but towards a part of the intelligentsia (both in the United States and in Europe) that has tolerated and even encouraged this type of discourse.

From Rorty (1991), *Objectivity, Relativism and Truth*, pp. 22–4, 32–4

Solidarity or Objectivity?

. . . Those who wish to ground solidarity in objectivity – call them "realists" – have to construe truth as correspondence to reality. So they must construct a metaphysics which has room for a special relation between beliefs and objects which will differentiate true from false beliefs. They also must argue that there are procedures of justification of belief which are natural and not merely local. So they must construct an epistemology which has room for a kind of justification which is not merely social but natural, springing from human nature itself, and made possible by a link between that part of nature and the rest of nature. On their view, the various procedures which are thought of as providing rational justification by one or another culture may or may not really *be* rational. For to be truly rational, procedures of justification *must* lead to the truth, to correspondence to reality, to the intrinsic nature of things.

By contrast, those who wish to reduce objectivity to solidarity – call them "pragmatists" – do not require either a metaphysics or an epistemology. They view truth as, in William James's phrase, what is good for *us* to believe. So they do not need an account of a relation between beliefs and objects called "correspondence", nor an account of human cognitive abilities which ensures that our species is capable of entering into that relation. They see the gap between truth and justification not as something to be bridged by isolating a natural and transcultural sort of rationality which can be used to criticise certain cultures and praise others, but simply as the gap between the actual good and the possible better. From a pragmatist point of view, to say that what is rational for us now to believe may not be *true*, is simply to say that somebody may come up with a better idea. It is to say that there is always room for improved belief, since new evidence, or new hypotheses, or a whole new vocabulary, may come along. For pragmatists, the desire for objectivity is not the desire to escape the limitations of one's community, but simply the desire for as much intersubjective agreement as possible, the desire to extend the reference of "us" as far as we can. Insofar as pragmatists make a distinction between knowledge and opinion, it is simply the distinction between topics on which such agreement is relatively easy to get and topics on which agreement is relatively hard to get.

"Relativism" is the traditional epithet applied to pragmatism by realists. Three different views are commonly referred to by this name. The first is the view that every belief is as good as every other. The second is the view that "true" is an equivocal term, having as many meanings as there are procedures of justification. The third is the view that there is nothing to be said about either truth or rationality apart from descriptions of the familiar procedures of justification which a given society – *ours* – uses in one or another area of inquiry. The pragmatist holds the ethnocentric third view. But he does not hold the self-refuting first view, nor the eccentric second view. He thinks that his views are better than the realists', but he does not think that his views correspond to the nature of things. He thinks that the very flexibility of the word "true" – the fact that it is merely an expression of commendation – insures its univocity. The term "true", on his account, means the same in all cultures, just as equally flexible terms like "here", "there", "good", "bad", "you", and "me" mean the same in all cultures. But the identity of meaning is, of course, compatible with diversity of reference, and with diversity of procedures for assessing the terms. So he feels free to use the term "true" as a general term of commendation in the same way as his realist opponent does – and in particular to use it to commend his own view.

However, it is not clear why "relativist" should be thought an appropriate term for the ethnocentric third view, the one which the pragmatist holds. For the pragmatist is not holding a positive theory which says that something is relative to something else. He is, instead, making the purely *negative* point that we should drop the traditional distinction between knowledge and opinion, construed as the distinction between truth as correspondence to reality and truth as a commendatory term for well-justified beliefs. The reason that the realist calls this negative claim 'relativistic' is that he cannot believe that anybody would seriously deny that truth has an intrinsic nature. So when the pragmatist says that there is nothing to be said about truth save that each of us will commend as true those beliefs which he or she finds good to believe, the realist is inclined to interpret this as one more positive theory about the nature of truth, a theory according to which truth is simply the contemporary opinion of a chosen individual or group. Such a theory would, of course, be self-refuting. But the pragmatist does not have a theory of truth, much less a relativistic one. As a partisan of solidarity, his account of the value of cooperative human inquiry has only an ethical base, not an epistemological or metaphysical one. Not having *any* epistemology, *a fortiori*, he does not have a relativistic one.

The question of whether truth or rationality has an intrinsic nature, of whether we ought to have a positive theory about either topic, is just a question of whether our self-description ought to be constructed around a relation to human nature or around a relation to a particular collection of human beings, whether we should desire objectivity or solidarity. It is hard to see how one could choose between these alternatives by looking more deeply into the nature of knowledge, or of man, or of nature. Indeed, the proposal that this issue might be so settled begs the question in favor of the realist, for it presupposes that knowledge, man, and nature *have* real essences which are relevant to the problem at hand. For the pragmatist, by contrast, "knowledge" is, like "truth", simply a compliment paid to the beliefs which we think so well justified that, for the moment, further justification is not needed. An inquiry into the nature of knowledge can, on this view, only be a socio-historical account of how various people have tried to reach agreement on what to believe.

The view which I am calling "pragmatism" is almost, but not quite, the same as what Hilary Putnam, in his recent *Reason, Truth, and History* (Putnam, 1981), calls 'the internalist conception of philosophy'. Putnam defines such a conception as one which gives up the attempt at a God's eye view of things, the attempt at contact with the nonhuman which I have been calling 'the desire for objectivity'. Unfortunately, he accompanies his defense of the antirealist views I am recommending with a polemic against a lot of the other people who hold these views – e.g. Kuhn, Feyerabend, Foucault, and myself. We are criticized as 'relativists' . . .

My suggestion that the desire for objectivity is in part a disguised form of the fear of the death of our community echoes Nietzsche's charge that the philosophical tradition which stems from Plato is an attempt to avoid facing up to contingency, to escape from time and chance. Nietzsche thought that realism was to be condemned not only by arguments from its theoretical incoherence, the sort of argument we find in Putnam and Davidson, but also on practical, pragmatic, grounds. Nietzsche thought that the test of human character was the ability to live with the thought that there was no convergence. He wanted us to be able to think of truth as:

a mobile army of metaphors, metonyms, and anthropomorphisms – in short a sum of human relations, which have been enhanced, transposed, and embellished poetically and rhetorically and which after long use seem firm, canonical, and obligatory to a people.

[Nietzsche, 1977b: 46–7]

Nietzsche hoped that eventually there might be human beings who could and did think of truth in this way, but who still liked themselves, who saw themselves as *good* people for whom solidarity was *enough.*

I think that pragmatism's attack on the various structure–content distinctions which buttress the realist's notion of objectivity can best be seen as an attempt to let us think of truth in this Nietzschean way as entirely a matter of solidarity. That is why I think we need to say, despite Putnam, that 'there is only the dialogue', only *us*, and to throw out the last residues of the notion of 'transcultural rationality'. But this should not lead us to repudiate, as Nietzsche sometimes did, the elements in our movable host which embody the ideas of Socratic conversation, Christian fellowship, and Enlightenment science. Nietzsche ran together his diagnosis of philosophical realism as an expression of fear and resentment with his own resentful idiosyncratic idealizations of silence, solitude, and violence. Post-Nietzschean thinkers like Adorno and Heidegger and Foucault have run together Nietzsche's criticisms of the metaphysical tradition on the one hand with his criticisms of bourgeois civility, of Christian love, and of the nineteenth century's hope that science would make the world a better place to live, on the other. I do not think that there is any interesting connection between these two sets of criticisms. Pragmatism seems to me, as I have said, a philosophy of solidarity rather than of despair. From this point of view, Socrates' turn away from the gods, Christianity's turn from an Omnipotent Creator to the man who suffered on the Cross, and the Baconian turn from science as contemplation of eternal truth to science as progress, can be seen as so many preparations for the act of social faith which is suggested by a Nietzschean view of truth.

The best argument we partisans of solidarity have against the realistic partisans of objectivity is Nietzsche's argument that the traditional Western metaphysico-epistemological way of firming up our habits simply isn't working anymore. It isn't doing its job. It has become as transparent a device as the postulation of deities who turn out, by a happy coincidence, to have chosen *us* as their people. So the pragmatist suggestion that we substitute a "merely" ethical foundation for our sense of community – or, better, that we think of our sense of community as having no foundation, except shared hope and the trust created by such sharing – is put forward on practical grounds. It is *not* put forward as a corollary of a metaphysical claim that the objects in the world contain no intrinsically action-guiding properties, nor of an epistemological claim that we lack a faculty of moral sense, nor of a semantical claim that truth is reducible to justification. It is a suggestion about how we might think of ourselves in order to avoid the kind of resentful belatedness – characteristic of the bad side of Nietzsche – which now characterizes much of high culture. This resentment arises from the realization, which I referred to at the beginning of this chapter, that the Enlightenment's search for objectivity has often gone sour.

The rhetoric of scientific objectivity, pressed too hard and taken too seriously, has led us to people like B. F. Skinner on the one hand and people like Althusser on the other – two equally pointless fantasies, both produced by the attempt to be "scientific" about our moral and political lives. Reaction against scientism led to attacks on natural science as a sort of false god. But there is nothing wrong with science, there is only something wrong with the attempt to divinize it, the attempt characteristic of realistic philosophy. This reaction has also led to attacks on liberal social thought of the type common to Mill and Dewey and Rawls as a mere ideological superstructure, one which obscures the realities of our situation and represses attempts to change that situation. But there is nothing wrong with liberal democracy, nor with the philosophers who have tried to enlarge its scope. There is only something wrong with the attempt to see their efforts as failures to achieve something which they were not trying to achieve – a demonstration of the "objective" superiority of our way of life over all other alternatives. There is, in short, nothing wrong with the hopes of the Enlightenment, the hopes which created the Western democracies. The value of the ideals of the Enlightenment is, for us pragmatists, just the value of some of the institutions and practices which they have created . . .

From Habermas (1987), *The Philosphical Discourse of Modernity*, Lecture XII, pp. 336–8

The Normative Content of Modernity

The radical critique of reason exacts a high price for taking leave of modernity. In the first place, these discourses can and want to give no account of their own position. Negative dialectics, genealogy, and deconstruction alike avoid those categories in accord with which modern knowledge has been differentiated – by no means accidentally – and on the basis of which we today understand texts. They cannot be unequivocally classified with either philosophy or science, with moral and legal theory, or with literature and art. At the same time, they resist any return to forms of religious thought, whether dogmatic or heretical. So an incongruity arises between these "theories", which raise validity claims only to renounce them, and the kind of institutionalization they undergo within the business of science. There is an asymmetry between the rhetorical gesture with which these discourses demand understanding and the critical treatment to which they are subjected institutionally, for example in the framework of an academic lecture. No matter whether Adorno paradoxically reclaims truth-validity, or Foucault refuses to draw consequences from manifest contradictions; no matter whether Heidegger and Derrida evade the obligation to provide grounds by fleeing into the esoteric or by fusing the logical with the rhetorical: there always emerges a symbiosis of incompatibles, an amalgam that resists "normal" scientific analysis at its core. Things are only shifted to a different place if we change the frame of reference and no longer treat the same discourse as philosophy or science, but as a piece of literature. That the self-referential critique of reason is located everywhere and nowhere, so to speak, in discourses without a place, renders it almost immune to competing interpretations. Such discourses unsettle the institutionalized standards of fallibilism; they always allow for a final word, even when the argument is already lost: that the opponent has misunderstood the meaning of the language game and has committed a category mistake in the sorts of response she has been making.

The variations of a critique of reason with reckless disregard for its own foundations are related to one another in another respect as well. They are guided by normative intuitions that go beyond what they can accommodate in terms of the indirectly affirmed "other of reason". Whether modernity is described as a constellation of life that is reified and used, or as one that is technologically manipulated, or as one that is totalitarian, rife with power, homogenized, imprisoned – the denunciations are constantly inspired by a special sensitivity for complex injuries and subtle violations. Inscribed in this sensitivity is the picture of an undamaged intersubjectivity that the young Hegel first projected as an ethical totality. With the counterconcepts (injected as empty formulas) of Being, sovereignty, power, difference, and nonidentity, this critique points to the contents of aesthetic experience; but the values derived therefrom and explicitly laid claim to – the values of grace and illumination, ecstatic rapture, bodily integrity, wish fulfillment, and caring intimacy – do not cover the moral change that these authors tacitly envision in connection with a life practice that is intact – and not only in the sense of reconciling inner nature. Between the declared normative foundations and the concealed ones there is a disparity that can be explained by the *undialectical* rejection of subjectivity. Not only the devastating consequences of an objectifying relation-to-self are condemned along with this principle of modernity, but also the *other* connotations once associated with subjectivity as an unredeemed promise: the prospect of a self-conscious practice, in which the solitary self-determination of all was to be joined with the self-realization of each. What is thrown out is precisely what a modernity reassuring itself once meant by the concepts of self-consciousness, self-determination, and self-realization.

A further defect of these discourses is explained by their totalizing repudiation of modern forms of life: Although they are interesting in regard to fundamentals, they remain undifferentiated in their results. The criteria according to which Hegel and Marx, and even Max Weber and Lukács, distinguished between emancipatory–reconciling aspects of social rationalization and repressive–alienating aspects have been blunted. In the meantime, critique has taken hold of and demolished the sorts of concepts by which those aspects could be distinguished from one another so that their paradoxical entanglement became visible. Enlightenment and manipulation, the conscious and the unconscious, forces of production and forces of destruction, expressive self-realization and repressive desublimation, effects that ensure freedom and those that remove it, truth and ideology – now all these moments flow into one another. They are not linked to one another as, say, conflicting elements in a disastrous functional context – unwilling accomplices in a contradictory process permeated by oppositional conflict. Now the differences and oppositions are so undermined and even collapsed that critique can no longer discern contrasts, shadings, and ambivalent tones within the flat and faded landscape of a totally administered, calculated, and power-laden world. To be sure, Adorno's theory of the administered world and Foucault's theory of power are more fertile, and simply more informative, than Heidegger's or Derrida's lucubrations on technology as an instrumental frame [*Gestell*] or on the totalitarian nature of the political order. But they are all insensitive to the highly *ambivalent* content of cultural and social modernity. This leveling can also be seen in the diachronic comparison of modern forms of life with pre-modern ones. The high price earlier exacted from the mass of the population (in the dimensions of bodily labor, material conditions, possibilities of individual choice, security of law and punishment, political participation, and schooling) is barely even noticed.

From Eagleton (1996), *The Illusions of Postmodernism*, pp. 131–5

The chief contradiction of postmodernism is a little like that of old-fashioned structuralism. Was structuralism radical or conservative? It is easy enough to see the ways in which it behaved as a kind of technocracy of the spirit, the final penetration of the rationalizing impulse of modernity into the inner sanctum of the subject. With its rigorous codings, universal schemas and hard-nosed reductionism, it reflected in the sphere of *Geist* a reification already apparent in reality. But this is only one side of the story. For in extending the logic of technocracy into the mind, structuralism scandalized the liberal humanism whose task was to preserve the life of the mind from any such vulgar reduction. And this liberal humanism was one of the dominant ideologies of technocratic society itself. In this sense, structuralism was radical and conservative at the same time, colluding with the strategies of modern capitalism in a way deeply at odds with its own sovereign values. It is as though by pressing a sort of technological determinism all the way through to the mind itself, treating individuals as the mere empty locus of impersonal codes, it irritated the way modern society actually treats them but pretends it does not, thus endorsing its logic while unmasking its ideals. "System", writes Roland Barthes, "is the enemy of Man" – meaning, no doubt, that for humanism the subject is always that which is radically irreducible, that which will seep through the cracks of your categories and play havoc with your structures.

There is a similar sort of contradiction built into postmodernism, which is also both radical and conservative together. It is a striking feature of advanced capitalist societies that they are both libertarian and authoritarian, hedonistic and repressive, multiple and monolithic. And the reason for this is not hard to find. The logic of the marketplace is one of pleasure and plurality, of the ephemeral and discontinuous, of some great decentred network of desire of which individuals seem the mere fleeting effects. Yet to hold all this potential anarchy in place requires strong foundations and a firm political framework. The more market forces threaten to subvert all stability, the more stridently one will need to insist upon traditional values. It is not unusual to find British politicians who support the commercialization of radio but are horrified by poems which don't rhyme. But the more this system appeals to metaphysical values to legitimate itself, the more its own rationalizing, secularizing activities threaten to strike them hollow. These regimes can neither abandon the metaphysical nor properly accommodate it, and they are thus always potentially self-deconstructing.

The political ambivalences of postmodernism match this contradiction exactly. One might venture, in a first crude approximation, that a lot of postmodernism is politically oppositional but economically complicit. This, however, requires some fine-tuning. Postmodernism is radical in so far as it challenges a system which still needs absolute values, metaphysical founda- tions and self-identical subjects; against these it mobilizes multiplicity, non-identity, transgression, anti-foundationalism, cultural relativism. The result, at its best, is a resourceful subversion of the dominant value-system, at least at the level of theory. There are business executives who have heard all about deconstruction and react to it much as religious fundamentalists do to atheism. In fact they are quite right to do so, since in its more politicized forms deconstruction is indeed an assault on much of what most businessmen hold dear. But postmodernism usually fails to recognize that what goes at the level of ideology does not always go at the level of the market.

If the system has need of the autonomous subject in the law court or polling booth, it has little enough use for it in the media or shopping mall. In these sectors, plurality, desire, fragmentation and the rest are as native to the way we live as coal was to Newcastle before Margaret Thatcher got her hands on it. Many a business executive is in this sense a spontaneous postmodernist. Capitalism is the most pluralistic order history has ever known, restlessly transgressing boundaries and dismantling oppositions, pitching together diverse life-forms and continually overflowing the measure. The whole of this plurality, need one say, operates within quite stringent limits; but it helps to explain why some postmodernists look eagerly to a hybridized future while others are persuaded that it has already arrived.

Postmodernism, in short, scoops up something of the material logic of advanced capitalism and turns this aggressively against its spiritual foundations. And in this it bears more than a passing resemblance to the structuralism which was one of its remote sources. It is as though it is urging the system, like its great mentor Friedrich Nietzsche, to forget about its metaphysical foundations, acknowledge that God is dead and simply go relativist. Then, at least, it might trade a modicum of security for a degree of actuality. Why not just confess that your values are as precariously ungrounded as anybody else's? It would hardly leave you vulnerable to attack, since you have just craftily demolished any vantage-point from which any offensive onslaught might be launched. In any case, the kind of values which are rooted in what you do, which reflect the unvarnished social reality rather than the highfalutin moral ideal, are likely to be a good deal more cogent than a lot of nebulous talk about progress, reason or God's special affection for the nation.

But it is all very well for pragmatist philosophers to argue in this way. Those who bear the burden of running the system are aware that ideologies are in business to *legitimate* what you do, not just to reflect it. They cannot simply dispense with these high-sounding rationales, not least because a great many people still credit them, indeed cling to them ever more tenaciously as they feel the ground shifting beneath their feet. The commodity, *pace* Adorno, cannot be its own ideology, at least not yet. One could imagine a future phase of the system of which this would be true, in which it had taken a course at some North American university, desperately or cheerfully jettisoned its own foundations and left behind it the whole business of rhetorical legitimation. Indeed there are those who claim that this is precisely what is afoot today: that 'hegemony' is no longer important, that the system does not care whether we believe in it or not, that it has no need to secure our spiritual complicity as long as we do more or less what it demands. It no longer has to pass through human consciousness to reproduce itself, just to keep that consciousness permanently distracted and rely for its reproduction on its own automated mechanisms. But postmodernism belongs in this respect to a transitional era, one in which the metaphysical, like some unquiet ghost, can neither resuscitate itself nor decently die. If it could manage to lapse from being, then no doubt postmodernism would pass away with it.

I must end, regretfully, on a minatory note. Postmodern end-of-history thinking does not envisage a future for us much different from the present, a prospect it oddly views as a cause for celebration. But there is indeed one such possible future among several, and its name is fascism. The greatest test of postmodernism, or for that matter of any other political doctrine, is how it would shape up to that. Its rich body of work on racism and ethnicity, on the paranoia of identity-thinking, on the perils of totality and the fear of otherness: all this, along with its deepened insights into the cunning of power, would no doubt be of considerable value. But its cultural relativism and moral conventionalism, its scepticism, pragmatism and localism, its distaste for ideas of solidarity and disciplined organization, its lack of any adequate theory of political agency: all these would tell heavily against it. In confronting its political antagonists, the left, now more than ever, has need of strong ethical and even anthropological foundations; nothing short of this is likely to furnish us with the political resources we require. And on this score, postmodernism is in the end part of the problem rather than of the solution.

Suggested further reading

McCumber, J (2000), *Philosophy and Freedom: Derrida, Rorty, Habermas, Foucault.* Bloomington: Indiana University Press

Bibliography

Adams, T. (1988), 'The Creative Feminine: Kristeva and the Maternal Body', in Seu, I. B. and Heenan, M. C. (1998), *Feminism and Psychotherapy. Reflections on Contemporary Theories and Practice*. London: Sage.

Althusser, L., with Balibar, E. (1970), *Reading Capital*. London: New Left Books.

Anderson, P. (1998), *The Origins of Postmodernity*. London and New York: Verso.

Anderson, W. T. (ed.) (1996), *The Fontana Postmodern Reader*. London: Fontana.

Appignanesi, L. (ed.) (1989), *Postmodernism: ICA Documents*. London: Free Association Books.

Arendt, H. (1961), *Between Past and Future*. New York: Viking.

Barratt, B. (1993), *Psychoanalysis and the Postmodern Impulse: Knowing and Being Since Freud's Psychology*. Baltimore, MD: The Johns Hopkins University Press.

Barthes, R. (1977), *Image/Music/Text*. London: Fontana.

Bataille, G. (1991), *The Accursed Share: An Essay on General Economy: Consumption* (trans. Hurley, R). New York: Zone Books.

Baudrillard, J. (1975) *The Mirror of Production*. St. Louis: Telors Press.

—— (1988), *Selected Writings* (ed. Poster, M.). Oxford: Polity Press.

—— (1993), *Symbolic Exchange and Death*. London: Sage.

—— (2002), *The Spirit of Terrorism*. London and New York: Verso.

Beauvoir, S. de (1953), *The Second Sex*. London: Jonathan Cape.

Becker, C. (1992), *Living and Relating*. London: Sage.

Benjamin, W. (1973), *Illuminations*. London: Fontana.

Benvenuto, B. and Kennedy, R. (1986), *The Works of Jacques Lacan: An Introduction*. London: Free Association Books.

Bernasconi, R. and Wood, D. (eds) (1988), *The Provocation of Levinas. Rethinking the Other*. London: Routledge.

Best, S. and Kellner, D. (1997), *The Postmodern Turn*. New York: Guilford Press.

Binswanger, L. (1963), *Being-in-the-World. Selected Papers of Ludwig Binswanger*. New York: Basic Books.

Bion, W.R. (1967), 'Notes on Memory and Desire', in Spillius, E. B. (ed.) *Melanie Klein Today. Developments in Theory and Practice. Vol.2: Mainly Practice*. London: Routledge, 1988.

Boss, M. (1963), *Psychoanalysis and Dasein Analysis*. New York: Basic Books.

Bottomore, T. (ed.) (1983), *A Dictionary of Marxist Thought*. Oxford: Blackwell.

Bouveresse, J. (1995), *Wittgenstein Reads Freud. The Myth of the Unconscious*. Princeton, NJ: Princeton University Press.

Brooke, R. (ed.) (1999), *Pathways into the Jungian World. Phenomenology and Analytical Psychology*. London: Routledge.

Buber, M. (1958), *I and Thou*. New York: Charles Scribner's Sons.

Butler, J. (1990), *Gender Trouble. Feminism and the Subversion of Identity*. London: Routledge.

Cahoone, L. (ed.) (1996), *From Modernism to Postmodernism*. Oxford: Blackwell.

Callinicos, A. (1990), *Against Post-Modernism: A Marxist Critique*. Basingstoke: Palgrave.

Campbell, J. (2000), *Arguing with the Phallus: Feminist, Queer and Postcolonial Theory: A Psychoanalytic Contribution*. London: Zed Books.

Centore, F. F. (1991), *Being and Becoming. A Critique of Post-Modernism*. Westport, CT: Greenwood Press.

Child, M. Williams, D. D., Birch, J. A. and Bordy, R. M. (1995), 'Autonomy or Heteronomy? Levinas's Challenge to Modernism *and* Postmodernism', *Educational Theory*, Vol. 45, No. 2, pp. 167–89.

Christy, D. (1998) 'The Science of Nonsense', *The Guardian*, 27 June.

Cixous, H. (1976), 'The laugh of the medusa', *Signs*, 1: 875–99.

—— (1986), 'Sorties', in Cixous and Clément (1986).

—— (ed. Sellers, S.) (1994), *The Hélène Cixous Reader*. London: Routledge.

Cixous, H. and Clément, C. (1986), *The Newly Born Woman* (trans. Wing, B.). Manchester: Manchester University Press.

Cohn, H. (1997), *Existential Thought and Therapeutic Practice*. London: Sage.

Collins, J. (2000), *Heidegger and the Nazis*. Duxford Cambs: Icon.

Connor, S. (1989), *Postmodernist Culture: An Introduction to Theories of the Contemporary*. Oxford: Blackwell.

Cooper, M. (2003), *Existential Therapies*. London: Sage.

Cooper, R., Friedman, J., Gans, S., Heaton, J. M., Oakley, C., Oakley, H. and Zeal, P. (1989), *Thresholds between Philosophy and Psychoanalysis*. London: Free Association Books.

Culler, J. (1986), *Ferdinand de Saussure*. Ithaca, NY: Cornell University Press.

Deleuze, G. and Guattari, F. (1984), *Anti-Oedipus: Capitalism and Schizophrenia*. (Preface by M. Foucault) London: The Athlone Press.

—— (1987), *A Thousand Plateaux*. Minneapolis: University of Minnesota Press.

Derrida, J. (1976 [1967]), *Of Grammatology*. Baltimore, MD: The Johns Hopkins University Press.

—— (1978b [1967]), 'Cogito and the History of Madness', in *Writing and Difference*. Chicago: University of Chicago Press.

—— (1987), 'Du tout', from *The Postcard. From Socrates to Freud and Beyond*. Chicago: University of Chicago Press.

—— (1995), *The Gift of Death*. Chicago: University of Chicago Press.

—— (1997a), *Adieu à Emmanuel Levinas: le mot d'acceuil*. Paris: Galilée.

—— (1997b), *Politics of Friendship*. London: Verso.

—— (ed. Wolfeys, J. L.) (1998), *The Derrida Reader: Writing Performances*. Edinburgh: Edinburgh University Press.

—— (2000), *États d'âme de la psychanalyse. Adresse aux États Généraux de la Psychanalyse (juillet 2000)*. Paris: Galilée.

—— (2001), *On Cosmopolitanism and Forgiveness*. London: Routledge.

DiCenso, J. (1998), *The Other Freud. Religion, Culture and Psychoanalysis*. London: Routledge.

Docherty, T. (ed.) (1993), *Postmodernism: A Reader*. New York: Columbia University Press.

Eagleton, T. (1996), *The Illusions of Postmodernism*, Oxford: Blackwell.

—— (2000), *The Idea of Culture*. Oxford: Blackwell.

Eco, U. (1984), *Semiotics and the Philosophy of Language*. London: Macmillan.

Elliott, A. (1999), *Social Theory and Psychoanalysis in Transition. Self and Society from Freud to Kristeva*. London: Free Association Books.

Elliott, A. and Spezzano, C. (eds) (2000), *Psychoanalysis at its Limits. Navigating the Post-Modern Turn*. London: Free Association Books.

Esteva, G. and Prakesh, M. S. (1998), *Grassroots Post-Modernity. Remaking the Soil of Cultures*. Basingstoke: Palgrave.

Evans, D. (1996), *An Introductory Dictionary of Lacanian Psychoanalysis*. London: Routledge.

Featherston, M. (ed.) (1988), *Postmodernism*. London: Sage.

Felman, S. (1987), *Jacques Lacan and the Adventure of Insight. Psychoanalysis in Contemporary Culture*. Cambridge, MA: Harvard University Press.

Fiumara, G. C. (2001), *The Mind's Affective Life. A Psychoanalytic and Philosophical Inquiry*. Hove: Brunner-Routledge.

Forrester, J. (1990), *The Seductions of Psychoanalysis. Freud, Lacan and Derrida*. Cambridge: Cambridge University Press.

Forrester, J. and Appignanesi, L. (1992), *Freud's Women*. London: Weidenfeld and Nicolson.

Foster, H. (ed.) (1985), *Post-Modern Culture*. London: Pluto.

Foucault, M. (1971a), *Madness and Civilization: A History of Insanity in the Age of Reason*. London: Tavistock Publications.

—— (1971b), 'The Discourse on Language' (trans. Swyer, R.), *Social Science Information*, April, 7–30.

—— (1972), *The Archeology of Knowledge*. New York: Pantheon.

—— (1973), *The Birth of the Clinic: An Archeology of Medical Perception*. New York: Random House.

Foucault, M. (1978), *The History of Sexuality, Vol. 1: An Introduction*. New York Pantheon.

Foucault, M. (1979), *Discipline and Punish: The Birth of the Prison*. New York Random House.

—— (1980), 'Truth and Power', interview with Fontana, A. and Pasquino, P., in *Power/Knowledge: Selected Interviews and Other Writings, 1972–77*. New York: Pantheon.

Foucault, M. (1985), *The History of Sexuality, Vol. 2: The Uses of Pleasure*. New York Pantheon.

Foucault, M. (1986a), *The History of Sexuality, Vol. 3: The Core of the Self*. New York Pantheon.

—— (1986b), *The Foucault Reader. An Introduction to Foucault's Thought* (ed. Rabinow, P.). Harmondsworth: Penguin.

Frankl, V. (1973 [1967]), *Psychotherapy and Existentialism. Selected Papers on Logotherapy*. Harmondsworth: Penguin.

Freud, S. (1900), *The Interpretation of Dreams, The Standard Edition of the Complete Psychological Works of Sigmund Freud*, London: The Hogarth Press, 1953–64. Vols IV and V.

Freud, S. (1901), 'On Dreams', *The Standard Edition of the Complete Psychological Works of Sigmund Freud*, London: The Hogarth Press, 1953–1964. Vol V.

—— (1905 etc.), *Three Essays on the Theory of Sexuality, The Standard Edition of the Complete Psychological Works of Sigmund Freud*. London: The Hogarth Press, 1953–1964. Vol. VII.

—— (1911), 'Formulations on the Two Principles of Mental Functioning', *The Standard Edition of the Complete Psychological Works of Sigmund Freud*. London: The Hogarth Press, 1953–1964. Vol. XII.

—— (1915), 'The Unconscious', *The Standard Edition of the Complete Psychological Works of Sigmund Freud*. London: The Hogarth Press, 1953–1964. Vol. XIV.

—— (1916–17), *Introductory Lectures on Psychoanalysis. The Standard Edition of the Complete Psychological Works of Sigmund Freud*. London: The Hogarth Press, 1953–1964. Vol. XVI.

—— (1921), *Group Psychology and the Analysis of the Ego. The Standard Edition of the Complete Psychological Works of Sigmund Freud*. London: The Hogarth Press, 1953–1964. Vol. XVIII.

—— (1924), 'The Dissolution of the Oedipus Complex', *The Standard Edition of the Complete Psychological Works of Sigmund Freud*. London: The Hogarth Press, 1953–1964. Vol. XIX.

Friedman, M. (ed.) (1964), *The Worlds of Existentialism. A Critical Reader*. Atlantic Highlands, NJ: Humanities Press.

Frosh, S. (1987), *The Politics of Psychoanalysis. An Introduction to Freudian and Post-Freudian Theory*. New Haven, CT and London: Yale University Press.

—— (1994), *Sexual Difference. Masculinity and Psychoanalysis*. London: Routledge.

Fukuyama, F. (1992), *The End of History and the Last Man*. London: Hamish Hamilton.

Gans, S. (1997) 'Lacan and Levinas: Towards an Ethical Psychoanalysis', *Journal of the British Society for Phenomenology*, Vol. 28, No. 1, January.

Garland, H. and Garland, M. (eds) (1976), *The Oxford Companion to German Literature*. Oxford: Clarendon Press.

Gay, P. (1995), *The Freud Reader*. New York: Vintage.

Giorgi, A. (1970), *Psychology as a Human Science: A Phenomenologically Based Approach*. New York: Harper and Row.

Gondek, H. (1995–6) 'Cogito and Separation. Lacan/Levinas', *Journal of European Psychoanalysis*, No. 2, Fall–Winter, pp. 133–68.

Gordon, P. (1999), *Face to Face: Therapy as Ethics*. London: Constable.

Grosskurth, P. (1987), *Melanie Klein*. London: Maresfield Library.

Grosz, E. A. (1986), 'Language and the Limits of the Body: Kristeva and Abjection', in Grosz, E. A., Threadgold, T., Kelly, D., Cholodenko, A. and Colless, E., *Futur*fall. Excursions into Post-Modernity*. Sydney: Power Institute of Fine Arts, University of Sydney.

—— (1990), *Jacques Lacan: A Feminist Introduction*. London: Routledge.

—— (1996) *Space, Time and Perversion – Essays on the Politics of Bodies*. London: Routledge.

Guattari, F. (1984 [1977]), *Molecular Revolution. Psychiatry and Politics*. Harmondsworth: Penguin.

Gutting, G. (2001), *French Philosophy in the Twentieth Century*. Cambridge: Cambridge University Press.

Habermas, J. (1972), *Knowledge and Human Interests*. London: Heinemann.

—— (1985 [1981]), 'Modernity – An Incomplete Project', in Foster (1985).

—— (1987), *The Philisophical Discourse of Modernity*. Cambridge, MA: MIT Press.

Harasym, S. (ed.) (1998) *Levinas and Lacan. The Missed Encounter*. New York: State University of New York Press.

Harvey, D. (1989), *The Condition of Postmodernity*. Oxford: Blackwell.

Harvey, P. (ed.) (1967), *The Oxford Companion to English Literature*. Oxford: Clarendon Press.

Hauke, C. (2000), *Jung and the Postmodern*. London: Routledge.

Heaton, J. (1990), 'What Is Existential Analysis?', *Journal of the Society for Existential Analysis*, No. 1.

—— (2000), *Wittgenstein and Psychoanalysis*. Duxford, Cambs: Icon Books.

Hegel, G. W. F. (1956), *The Philosophy of History*. New York: Dover.

—— (1977), *Phenomenology of Spirit* (trans. Miller, A. V.). Oxford: Oxford University Press.

Heidegger, M. (1963 [1927]), *Being and Time* (trans Macquarrie, J. and Robinson, E.). New York: Harper and Row.

—— (1993a), *Martin Heidegger. Basic Writings* (ed. Krell, D. F.). London: Routledge.

—— (1993b [1947]), 'Letter on Humanism', in Heidegger (1993a).

—— (2001), *The Zollikon Seminars* (ed. Boss, M.). Evanston, IL: Northwestern University Press.

Hoeller, K. (ed.) (1993), *Merleau-Ponty and Psychology*. Atlantic Heights, NJ: Humanities Press.

Hollingdale, R. J. (1969), Introduction to Nietzsche, F., *Thus Spoke Zarathustra*. Harmondsworth: Penguin.

Horkheimer, M. and Adorno, T. (1979), *Dialectic of Enlightenment*. London: Verso.

Howard, A. (2000), *Philosophy for Counselling and Psychotherapy. Pythagoras to Postmodernism*. Basingstoke: Palgrave.

Husserl, E. (1960 [1931]), *Cartesian Meditations. An Introduction to Phenomenology* (trans. Cairns, D.). The Hague: Martinus Nijhoff.

Irigaray, L. (1981), 'This Sex Which Is Not One' (trans. Reeder, C.), in Marks and de Courtivron (1981).

—— (1985a), *Speculum of the Other Woman*. Ithaca, NY: Cornell University Press.

—— (1985b), *This Sex Which Is Not One*. Ithaca, NY: Cornell University Press.

—— (1992), *The Irigaray Reader* (ed. Whitford, M.). Oxford: Blackwell.

—— (1994), *Thinking the Difference*. London: Routledge.

Jakobson, R. (1980), *Selected Writings – III. The Poetry of Grammar and the Grammar of Poetry*. The Hague and Paris: Mouton.

Jameson, F. (1985), 'Postmodernism and Consumer Society', in Foster (1985).

Jameson, F. (1996), *Postmodernism, or, The Cultural Logic of Late Capitalism*. London and New York: Verso.

Jameson, F. (1998), *The Cultural Turn: Selected Writings on the Postmodern, 1983–1998*. London and New York: Verso.

Jencks, C. (ed.) (1992), *The Postmodern Reader*. London: Academy Editions.

—— (1996), *What Is Post-Modernism?* New York: Wiley.

Kearney, R. (1995), *States of Mind. Dialogues with Contemporary Thinkers on the European Mind*. Manchester: Manchester University Press.

Kearney, R. and Rainwater, M. (1996), *The Continental Philosophy Reader*. London: Routledge.

Kemp, S. and Squires, J. (1997), *Feminisms*, Oxford: Oxford University Press.

Kierkegaard, S. (1944) [1848], *The Concept of Dread* (trans Lowry, W.). Princeton, NJ: Princeton University Press.

—— (1954) [1848, 1849], *Fear and Trembling and Sickness unto Death* (trans Lowry, W.). New York: Doubleday Anchor.

Klein, M. (1975a [1930]), 'The Importance of Symbol Formation in the Development of the Ego', from *The Writings of Melanie Klein*, Vol. I. London: The Hogarth Press and the Institute of Psycho-Analysis.

—— (1975b [1946]), 'Notes on some Schizoid Mechanisms', from *The Writings of Melanie Klein*, Vol. II. London: The Hogarth Press and the Institute of Psycho-Analysis.

Kojève, A. (1980), *Introduction to the Reading of Hegel* (trans. Nichols, J.). Ithaca, NY: Cornell University Press.

Koning, A. J. J. and Jenner, F. A. (1982), *Phenomenology and Psychiatry*. London: Academic Books.

Kristeva, J. (1982), *Powers of Horror. An Essay on Abjection*. New York: Columbia University Press.

—— (1986), *The Kristeva Reader* (ed. Moi, T.). Oxford: Blackwell.

—— (1994), *Strangers to Ourselves*. New York: Columbia University Press.

—— (1998), *L'avenir d'une révolte*. Paris: Calmann-Lévy.

Kroker, A., Kroker, M. and Cook, D. (1994 [1984]), *Panic Encyclopaedia. The Definitive Guide to Postmodernism*. London: Macmillan.

Kvale, S. (1992), *Psychology and Postmodernism*. London: Sage.

Lacan, J. (1977), *Écrits. Selected Writings* (trans. Sheridan, A.) London: Routledge.

—— (1988), 'Overture to the Seminar' and 'The Topic of the Imaginary', in *The Seminar of Jacques Lacan, Book 1, Freud's Papers on Technique 1953–1954* (trans. Forrester, J.). Cambridge: Cambridge University Press.

—— (1993), *The Seminar of Jacques Lacan. Book III. The Psychoses, 1955–56* (trans. Grigg, R.). London: Routledge.

Laing, R. D. (1965 [1960]), *The Divided Self. An Existential Study in Sanity and Madness*. Harmondsworth: Penguin.

Laplanche, J. (1996) 'Psychoanalysis as Anti-Hermeneutics', *Radical Philosophy*, 79 (Sept/Oct).

Laplanche, J. and Pontalis, J-B. (1988 [1967]), *The Language of Psychoanalysis*. London: Karnac.

Layton, L. (1999), *Who's That Girl? Who's That Boy? Clinical Practice meets Postmodern Gender Theory*. New York: Jason Aronson.

Lechte, J. (1994), *Fifty Key Contemporary Thinkers. From Structuralism to Postmodernity*. London: Routledge.

Levinas, E. (1969 [1961]), *Totality and Infinity. An Essay on Exteriority* (trans. Lingis, A.). Pittsburgh: Duquesne University Press.

—— (1985), *Ethics and Infinity. Conversations with Philippe Nemo* (rans. Cohen, R.). Pittsburgh: Duquesne University Press.

—— (1989) *The Levinas Reader* (ed. Hand, S.). Oxford: Blackwell.

—— (1995 [1981]), 'Ethics of the Infinite', in Kearney (1995).

Lévi-Strauss, C. (1963 [1958]), *Structural Anthropology*. New York: Basic Books.

Lispector, C. (1992 [1977]), *The Hour of the Star* (trans. Pontiero, G.). Manchester: Carcanet.

Loewenthal, D. (1996) 'The Post-modern Counsellor: Some implications for practice, theory, research and professionalism', *Counselling Psychology Quarterly*, Vol. 9, No. 4, pp. 373–81.

Loewenthal, D. and Snell, R. (2001), 'Psychotherapy as the Practice of Ethics', in Palmer-Barnes, F. and Murdin, L. (eds), *Values and Ethics in the Practice of Psychotherapy and Counselling* Buckingham: Open University Press.

Løvlie, L. (1992), 'Postmodernism and Subjectivity', in Kvale (1992).

Lyotard, J-F. (1984), *The Post-Modern Condition: A Report on Knowledge*. Foreword by F. Jameson. Manchester: Manchester University Press.

—— (1988) *The Differend: Phrases in Dispute*. Manchester: Manchester University Press.

—— (1989), *The Lyotard Reader* (ed. Benjam, A. E.). Oxford: Blackwell.

—— (1991 [1988]), *The Inhuman: Reflections on Time* (trans. Bennington, G. and Bowlby, R.). Blackwell: Oxford.

—— (1992), *The Postmodern Explained to Children. Correspondence, 1982–1983*. Sydney: Power Institute of Fine Arts.

Lyotard, J-F. and Thébaud, J-L. (1979), *Just Gaming*. Minneapolis: University of Minnesota Press.

McCall, R. J. (1983), *Phenomenological Psychology. An Introduction, with a glossary of some key Heideggerian terms*. Madison: University of Wisconsin Press.

McCumber, J. (2000), *Philosophy and Freedom: Derrida, Rorty, Habermas, Foucault*. Bloomington: Indiana University Press.

McLuhan, M. and Fiore, Q. (1967), *The Medium is the Massage. An Inventory of Effects*. Harmondsworth: Penguin.

MacQuarrie, J. (1972), *Existentialism*. London: Hutchinson.

Magnus, B. and Higgins, K. M. (eds) (1996), *The Cambridge Companion to Nietzsche*. Cambridge: Cambridge University Press.

Malson, H. (1997), *Feminism, Post-Structuralism and the Social Psychology of Anorexia Nervosa*. London: Routledge.

Marcuse, H. (1955), *Eros and Civilization*. London: Allen Lane.

Marks, E. and de Courtivron, I. (1981), *New French Feminisms* (trans. Reeder, C.). Brighton: Harvester.

Matthews, E. (1996), *Twentieth-Century French Philosophy*. Oxford: Oxford University Press.

May, R. (ed.) (1961), *Existential Bases of Psychotherapy*. New York: Random House.

Merleau-Ponty, M. (1956 [1945]) 'What is Phenomenology?', preface to Merleau-Ponty, M. (1945), (Trans. Bannan, J. F.), *Cross Currents*, Vol. VI, No. 1 (Sept. 1956).

—— (1994 [1945]), *Phenomenology of Perception*. London: Routledge.

—— (1964) *L'œil et l'esprit*. Paris: Gallimard.

Mitchell, J. and Rose, J. (eds) (1982), *Feminine Sexuality: Jacques Lacan and the école freudienne*. London: Macmillan.

Moi, T. (1987), *French Feminist Thought. A Reader*. Oxford: Blackwell.

—— (1990), *Feminist Theory and Simone de Beauvoir*. Oxford: Blackwell.

Moran, D. (2000), *Introduction to Phenomenology*. London: Routledge.

Moss, S. (2000), 'A Staggeringly Post-Modern Work of Literary Trickery', *The Guardian*, 9 August.

Myerson, S. (2001), *Ecology and the End of Postmodernism*. Duxford, Cambs: Icon.

Nietzsche, F. (1969), *Thus Spake Zarathustra*. Harmondsworth: Penguin.

Nietzsche, F. (1974), *The Gay Science* (ed. and trans. Kaufmann, W.). New York: Vintage.

—— (1977a), *A Nietzsche Reader* (ed. Rieu, E. V.). Harmondsworth, Middlesex: Penguin.

—— (1977b), 'On Truth and Lie in an Extra-Moral Sense', in *The Portable Nietzsche* (ed. and trans. Kaufmann, W.). New York: Viking.

—— (1989), *Beyond Good and Evil* (trans. Kaufmann, W.). New York: Vintage.

Norris, C. (1987), *Derrida*. London: Fontana.

—— (1992), *Uncritical Theory: Postmodernism, Intellectuals, and the Gulf War*. London: Lawrence and Wishart.

O'Connor, N. and Ryan, J. (1993), *Wild Desires and Mistaken Identities. Lesbianism and Psychoanalysis*. London: Virago.

Owens, C. (1985 [1983]), 'The Discourse of Others: Feminists and Postmodernism', in Foster (1985).

Parker, I. (1999), *Deconstructing Psychotherapy*. London: Sage.

Payne, M. (ed.) (1998), *A Dictionary of Cultural and Critical Theory*. Oxford: Blackwell.

Peperzak, A. (1993), *To the Other: An Introduction to the Philosophy of Emmanuel Levinas*. West Lafayette, IN: Purdue University Press.

Peperzak, A., Critchley, S., and Bernasconi, R. (1996), *Emmanuel Levinas. Basic Philosophical Writings*. Bloomington and Indianapolis: Indiana University Press.

Phoca, S. and Wright, R. (1999), *Introducing Postfeminism*. Duxford, Cambs: Icon.

Putnam, H. (1981), *Reason, Truth and History*. Cambridge: Cambridge University Press.

Ree, J. and Chamberlain, J. (eds) (1998), *Kierkegaard: A Critical Reader*. Oxford: Blackwell.

Reid, J. M. H. (ed.) (1976), *The Concise Oxford Dictionary of French Literature*. Oxford: Clarendon Press.

Robinson, D. (1999), *Nietzsche and Postmodernism*. Duxford, Cambs: Icon.

Rogers, C (1967 [1961]), *On Becoming a Person. A Therapist's View of Psychotherapy*. London: Constable.

Rorty, R. (1991), *Objectivity, Relativism and Truth*. Cambridge: Cambridge University Press.

Rosenau, P. (1991), *Post-Modernism and the Social Sciences*. Princeton, NJ: Princeton University Press.

Roudinesco, E. (1999), 'Rencontres de Rabat avec Jacques Derrida', *European Journal of Psychotherapy, Counselling and Health*, Vol. 2, No. 2, August.

Roudinesco, E. and Plon, M. (1997), *Dictionnaire de la psychanalyse*. Paris: Fayard.

Russell, B. (1999 [1961]), *History of Western Philosophy and its Connection with Political and Social Circumstances from the Earliest Times to the Present Day*. London: Routledge.

Rycroft, C. (1971), *Reich*. London: Fontana.

Samuels, A. (2000), *The Political Psyche*. London: Routledge.

Sartre, J-P. (1956 [1943]), *Being and Nothingness*. New York: Philosophical Library.

—— (2001 [1945]), *The Reprieve*. London: Penguin.

Sarup, M. (1993), *An Introductory Guide to Post-Structuralism and Postmodernism*. Hemel Hempstead: Harvester Wheatsheaf.

Sass, L. A. (1992), 'The Epic of Disbelief: The Postmodernist Turn in Contemporary Psychoanalysis', in Kvale (1992).

Saussure, F. de (1966 [1916]), *Course in General Linguistics*. New York: McGraw-Hill.

Scott, A. (1996), *Real Events Revisited. Fantasy, Memory and Psychoanalysis*. London: Virago.

Shamdasani, S. and Munchow, M. (eds) (1994), *Speculations after Freud. Psychoanalysis, Philosophy and Culture*. London: Routledge.

Shiach, N. (1991), *Hélène Cixous: A Politics of Writing*. London: Routledge.

Sim, S. (ed.) (1998), *The Critical Dictionary of Postmodern Thought*. Duxford, Cambs: Icon Books.

—— (2001), *Lyotard and the Inhuman*. Duxford, Cambs: Icon Books.

Smith, A-M. (1998), *Julia Kristeva: Speaking the Unspeakable*. London: Pluto Press.

Sokal, A. and Bricmont, J. (1998), *Intellectual Impostures*. London: Profile.

Spinelli, E. (1989), *The Interpreted World. An Introduction to Phenomenological Psychology*. London: Sage.

Steuerman, E. (2000), *The Bounds of Reason: Habermas, Lyotard, and Melanie Klein on Rationality*. London: Routledge.

Sturrock, J. (1998), Review of Sokal A., and Bricmont, J., *Intellectual Impostures. London Review of Books*, Vol. 20, No. 14, 16 July.

Symington, N. (1986), *The Analytic Experience. Lectures from the Tavistock*. London: Free Association Books.

—— (1999), *Emotion and Spirit. Questioning the Claims of Psychoanalysis and Religion*. London: Karnac.

Timimi, S. (2002), *Pathological Child Psychiatry and the Medicalization of Childhood*. Hove: Brunner-Routledge.

Timpanaro, S. (1976), *The Freudian Slip*. London: New Left Books.

Tucker, R. (ed.) (1978), *The Marx-Engels Reader*. New York: Norton.

Van Deurzen-Smith, E. (1996), *Everyday Mysteries. Existential Dimensions of Psychotherapy*. London: Routledge.

Van Deurzen, E. (2001), *Existential Counselling and Psychotherapy in Practice*. London: Sage.

Weber, M. (1974), 'Science as a Vocation' (ed. Gerth, H. H. and Mills, C. W.), *From Max Weber: Essays in Sociology*. New York: Free Press.

West, D. (1998), *An Introduction to Continental Philosophy*. Oxford: Polity Press.

Whyte, L. L. (1979), *The Unconscious before Freud*. London: Julian Friedmann.

Williams, C. (2001), *Contemporary French Philosophy. Modernity and the Persistence of the Subject*. London: The Athlone Press.

Williams, R. (1965 [1961]), *The Long Revolution*. Harmondsworth: Pelican.

—— (1976), *Keywords. A Vocabulary of Culture and Society*. London: Fontana.

Winnicott, D. W. (1958 [1951]), 'Transitional Objects and Transitional Phenomena', *Through Paediatrics to Psychoanalysis. Collected Papers*. London: Tavistock.

Wittgenstein, L. (1965), 'Lecture on Ethics', *The Philosophical Review*, Vol. 74, No. 1 (January), pp. 3–12 in Cahoone (1996).

—— (1998), *Culture and Value* (revised 2nd edition, ed. von Wright, G. R.). Oxford: Blackwell.

—— (2001 [1958]), *Philosophical Investigations*. Oxford: Blackwell.

Wolfenstein, E. V. (1993), *Psychoanalytic Marxism. Groundwork*. London: Free Association Books.

Woods, D. (ed.) (1992), *Derrida: A Critical Reader*. Oxford: Blackwell.

Worsley, R. (2001), *Process Work in Person-Centred Therapy. Phenomenological and Existential Perspectives*. Basingstoke: Palgrave.

Wright, E. (1998), *Psychoanalytic Criticism* (2nd edition). Cambridge: Polity Press.

—— (2000), *Lacan and Postfeminism*, Duxford, Cambs: Icon.

Young, R. (ed.) (1981), *Untying the Text: A Post-Structuralist Reader*. London: Routledge.

Žižek, S. (1991), *Looking Awry: An Introduction to Jacques Lacan through Popular Culture*. Cambridge, MA: MIT Press.

—— (1999), *The Žižek Reader* (ed. Wright, E. and Wright, E.). Oxford: Blackwell.

—— (2001), *On Belief*. London: Routledge.

—— (2002), *Welcome to the Desert of the Real! Five Essays on September 11th and Related Dates*. London and New York: Verso.

Index

CPSIA information can be obtained at www.ICGtesting.com
Printed in the USA
LVOW04s1411010914